MASSIVELY VIOLENT & DECIDEDLY AVERAGE

LEE HOWEY

WITH TONY GILLAN

\ R b\

First published in Great Britain in 2018 by
Biteback Publishing Ltd
Westminster Tower
3 Albert Embankment
London SE1 7SP
Copyright © Lee Howey and Tony Gillan 2018

ISBN 978-1-78590-350-2

10 9 8 7 6 5 4 3 2 1

A CIP catalogue record for this book is available from the British Library.

Set in Minion Pro

Printed and bound in Great Britain by
CPI Group (UK) Ltd, Croydon CR0 4YY

MIX
Paper from
responsible sources
FSC
www.fsc.org   FSC® C020471

To Maz

*Thank you so much for all you do for me and for your support
and encouragement to write this book. I would have never had
the belief to even start this project without your confidence in me.
You and our boys Joseph and Christopher give me strength and
purpose every day.*

*Also in memory of my father-in-law, Denis 'Denny' Spillane,
1937–2017. Dearly missed – 'Up the Kingdom.'*

ACKNOWLEDGEMENTS

My thanks go to all the people who helped me to become a footballer, especially Norman Howey.

Information for this book provided by Paul Watson and Laurent Degueldre (AS Hemptinne), Pat Godbold (Ipswich Town), Rob Mason (Sunderland), Bobby (surname unknown, of Buckingham Town), Brian Porter (Daventry Town) and Phil Curtis at the Sunderland Antiquarian Society was invaluable.

Thanks too to Kevin Ball, Gary Bennett and Niall Quinn for the cover quotes. Also to proofreaders Keith Nixon, Alan Smith and Dave Turner. A mention too for Liz Gillan, for generally putting up with things.

Finally to Tony Gillan, who has been a great support to me in putting this book together. My memory for details was a little vague, but you were able to fill in the gaps with research and humour.

CONTENTS

Introduction   ix

1.   In the beginning…   1
2.   Ipswich   25
3.   Belgium   51
4.   Big break   79
5.   Making a mark   103
6.   There's a song about me, you know   129
7.   Punch-ups, my goal of the century and Klinsmann   147
8.   The season couldn't end quickly enough   171
9.   Progress and Peter Reid   181
10. We didn't want the season to end   217
11. Premier League   243
12. Frustration   269
13. Burnley: oh dear   291
14. Northampton, downwards and the end   321
15. And now…   341

Index   349

INTRODUCTION

So many memories from the pinnacle of football. The Champions League, the FA Cup final, the World Cup, England versus Brazil – I've watched them all.

International fame, an MBE, streets named in my honour, documentaries about my career and the acquisition of a few million quid to keep me amused in my autumn years; these are just some of the things that never happened to me.

Medically speaking, I really ought not to have played football beyond the age of nineteen, but I continued until well into my thirties. As a consequence my paso doble is not as acclaimed as it once was; I creak more than a little and not all of me is original, with various parts now composed of metal and plastic. A bolt through the neck might be my next procedure. It may as well be; a triple bypass and a hysterectomy are about the only other operations I have yet to undergo.

Something else I had to contend with was deep, deep anxiety. Fear of a failure to perform and a feeling of massive responsibility to succeed, especially at my home town club.

It all ended on a dark, freezing March evening in 2006 in an Eagle Bitter United Counties League Premier Division game for Buckingham Town at Ford Sports Daventry in miserable, driving rain. But this momentous occasion is not widely remembered outside my house.

All of this brought me to where I am today – the payments industry with Judopay.

But the chances are that you envy me.

You may now be thinking how arrogant the previous sentence makes me sound. You may be asking yourself: 'Who does he think he is? And why is he writing his story anyway? He was hardly Bobby Moore.'

Allow me to explain. The fact that you have read even this far means that you are probably a football fan. If Paul Scholes or Tony Adams or even Kevin Ball happens to be reading this then OK, they aren't likely to be too seriously stricken by the green-eye. But if, like most of my friends, you were never given the opportunity to play professional football, then it is only natural to feel a tinge of envy (which incidentally is not the same as jealousy).

I don't mean envious to an unhealthy level that disrupts your sleep, puts you off your food or makes you wish for another person to fall down a well. Just a small and natural dose of envy, such as you might feel for someone who can mend motor vehicles, or perform card tricks. As a football fan, you will inevitably feel more envy for Mario Götze than you do for me. He scored an extra-time winner, the only goal in the 2014 World Cup final for Germany against Argentina in the Maracanã Stadium. But I once scored an extra-time winner too, the only goal in an FA Cup third round replay for Sunderland against Carlisle United at Brunton Park.

There were almost 75,000 spectators to witness Mr Götze's goal first hand, including world leaders and Hollywood stars, with billions more watching on television to see his effort land the biggest prize in football. He must have felt sensational.

But my little goal at Carlisle, a six-yard side-footer from a corner immediately in front of our own supporters, felt pretty damn good too. Although it has been largely forgotten and the ultimate prize for it was a 2–1 fourth round defeat at Wimbledon, I still say that it is, for most readers of this book, a small source of envy. It's on YouTube, should you care to relive the moment (it has at least a dozen hits).

There were more glamorous days in my career than that cup tie in Cumbria. I did win a First Division Championship medal. I got to play Premier League football in some of the country's most famous grounds, against some of the most celebrated names in English football in the 1990s – including Jürgen Klinsmann, Ryan Giggs, Eric Cantona, Gianfranco Zola, Peter Schmeichel, Ian Wright, Alan Shearer and Fabrizio Ravanelli – and not always unsuccessfully. It wasn't all assaults upon the kneecaps on wet Tuesday nights in Hartlepool.

Returning to the question of why I have written this book, I have been inspired by several autobiographies of other footballers, past and present; household names with glory-laden careers whose exploits on the pitch will simply never be forgotten. I won't name names and I am not referring to *all* football memoirs. But some of them have, despite access to such fabulous raw material, produced bloody awful books; predictable, plodding, repetitive, vain, self-important, expletive-strewn and just plain boring. So I was encouraged by these people negatively. They were far better footballers than I, but this is a more enjoyable book.

Trust me when I say that is not a massive boast.

This book does not end with an unforgettable game at Wembley, or a 100th England cap, or even scoring the goal that averted a relegation. But I sincerely hope that it ends with the reader having had an insight into our beloved game when it was still imbued with some semblance of reality. I hope, more importantly, that it ends with the reader having had a good time. Despite the numerous setbacks, the abuse and the dodgy knees, I had a *great* time.

Even if I could, I wouldn't change a thing.

I'm glad to say that football supporters who are old enough still remember me. In August 2015 I was invited to take part in an event at the Roker Hotel in Sunderland, to commemorate the famous football documentary *Premier Passions*. I joined Peter Reid, Richard Ord, Kevin Ball, Martin Smith, Bobby Saxton and Niall Quinn. Each one of us was introduced with a big build-up by the compère, Peter Daykin.

Peter Reid got: 'The man who transformed a failing football club as a manager; as a player he represented his country, won two league titles...'

Niall Quinn was described as: 'Sunderland's messiah. A legendary goal scorer and a man who graced two World Cups...'

Richard Ord was: 'A classy defender, respected throughout football with over 250 appearances in the famous red and white shirt...'

And so on, until it was my turn. Last and evidently least.

'Never forget that this man had the distinction of serving his club at centre-back as well as striker. In both roles he is widely regarded as not just massively violent, but also as decidedly average.'

Oh well – if the cap fits. Not that I won any caps.

Still, far better 'decidedly average' than not there at all.

Lee Howey, 2018

CHAPTER I

IN THE BEGINNING...

Don't worry. This is a memoir, not an autobiography.

The main difference between the two is that memoirs give you only the goods, the juicy stuff, rather than being weighed down by unnecessary detail about how the author likes his eggs, the destination of his first holiday or his favourite films. This book will have none of that. Nor will it contain emetic passages about the gladness of my fluffy heart when my children were born, or purple prose descriptions of the languid sun setting behind Booze Buster on Fulwell Road, or how the twinkling stars in the dark skies above Roker Park inspired such stirring poetry in me during a goalless draw with Grimsby while some bastard was stamping on my ankle.

No, none of that old guff. However, a bit of background may be in order. I can't relate first-hand any events for this book from any earlier than 1 April 1969. That was when this particular Howey first saw planet Earth, from Sunderland General Hospital.

I arrived without fanfare. This was by request as my mother hated trumpets, especially at a time like that. But both of my parents were apparently quite chuffed with the advent of their first-born and it is widely reported to have gladdened their fluffy hearts. My parents, Norman and Yvonne Howey, née Drummond, are still together and living in Sunderland. It hasn't been a marriage abundantly laden with chocolates, flowers and candlelit dinners. This is despite my father being a former shipyard labourer from Pennywell. The tales you may have heard about the incurably romantic nature of Wearside's maritime workers are largely apocryphal. But after a few decades of, well, each other, they're still together. In most people's experience, this is about as successful as marriage gets.

Historians among you will of course immediately recall that Marvin Gaye was at number one with 'I Heard It Through the Grapevine' when I first appeared. Sunderland's most recent game was a 1–1 draw at Newcastle United (doubtless you will also know that Colin Suggett scored for Sunderland, Jackie Sinclair for Newcastle), President Eisenhower had died three days earlier, John had just married Yoko, men were about to walk on the moon, fashion was getting worse and voters were about to get younger; from twenty-one to eighteen.

That's enough scene setting I think. It's not as though I remember any of it. What I do recollect vividly is the omnipresence of football. My father Norman played semi-professionally in the Northern and Wearside Leagues. This was football of a pretty decent standard, as well as bringing in a useful few quid. My mother Yvonne's hairdressing career was scuppered by babies.

In London it has always been possible to choose which club to support, which means a selection of about a dozen clubs in the capital, plus (let's be honest) Liverpool and Manchester United. There can be very few Sunderland supporters, ever, who made a conscious decision that SAFC was the club for them. The 'decision' is made by genetics at the point of conception. So it was with my dad, and then me.

Sunderland's rivalry with Newcastle United back then was not as we know it today. It has always been the case that when one of the two clubs is at home, the other is automatically away. When I was born it was common practice among many in the North East to watch the home games of both. Norman did this. He was Sunderland daft but just loved football and, with so little of it on television, he would stand with his friends in St James' Park every other week and happily watch Newcastle – albeit occasionally enlivening a dull game by verbally winding up those around him in the Gallowgate End in black and white livery. But it never went beyond banter. For those only familiar with the current relationship between the respective followers of the clubs, this may seem a mite difficult to believe, akin to the Orange Order arranging a bus trip to the Vatican. But I can assure you that it happened.

We lived in a high-rise block in Gilley Law in the south of Sunderland. As far back as I remember I was kicking a ball around in the streets. At every school playtime and lunchtime, I played football. Then, at the end of a trying day of education, I would go home and unwind by playing a relaxing game of football. The weather was never a cause for postponements in the streets of Gilley Law, although there was the occasional breather from relentless football when we would trail our mucky feet back indoors to watch a bit of television – especially if there was football on.

Lest you should think I was an obsessive child and not a properly rounded individual, I should point out that I was also an avid reader, and not just of *Shoot!* I was also an occasional subscriber to *Match* weekly, *Roy of the Rovers* and everything in between.

Aged around five, I was the youngest player in the neighbourhood, so a specific natural law was upheld. The sacred codes of jumpers-for-goalposts football and universally cognisable human reason are inextricably entwined: i.e. they made me go in goal.

I was desperate to join in and accepted my lot until such time as an even younger and smaller partaker would slither his way into the game. More of him in a while. It was a sort of apprenticeship. The venue was usually a 'pitch' that is still there today. It was a nearby field with a 1:3 gradient, which thereby presented an obvious advantage to whichever team was defending the summit.

Keeping goal at base camp was rather less appealing, but I persevered. Only the dark could end the game, at which point I was thrown into the bath to be pristine and presentable for Yvonne when I arrived at school the following day.

The People's Republic of Gilley Law and its surrounding dependencies would later prove to be something of a stellar neighbourhood. Many of the regular participants in our games were then of approximately school leaving age. They all had about ten years on me and projected carefree confidence and, so it seemed at the time, a dash of sophistication. Several of them would achieve much in the game. They included Kevin Dillon, who became part of the renowned team of hard-nuts at Birmingham City in the 1980s and the last player to be given a debut by Sir Alf Ramsey.

Then there was Mick Harford, later capped by England and a League Cup winner with Luton Town. He also played for Newcastle, Derby County and Chelsea, and was ever so briefly a colleague of mine at Sunderland. His Premier League career (the league didn't start until 1992) lasted for a total of fifteen minutes, during which time he scored the winner for Coventry City against Newcastle at Highfield Road in 1993. He was also another of the renowned team of hard-nuts at Birmingham City in the 1980s.

Mick Smith was not one of the renowned team of hard-nuts at Birmingham City in the 1980s. He joined Wimbledon in 1979 when they were in the Third Division, and played for them over 200 times as part of the incipient 'Crazy Gang.' By the time he left them in 1986 they had been promoted to the old First Division.

Occasionally we were joined by Mick Hazard, who would sometimes wander over from Thorney Close. He would go on to play for Tottenham in two winning cup finals: the FA Cup of 1982 and the UEFA Cup of 1984. He also spent years at Chelsea, then Swindon, where he played in their only Premier League season. If he harbours disappointment at never having been part of the

4

renowned team of hard-nuts at Birmingham City in the 1980s, he has never made it public.

As far as kids' kick-abouts go, this must be about as lofty as it gets. I wasn't going to be allowed out of goal in a hurry. It made me dream of possibilities for myself. Four older lads from my neck of the woods would forge successful careers, and one of them wasn't even called Mick.

If only to temporarily stem my compulsion to constantly play football, football and then more football, my dad began to take me to Sunderland home games in his battered old van. Like the first record you bought, most fans have an eidetic memory of their first game. I'm afraid that mine is a little sketchier. I do remember that it was in the dark during the freezing pit of winter when I was about five. Looking at the record books, the favourite would appear to be a floodlit Division Two game against Manchester United at Roker on 18 January 1975, in front of 46,000 people, but I can't be certain. Whatever the fixture was, there and then I became even more hooked on the game and a very easy child to buy birthday and Christmas presents for: Sunderland shirt, Sunderland tracksuit, Sunderland pennant, a ball, *Shoot!* annual, etc. (I would eventually do one of those cheesy Q&A sessions for *Shoot!*: favourite meal, best friend in football, pet hates and so on – a load of old moon juice of course, but still a strangely proud moment.)

• • •

I exaggerate how much football I played. Slightly. My mates and I did have a wide range of academic interests, such as climbing trees, jumping off walls, riding our bikes, rummaging round building sites and being a general nuisance. We were just let out like semi-feral cats and away we went, as did millions of other kids the same age. It was simply the norm. I tell this to my children now and it truly seems like a different world. In many ways, it was. I'm fairly sure that perverts had been invented long before the 1970s, but they didn't have today's high profile.

My best friend was John Sproates. We were virtually inseparable and our friendship even survived the time that I killed his dog. Geoff Thomas may now be reading this with knowing cynicism, so I must stress that it really was a complete accident. I was calling the dog to come to the other side of the road where I was standing. My voice was the last thing that poor Smokey heard. The last thing he saw was the radiator of a Ford Cortina. May God have mercy upon his soul.

John is over it now. As he is today a highly trained British serviceman and recently to be found bobbing around the Indian Ocean looking for Somali pirates, I certainly *hope* he's over it. Animal lovers and advocates of karma may be heartened to learn that I was run over myself six weeks later. John also mentioned that it served me right. Happily, it was for a relatively short period of time that I was known as the Wearside Dog Murderer.

My formative years were for the most part quite normal. But as the poem says, into each life some rain must fall. When I was two-and-a-half, there was a sustained deluge when my precious little brother Steven was born; as far as I know, my only sibling.

Aged seven or so, I would scamper out of the flat to join my cohorts, usually to play football or possibly to attend to one of our other projects, such as smashing things. My brother would indulge in some high-pitched wailing because he had been left out. So our mother would open the window and shriek after me: 'Take your little brother! Take your little brother!'

Steven's inveterate career as a monumental pain in the arse began early. He was a spectacular whinger in those days and his related talent for twisting his face almost round to the back of his small, petulant head was unsurpassed. I say 'in those days': the child is indeed the father of the man and this is a gift he retains. It is reassuring to note that there are still a few constants in this ever-changing world of ours. He was, in fact, known unaffectionately as the 'Ginger Whinger' as he then had this peculiar excrescence of strawberry blond hair, which did at least distract some attention from his permanently wobbling bottom lip.

The whinging was constant. It didn't matter what was on the agenda; it would be met with a whinge. The accepted rite of passage alluded to earlier, that the youngest and snottiest should play in goal, was not respected by Steven, who would whinge about this duty and demand to be outfield, even though a casual glance could confirm his youth and his snot (indeed, he tended to be festooned in mucus; these candlesticks, along with his alarming hair colour, made him resemble something from the Book of Revelation).

Had to go in goal? Whinge. Lost the game? Whinge. No one would pass to him? Whinge. Punk rock hits the charts? Whinge. United Nations announce that smallpox has been eradicated? Whinge, whinge, whinge. I recall very few events that Steven greeted with warmth and an appreciative smile. It's enshrined in Magna Carta or something that the youngest goes in goal. This made Steven's whinging on the matter particularly irksome, as I had served my time uncomplainingly.

He did like his football, but was not the automatic, unquestioning Sunderland supporter that I was. He was a fickle fan. For example, he had a flirtation with Tottenham Hotspur during their Ossie Ardiles and Glenn Hoddle era, before moving on to some other club, then another and another that he had no connection with. I think he did eventually want to support Sunderland, but he never had a deep affinity with any team. He possibly attended the occasional match, but I don't remember it.

His disagreeability was non-stop and he would often make my life hell. Our first school was St Leonard's Primary in Silksworth where, aged seven, I was told I could have a trial for one of the football teams and was therefore quite giddy with excitement. However, during the lunchtime before the trial I was summoned to see the headmaster, Mr Conroy.

A prefect had informed Mr Conroy that I had been nabbed in the course of acting the goat on the school bus. Goat acting was one of the less socially acceptable crimes of the era and would have been specifically prohibited by an Act of Parliament if Mr Conroy had had his way. The sentence in this instance was to sit outside his office all afternoon, missing the trial in its entirety. I was distraught; more so because while I was not averse to reprehensible behaviour myself, I had no idea what I was supposed to have done on that bus. I rummaged through my mind for some memory of any goats I may have recently acted, but could think of none.

Eventually Mr Conroy called for the prefect, who looked at me and immediately confirmed: 'That's not 'im.' The goat had in fact been acted by my delightful brother, who upon apprehension had told the prefect that his name was Lee in an attempt to evade justice. While this was at least evidence of a sort of low cunning from a boy in his first year at school, we were to later reflect that a more gifted child would have also given the authorities a false surname. You may be familiar with the passage in the Old Testament, when the skulduggery of Cain prevented Abel from getting on the footy team. Well now I knew how Abel felt.

When I was eight we moved to Thorney Close, where I would take Steven for a kick-about with certain unwritten laws evolving because he was so much smaller than me and susceptible to a tantrum if he should lose. We would play across the street with the openings to two narrow, cross-sectioning back lanes (ginnels, snickets, pathways, cuts, depending on where you're from) on either side of the street which served as goals. I had to chip the ball softly into the air rather than belt it: 'nee blammers' being the most important rule. If

I miskicked a chip and the ball went low into the corner of the goal, he would cry like a mistreated Scarlett O'Hara. Then, oblivious to my pleading, he would run into the house and inform the relevant powers-that-be, usually resulting in a good roaring in my direction.

He became aware that tale-telling of this sort was likely to mean a severe lambasting for his elder brother and he began to maximise this vicarious power. On one occasion, because he had created so much parental gyp for me and I knew he had done so deliberately, I mentally snapped and chased him all over the estate with the express purpose of administering him a rigorous wedging. However, as he accelerated along Tay Road, I decided instead to upgrade the retribution and that I would simply kick his fucking head in. If I was going to cop it for supposedly picking on him, I decided that I may as well have my money's worth. The pursuit lasted for quite a distance until his eventual capture. I had my knees on his arms and was happily and repeatedly whacking him.

Unless he was about to bite me on the bollocks, his escape was impossible.

So he bit me on the bollocks. In later years I would play against some horribly dirty footballers, but would never scream like that again. Having effected his escape, Steven then (understandably in the circumstances) managed to beat me back to the house where his version of events meant that I was given a proper clip myself. Oh, the injustice.

Incidentally, my brother's name is Steven and not 'Stephen' as it says in just about every book that mentions him. They even gave the wrong spelling on *Pointless* a couple of years ago – and we expect better from them.

Anyway, while Steven was hardly a Sunderland fanatic, as I've said, I would attend matches as often as time and money would allow. I still do. The disappointment of watching Sunderland lose limply to Norwich City in the 1985 League Cup final is undiminished; ditto with the awful 1990 Wembley play-off final against Swindon, just three years before I became a Sunderland player myself.

Still, then as now there was the occasional glory day (sadly no trophies since the FA Cup win when I was four). My absolute idol as a kid was Gary Rowell. I just loved him. He was a lethal finisher, scoring over 100 goals for Sunderland including a hat-trick against Arsenal in 1982. But his most famous hat-trick was at St James' Park in 1979 and I was at the game, five weeks before my tenth birthday. I travelled on the football train with my dad, followed by a police escort up to the ground. I could describe a walk through the town with the natives lining the streets to sportingly applaud their Wearside cousins as they gave a rousing chorus of 'May the Best Team Win', but that would be a clunking great lie. It remains my most terrifying experience.

Rowell was particularly adept at penalties. If he was about to take one you could nip out to the toilet. You didn't need to watch because it was going to be a goal and the keeper was about to dive the wrong way. Unfortunately, a bad injury when he was twenty-two seemed to deprive him of some speed. He was still a fine striker when he came back, but he could have been better still with that extra touch of pace. Other inspirations included Shaun Elliott, Stan Cummins, the late Rob Hindmarch and the incomparable Joe Bolton; a talented left-back often described as 'uncompromising'. We all know what that means, but there was more to his game than that and he gave everything on the pitch – or 110 per cent as they say in dull society.

• • •

It was just as I was about to enter year three (first-year juniors in old money) that the Howeys tunnelled out of Gilley Law and defected to Thorney Close, a council estate a short distance away on the other side of Durham Road. This put Steven and me in a different primary school catchment area. We switched to St Cuthbert's on Grindon Lane as it was the nearest Catholic school (for we were a family of Rome). This is tough for any child, but I adapted quite well, helped by being friends with Vincent Marriner, who was already at the school (and a good goalie). As expected, football was a terrific icebreaker. I don't remember much about the early days, so it must have been OK.

St Cuthbert's has always had a big reputation for football. Apart from a couple of Howeys plus Messrs Dillon, Hazard and Harford, alumni also include Kevin Young, a midfielder for Burnley, Port Vale and Bury. The school continues to lift trophies, and these days that includes the girls.

It did not occur to me yet that I was all that good at football. My first break into the St Cuthbert's team only came about because, in a recurring theme of my life up to that point, someone had to go in goal. I just wanted to play and was willing to take any position on the field. My instinct in goal was to flick the ball with my foot up into my hands, rather than just catch it. The young teacher, Ray Stewart, asked me what the hell I thought I was doing, but soon realised that I was not really a goalie and allowed me to play outfield. Within a year I was playing for the first, second and third teams. I would play a game for one team, change strip and then play a game for another.

And I still played footy when I got home.

Mr Stewart was the main football teacher, although he was also obsessed with trains (or should that be locomotives? Or railways? That lot are easily offended, so I apologise if I have used the wrong terminology). He was gradually replacing the fourth-year juniors (year six, these days) teacher, Jimmie McAuliffe, as the main football bod. The teachers were quite strict but Mr McAuliffe was fine with me – when I wasn't in his class. Approaching his sixties by then, he once took me aside for some or other misdemeanour and informed me, with nothing like uncertainty: 'You had better stick in at your lessons because I'll tell you now: I've seen some players come through this school – and you will *never* make a footballer.'

This was a serious, humiliating, proverbial kick in the nuts, exacerbated by the ensuing laughter in the classroom. I was not a model pupil and he wanted to make a point. But what a way to do it. Aside from the fact that he turned out to be wrong, this was a hell of a thing to say to a child. Neither did it have any connection to whichever piece of arsing about he had caught me doing.

Perhaps he did me an inadvertent favour. The school had a game a couple of days later and I scored in it, so I thought 'bollocks to him' and continued with the rest of my life. Years later when I did make it in football I was tempted to contact him and stick the ancient incident right up his nose. But he was an old bloke by then and I thought: 'What would that achieve?' I'm glad I resisted the temptation as it would have been utterly childish and besides, he must have known. He died aged eighty-four in 2006.

I played on the right wing at St Cuthbert's because (and this may surprise a few who only remember me as a professional) I was extremely quick. Whether by nature or nurture, this was a primary school team that was almost freakishly skilful. Other players included Jonathan Common (known to this day as Archie for reasons that remain obscure), Paul Redman, Jonathan Whelan, Lee McNally, David Simpson and the aforementioned Vincent Marriner.

Between them they would be given trials and apprenticeships at a number of Football League clubs. There is a variety of explanations as to why none of them made it professionally, although absent among these reasons was a lack of talent. Paul Redman, for example, was academically gifted and always had more possibilities than just football. He is now head of media at FIFA Films in Zurich (their media arm; he had nothing to do with that bloody awful *United Passions* film with Tim Roth perplexingly cast as Sepp Blatter).

Until this time there was no more to my football than the sheer joy of playing it. However, if you are a member of a side that wins virtually every game and one of the best players in it, a certain realisation will come. I was rattling in many, many goals and was not even a main striker. It got to the point where Mr Stewart would ban us from shooting inside the penalty area, just to make a game of it against some of the weaker opposition. Goals from within the box were simply disallowed in those games. I was pretty confident too. The only issue at that stage was whether or not I was the best player at St Cuthbert's. Archie Common and I had a scuffle or two over the issue because it's a highly important matter at that age. Archie was a completely different type of player to me and one of the most naturally gifted teammates I ever had. As I would eventually play alongside Chris Waddle, this is not something I say lightly.

• • •

A year or so after it had dawned on me that I was a pretty good player, my dad had an epiphany in this regard too.

Anyone who loves football will tell you that a game will draw you in. Any game. You can be driving past a playing field that is staging a match between two flabby pub teams; the outcome of the match is not going to affect your future happiness and yet, if one team is awarded a corner or free kick, you are compelled to keep watching to see if it leads to a goal. It's that addictive.

So it was when Norman was strolling along Grindon Lane one summer's day, running a substantial risk of treading in dog shit because he was using his peripheral vision to watch a kids' game on an adjacent pitch. One lad controlled the ball beautifully from a high pass, beat several defenders and then stroked it into the bottom corner with the much coveted 'good touch for a big man'. Norman thought: 'Bloody hell. He can play.'

It was only after some additional squinting that he realised he was watching his eldest son. This was when football became significantly more serious in the Howey household. From that moment on, my father would do what he considered to be the best he possibly could to help me to become a footballer. He would later do the same for Steven. However, such were my dad's methods that the amount of help he ultimately provided is a matter of some conjecture.

A theory called the 10,000 Hour Rule has emerged in recent years stating that in any sphere of human activity, but especially sport, 10,000 hours of practice will produce expertise. You may feel that the premise is sheer flapdoodle, as there is usually at least one person in your class at school who is so uncoordinated that they would require something closer to a million hours just to have an outside chance of touching their own nose, let alone playing professional sport. Nevertheless, there is no doubting the value of work ethic, practice and dedication, and Norman's ideas were very much along those lines; constant hard work and football, football, football.

He had read biographies of the likes of Bobby Charlton and Brian Clough, which would outline their sheer devotion to the game when they were growing up in the '40s and '50s, spending hour upon hour kicking a ball against a wall with either foot. It clearly hadn't done either of them any harm and so my dad saw that as the way forward. Therefore all my spare time was used at his behest to practise, practise, practise.

I maintain that a twelve-year-old can only kick a ball against a wall for so long before the benefits, as well as the brain, become nullified. My friends had other things in their lives that they invited me to become involved with, such as playing space invaders, chasing girls, watching *The Young Ones* and other invaluable enterprises. But I declined to join them as I had to plod on with practice to avert a strenuous shouting at and/or bedroom banishment when I returned home. This rendered me as something of an outsider among my peers; someone out of the clique. Similar reprisals would occur if Norman thought I had in any way shirked during a match, the theme being that I had let him down and what was I thinking of – that sort of approach. He was extremely vociferous on the touchline, and not just with me. He would also holler at the referee and other spectators. If another parent said anything untoward about me, he would limber up for a fight.

My mates thought he was great. They loved his enthusiasm. If I had performed well then he was pleasant to be with, but my mates weren't in our house an hour after a game when I was being energetically berated if I had played indifferently. The pressure at times was intense. I didn't necessarily have to score or be man of the match, but Norman demanded maximum effort, and my being a mere child with the attendant physical difficulties of growing was never going to be any reason to fail to try my hardest.

I did not therefore always have the greatest fun playing football as a schoolboy under this regime – and I use the word advisedly. But there was a pay-off that came years later. No matter how aggressive, scathing or downright unreasonable a coach was being towards me, at any level I played at, it was water off the wildfowl of your choice. At youth level, other lads would pack in and go home, but not me. Sticks and stones and the occasional two-footed lunge may break your bones; name-calling, however, had long ceased to have any effect. At least I eventually got to have insults screamed at me by professional coaches, and Norman's role in this is not to be underestimated. He had correctly identified something

15

that Jimmie McAuliffe hadn't. It was difficult growing up in these circumstances, but it was not without its rewards.

He wasn't so tough on my brother. He would play with Steven more himself, practising shots and crosses with another kid and his dad, which looked far more like fun to me, whereas I was expected to do my stuff alone. Perhaps his experiences with me had encouraged him to adopt a slightly different approach.

Norman was a big strong bloke and it would be some years before I showed anything like rebellion. When I was eleven, I watched him play in a Sunday league game. He'd had a tussle with an opponent, so he waited until everyone's attention was diverted by another incident that the referee was dealing with, upon which he seized his opportunity to punch his unfortunate adversary clean out. The poor chap then rolled silently down an adjacent bank. Had the man ended the incident in a water trough it would have been very much along the lines of a fight featuring Clint Eastwood or John Wayne.

My dad then jogged nonchalantly back to position to carry on the game before anyone else had even noticed. Tough with me though he was, he was not in the habit of punching his offspring. But the incident reinforced that he was not a father whose will was to be lightly ignored. The downside of this for Norman's own football was that he gathered a reputation, justly as it happens, as someone who could be easily aggravated into earning a red card. His fuse on the football field was not so much short as barely discernible.

That was how he wanted me to play, but I was never like him in that regard. They could kick me if they pleased. I was nowhere near soft, but I was by then a centre-forward and I extracted justice by inserting the ball into the net, whereas my dad wanted me to thump people. He would ask why I hadn't smashed a defender who had been overly physical and I would reply: 'I scored two goals.' The physical side of my game would develop at professional clubs – as you will see.

I must reiterate. He did help, but not as much as he had intended. He did everything he thought was beneficial and had an enormous knowledge of football. It's just that it all instilled in me a fear of failure in my performance, something I still feel today in a separate career in an entirely different industry. Before playing in Sunderland games I would feel physically sick and wouldn't be able to feel my legs. My first time in the starting XI was at Derby County in 1993. I was wrung out and could barely walk onto the pitch at the old Baseball Ground for a match that we would lose 5–0. I'm considerably better read now and I firmly believe that these anxiety issues go back an awfully long way.

By the time I was at Sunderland, Norman had mellowed and was more of a mate than he had been previously. Then we could discuss football more rationally. We still can. There isn't a problem – now. He always meant well and I won't allow anyone to speak ill of my dad.

• • •

Divine intervention may have played a part in St Cuthbert's success.

In the late 1970s my Uncle Tom was working as a joiner in Warsaw. He had done an initial six-week stint before two weeks' leave back in Blighty. Prior to his return to Poland we had a discussion about football boots. He made me stand in the kitchen on a sheet of paper in my stockinged feet and drew around them with a felt tip. He then took the piece of paper back to Poland where he said he could have a first-rate pair of boots knocked up for me by a local shoemaker for a fraction of what they would cost in the UK. The modern reader may be shocked to learn that in those days, we Brits had no compunction about utilising cheap Polish labour, but it did happen.

In September 1978 Pope John Paul I died after just thirty-three days in the job (bear with me, it's all connected). Following a three-day interview in the Sistine Chapel, he was replaced by Karol Wojtyła (himself a decent goalkeeper back in the day),who gave himself the papal name of John Paul II, thereby disappointing the waggish element of Thorney Close who had mooted the possibility of a John Paul being succeeded by a George Ringo. John Paul II was the first non-Italian pope since 1523. He was Polish and his second official visit as pope outside of Italy was to his native land. He arrived there in the summer of 1979 with the express intention of meeting up with Tom Howey for a few jars. It didn't take long for the Pope to track him down and when he did, Uncle Tom asked his Holiness to sanctify my new boots. The story went something like that anyway; the boot blessing part is certainly true. I would like to say that following this blessing I went on to score my hundredth goal of the season before 70,000 fans at Wembley Stadium.

And I did.

In 1980, St Cuthbert's was one of four teams to reach the finals of a national six-a-side tournament run by Smith's Crisps; sport and junk food have always had this symbiotic relationship. The games were played across the Wembley pitch on Saturday 7 June. Mr Stewart's coaching skills had guided us there and he was justifiably very proud. Such were the financial constraints that we travelled to London by bus. Had we gone by steam train I suspect it would have been the pinnacle of his entire life.

We were a sort of support act to an England–Scotland schoolboy international (a great game, which featured Paul McStay, Alistair Dick and Paul Rideout, who scored a screamer to complete a hat-trick for England, although Scotland won 5–4). Our semi-final was a 2–0 win over a southern team, with goals from Archie and me. We lost the final 2–1 to a school from Manchester, but I scored in that game too and the goal was my hundredth of the season, from the right boot of the pair blessed by the Pope the previous year. I never wore them again, although I still have them, replete with decaying blades of decades-old Wembley grass.

One in the eye for Professor Richard Dawkins there then. Thirty-three years after we played at Wembley, Sunderland were bottom of the Premier League with one point from their first eight games, when Pope Francis was photographed in St Peter's Square holding an SAFC home shirt. Two days later Sunderland beat Newcastle and went on to avoid relegation, as well as reach the League Cup final. If that, along with the tale of my old boots, doesn't dispense with atheism, then I don't know what will.

• • •

I left primary school on a high. In my last year at St Cuthbert's we won everything, and I scored 109 times. I then trotted off to comprehensive school, the all-boys St Aidan's RC Secondary. My first year of 1980–81 was spent at a place called Havelock, three miles from the rest of the school. For some reason, everyone had a much worse time at Havelock than at the main section. Mine was the last year to be educated there, which was excellent news for the lads in the year below. Should you find my description of the place to be somehow lacking, pop on a DVD of *The Shawshank Redemption* and you'll get the broad idea. If you're still not sure, then nip down to the library and borrow a copy of *Lord of the Flies*. If that doesn't do the trick, just punch yourself.

Havelock was dirty and brutal. There was just something about that place, the building and the atmosphere, that was worse than the main part of the school in Ashbrooke. It was so manky that I thought it should have been napalmed, but as the years passed I decided that that would have been too agreeable a fate. Violence was institutional. St Aidan's was then run by the Congregation of Christian Brothers and their accompanying loving tenderness.

They weren't all bad, but one of them, whose name my memory has refused to store, was a total sadist. He had two main hobbies: scripture recital and corporal punishment. There are passages in two of the gospels that say 'Suffer little children'. This bloke had clearly misinterpreted them. I recall Brother O'Twatt, or whatever his name was, dragging one David Leonard by the hair over several desks as a light-hearted prelude to kicking his head in. The same bloke would jump from a chair when administering a leather strap in order to gain more purchase, because obviously you just can't hit an eleven-year-old child hard enough. He left soon after his assault on David Leonard, possibly transferred before he could be prosecuted. This was sad in a way, as he would never be able to take a class of kids with Steven in it. There was another teacher called Weston, a nasty piece of work who never quite grasped the distinction between discipline and recreational bullying. It isn't simply a case of 'They couldn't do that now' – they really weren't supposed to do it then either.

As ever, a respite from life's unpleasantries came from football. I had no difficulty in making the school team. St Aidan's has always won a good portion of trophies and is proud of its achievements in sport. The fact that it was an all-boys school and therefore had double the number of players from which to choose is something they tend not to refer to. But our year did have a very good side. We had a choice between two great goalies in Vincent Marriner and Eddie Harrison (who might have made it had he been slightly taller, although he did go on to play in an England firemen's XI). Outfielders included Archie, Gavin Ledwith, David Simpson, Damian Adamson, James Duncan and Mickey Robinson, who eventually played for Darlington.

The team coach was Damian's dad, a gifted maths teacher called Tony Adamson who once sent Damian off for overuse of the mouth. In contradistinction to certain colleagues of his, the expression 'laid-back' does not provide a sufficiently accurate description of Mr Adamson, who would smoke fags in the classroom while he was teaching.

On colder days he would referee our matches from the interior of his car, parking his light blue hatchback at the side of the pitch. Assuming he could still see the game through a fug of cigarette smoke, he would toot his horn to signify a free kick and use the indicators to denote which team had received it. And he was still a better referee than Andre Marriner. Mr Adamson's officiation of matches from behind the wheel of a stationary 1975 Austin Princess did not strike anyone at the time as peculiar or even worthy of comment. I have to say now that despite all the goals and the trophies we won, this is one of my greatest memories of school football.

Another great memory is of setting a record that I believe still stands. When I was fifteen, we played the nearby Southmoor School. We won 10–2 and I scored all ten of our goals, five in each half, and even made the back page of the *Sunderland Echo* on the strength of it. I was marked that day by Philip Coxall, who was centre-half for England schoolboys. He got so pissed off at 8–0 that he went up front and scored their two. Scoring ten is an unusual occurrence at any level of football, and in case you were wondering, I can tell you that the tenth felt as good as the first. I loved scoring goals.

My dad wasn't there.

• • •

For our second year at St Aidan's, 1981–82, we were moved from Stalag Havelock to the more salubrious setting of Ashbrooke, where we continued to play football at every given opportunity. As soon as our lunches had gone south, we would charge into the yard and immediately divide into pairs, with all five or six pairs attacking the same goalkeeper (usually Vincent Marriner), but with each twosome for themselves. Now in our teens, we began to take an interest in fashion and made such assiduous efforts to be individuals that we all looked exactly the same. Fans of Madness one and all, we wore Fred Perry T-shirts, Farah trousers, white socks and black brogues with steel segs. It soon became apparent that black brogues with steel segs were not conducive to playing football in a concrete yard.

Like millions of dads, mine was on the dole for much of that decade, so my own brogues were the best that my mother's Providence cheque could purchase from a particular shop where such currency was accepted. Not a first-division pair. However, they were still as perilous as any other brogues when playing football. Brogues must have been the biggest cause of football injuries in the 1980s (although I suppose we should be grateful that we were not five years older, because playing football in platform shoes must have been positively lethal). An informal ban was therefore agreed among ourselves; trainers only for football. The universal trainer of choice was Dunlop Green Flash – so we were still all dressed identically. From then on, yard football was played alongside an extensive line of gleaming brogues that had been dutifully removed in the interests of our general wellbeing. It was an eminently sensible piece of schoolboy self-governance. These days they would contact the Health & Safety Executive.

As well as representing the school, I played for a Sunday team called Blackthorn for a couple of years. In the first year, the team was run by a gentleman called Ray Lindstedt. In the second year, the team was run by a gentleman called Norman Howey.

Those of you who have been paying attention will have guessed that I was not wholeheartedly pleased with the appointment of the latter. He was his usual exacting self; more so because I was the best player on the team.

I was responsible for taking free kicks, throw-ins, corners, penalties and was the main goal scorer. Because he did not go so far as to expect me to head in goals from my own corners, Norman thought that his demands upon me were wholly reasonable, but he was shovelling on even more pressure than usual. I have a glaring memory of eliciting his fury by missing a penalty; over the bar during a 1–0 defeat. This was not, to put it mildly, a pleasant afternoon. We didn't have a car then, but were given a lift home by one of the other dads. The silence in that car was an ominous prelude to the sonic bollocking I was about to receive in the house. It was tough love.

For obvious reasons, the following season I went off to play for another Sunday team called Moorside, where I was up front with Clive Mendonca, who would haunt his home town club with a hat-trick in the extraordinary 1998 play-off final between Charlton and Sunderland. Another teammate was Gary Coatsworth, who later joined Barnsley, Darlington and Leicester City.

In 1998 the BBC broadcast a famous fly-on-the-wall documentary about Sunderland AFC called *Premier Passions*, which I featured in. It is probably best remembered for the ranting of the manager, Peter Reid, when things were going badly as we fought in vain to keep the club in the Premier League. There were often similar scenes in our house in Tintagel Close.

Peter Reid was a professional doing a high-pressure job in a multi-million-pound industry. Blackthorn was a kids' Sunday team. But Norman did not make that distinction because he took all football extremely seriously. However, like Mr Reid, he would also give effusive praise if he thought it was merited. I say yet again – he always did what he thought was best and, despite my misgivings, both of his sons would become professional footballers. So who was right?

CHAPTER 2

IPSWICH

Some very good schoolboy footballers of my age were based in and around Sunderland. Those who remember the town at that time (it became a city in 1992) may recall the names of – with apologies to anyone I may have missed out – Philip Coxall, Archie Common, David Pringle, Paul Redman, Gary Breeds (another England youth player), Neil Foster, Ian Dipper, Mickey Robinson, Grant Brown and Clive Mendonca, with Richard Ord a few miles down the A19 in Murton.

Although they were all tipped to become professionals, only Brown (Leicester and Lincoln City), Mendonca (Charlton Athletic, Rotherham and Grimsby), Ord (Sunderland) and I would properly make it. Some of the others became apprentices and Mickey Robinson did play once in the Football League for Darlington. Ian Dipper is now a respected kids' coach. But the overall story of that bag of players is quite typical. The moral is that the chances of making a living from the game are minimal. Despite this, there will never be a shortage of lads who assume that they will rise to the top because they are a cut above on the football pitch as teenagers. Oh, life.

When I was fourteen, I trained with the younger players at Sunderland, who then included Gary Owers and Gordon Armstrong. The manager of the time was Alan Durban, but we were coached by George Herd, a former Sunderland inside-forward who also played for Scotland. He was a great man (still is, now in his eighties), a wonderful coach with infectious enthusiasm and a tremendous player. He was then nudging fifty years of age, but was doing stuff with a ball that we could only watch with slack-jawed admiration.

However – allow me to indulge in a cliché here – a dream come true was not to be. I was not physically prepossessing at that stage; on the lanky side and with the added disadvantage of still developing bodily. I was also, relative to other players, not quite as quick as I had been. George took me to one side and informed me that they had just signed a lad who lived in Newcastle. I don't recall the name of the fellow in question, but he was ginormous, about 6ft 7in. He was in the Andy Carroll mould without being anywhere near as good (think of the Honey Monster, only slightly better at set-pieces), but he was deemed good enough for me to be offloaded. They could only offer terms to seven kids and it seemed that I was the eighth. The gist of it was: 'We've got our centre-forward and it isn't you. Off you pop then, there's a good chap.' Devastated is the *mot juste*.

Several weeks later I received a call from Newcastle United, asking if I wanted to try my luck there. At the behest of the youth coach Colin Suggett (the same bloke who scored for Sunderland against Newcastle ten days before I was born), I had deigned to train with them a few times during the summer.

Jack Charlton was the manager, but more memorable was the presence of a young Paul Gascoigne who was two years older than me.

Only six years later, the World Cup would make him globally famous and recognised as arguably the most naturally gifted footballer on the planet. At Benwell in 1984 he was far better known as a pain in the arse. He was a dumpy little right-back and the professionals at the club couldn't stand him. He had a bit of skill but didn't seem like anything out of the ordinary (other than being visibly off his onion), yet that wouldn't prevent him from throwing buckets of ice into the communal bath. At least *he* thought it was funny.

My time at Newcastle came to nothing, although I did play one game. I insisted on wearing a T-shirt beneath the strip (difficult to remember now, but I believe they play in black and white stripes or whatever). I never usually wore a T-shirt, but wearing a Newcastle strip directly against your skin results in burns, cutaneous disease, hives, leprosy, cryptosporidiosis and nob-rot. It's a well-known medical fact. Still, I played well in that game and was soon afterwards telephoned by John Carruthers, who was scouting for Ipswich Town. I was about to be given my first big break in football.

During the Easter holidays, John would run a minibus to Suffolk, packed with youngsters from Scotland and the north of England. Just turned fifteen, I was off to participate in three trial matches, plus another one in the gym. These were North v South affairs and were not exactly played in the Corinthian spirit. My word, it was vicious. My dad would have loved it. I was marked by a lad called Danny Mayhew, a nice fellow as it turned out. He would also be given a contract, but only after I had smashed him all over the pitch during the trials.

I was determined to get to every ball possible and, in common with everyone else there, was not especially scrupulous as to how I would achieve this. (Danny never made it as a footballer, but he did become the *Clothes Show* Model of the Year for 1990.) The North would tend to gain the upper hand during the sporadic mass brawls and I have to confess that I loved it; the real physicality of it. More importantly, I played well and the coaching staff were impressed. They included the youth team coach Peter Trevivean, assistant manager Charlie Woods (a former Ipswich and Newcastle player) and the club's reserve team coach and physio, Brian Owen.

Bobby Ferguson was Ipswich Town's manager. He sat me down and said: 'I like what I'm seeing, son. I want you to sign for us.'

Younger readers may not realise what a big deal Ipswich were in 1984. They were never a massive club, but were certainly at that time a big team.

Bobby Robson had left the club two years earlier to become manager of England. They had peaked, but remained a well established top-flight club and they still had the remnants of that great 1981 UEFA Cup winning side. These were the days when the UEFA Cup was worth winning, and lifting that trophy meant you were one of the best teams in Europe. That same season, they perhaps should have been champions of England but were ultimately squeezed out by Aston Villa (in the last season of two points for a win). George Burley, Russell Osman, Terry Butcher, Paul Cooper, Steve McCall, Ian Atkins, Mich d'Avray and Eric Gates were all still around when I arrived. Recent departees included John Wark, Frans Thijssen, Arnold Mühren, Paul Mariner and Alan Brazil.

When I was offered that contract I was so happy I almost cried. I went home, returned to East Anglia with my parents shortly afterwards and signed the forms.

You can imagine what this did for my schoolwork. At the time we had the old O Levels, which were similar to GCSEs, but difficult. I was put in for eleven O Levels and passed English language, maths and economics: the only subjects that I personally did not need to revise for (I have always been interested in economics and how the world works).

So I attained three O Levels, or to put it another way, almost ten. To explain, I got seven D grades (plus a U in biology, from which I gleaned some inverted pride, as I didn't like the teacher). They would have been Cs or better and therefore passes had I been sufficiently interested – but I wasn't. Never the most diligent student in the first place, with a year remaining at school I was told that I was going to be an apprentice at a First Division football club and the result was that my already negligible interest waned further. The standard of my homework became ever flimsier and exams were simply not as important to me as footy.

Fortunately, the long-term consequences of this were not as disastrous as they have been for many others who wrongly thought: 'I'm sorted.'

Like most people, I do not curl up of an evening with *A Brief History of Time*. But being distracted by impending professional football as a teenager does not make me a thicky. The notion that *all* footballers are stupid is in itself just that – stupid. The idea that anyone with a facility for kicking a ball must by definition be unintelligent, has as much credence as claiming that every person who is left-handed, or 5ft 7in., or good at shorthand is unintelligent too. The division of footballers into categories such as 'very intelligent', 'quite intelligent' and so on, all the way down to 'would rather have the dog on my quiz team', is identical to that of the rest of society.

My situation was typical. I was too obsessed with the game to take my studies seriously. I was then thrown into an all-male environment with a lot of other working-class lads who were all determined to become footballers. How educated did anyone expect us to become? This applies even more so today when Premier League players can become millionaires before they reach twenty. What would you be doing in their situation? Enrolling in a philosophy degree at the Open University, or whooping it up?

The public's low estimation of footballers' intellect has been compounded in recent years by the absurd ranting of Joey Barton in his badly worded, badly spelled, badly punctuated and badly thought-out Tweets, attempting to pass himself off as an intellectual because he can cut and paste quotes from Nietzsche. Like a dog that thinks it's human, Joey actually believes himself intelligent, and was not even disabused of this notion after making a complete tit of himself on *Question Time*.

But please, please do not confuse 'uneducated' with 'unintelligent'. I can assure you that I and many other players have read a book or two since leaving school.

• • •

On Monday 15 July 1985, two days after Live Aid, I was packed off to start a new life at Ipswich Town FC.

I travelled by train with Neil Emmerson from Gateshead and, happily, a friend of mine from St Aidan's called Martin Young, who was a goalkeeper (years later I saw him while he was working as an undercover policeman, attempting to infiltrate a gang of football hooligans in Sunderland city centre. I didn't realise he was in disguise and almost inadvertently ruined the operation by greeting him warmly, slapping him on the back and calling him audibly by his first name in the middle of a bustling John Street. It can't have been much of a disguise).

When I arrived I met Danny Olson from Whitley Bay and another gentleman of my acquaintance from the North East known as Toast, who was a year ahead of me and would play for the first team a few times. His real name was Chris O'Donnell; a perfectly serviceable name if you ask me, so I have no idea why he was called Toast. A few familiar faces in a new environment will usually help, even if they do have silly names.

Apprentices a year or two ahead of me and on the verge of the first team included Craig Forrest from British Columbia, who would play over 300 games in goal for the club and fifty-six times for Canada. There was also Michael Cole, who made it at Ipswich and Fulham. I shall return shortly to some of the other star apprentices, although not for the best of reasons.

Being transported to a smaller town at the age of sixteen, almost 300 miles from home and away from familiar surroundings for the first time, is never easy; certainly not to begin with. This is before considering the regime I lived under at Ipswich. On my first day I arrived at Portman Road in the morning, was introduced to all the relevant people and, along with all the other newbies, was assigned my digs. The club didn't own a hostel or any other accommodation; they just asked people in the area if they would be willing to take in a young footballer. This may sound distinctly dodgy in the present era, but that was how it worked – rather like the Sorting Hat at Hogwarts.

I was lucky. I was taken in by a lovely couple called Roy and Steph. Roy was a director at Ransomes, the turf care equipment company and club sponsor (in 2013 they developed the first triplex mini flail mower, straight up). The club paid for my £40 per week accommodation which included breakfast, evening meals and as much lawnmower oil as I could drink.

We had to arrange our own lunches and, being teenagers, we ate exactly the same meal every day for two years. After training we would file into the club cafe in the Portman Stand called the Centre Spot, where I would guzzle two slices of toast, a tin of beans with cheese on top and brown sauce, washed down with blackcurrant and soda water. Food of the gods – although I wouldn't like to say in which mythology.

Football's performance nutritionists of today would have a coronary thinking about this meal, let alone eating it every day for two years. However, its lack of dietetic advantages had to be considered against the fact that it only cost a quid – and I was on £25 per week in my first year, although this later soared to £27.50. There was no chance of any money arriving from home. My dad was still unemployed so the Red Cross was more likely to oblige. I therefore had to be somewhat elastic with my income. Still, I rather enjoyed my lunches in that cafe and, if you are ever in Suffolk and should wish to whisk that special someone off for two slices of toast, a tin of beans with cheese on top and brown sauce, washed down with blackcurrant and soda water, I know just the place.

Cancel that. My research has just revealed that they converted the Centre Spot into Ipswich's hall of fame in 2013. Philistines. They paved paradise...

The combined joy of football and *haute cuisine* aside, it was still the case that I was a far-from-home youngster in an alien environment, not well remunerated and with a physically demanding job that was overseen by disciplinarians. The question is later asked of anyone in such circumstances: Were such difficulties insuperable and did you miss home life and your affectionate family? In my case the answer is a complex one that I can only attempt to explain to the reader; an answer to be gamely attempted and hopefully accomplished in the next paragraph.

No.

I loved being away from home and from Norman in particular. Harsh, but true. For me, being in Ipswich wasn't only about the football. Dad wasn't just strict about my development as a player; he was also a stickler about what time I should be home and a raft of other issues. Again, he did me a favour in the longer term because it made me strict with myself about fitness, sleep and not socialising too much. But the fact that I now had the *freedom* to do things, even things I had absolutely no intention of doing, felt wonderful.

I didn't often socialise as a teenager in Sunderland. Occasionally I would put on my little leather tie and frequent a local dump-o-teque called Genevieve's in Monkwearmouth (finally demolished in 2012 and replaced by another eyesore called Tesco), but that was about it.

Ipswich had less than half the population of Sunderland. Life was quieter there. But we still made the occasional sortie into the local fleshpots. One early expedition I was invited to came when I had been there for about three weeks. It was at the instigation of the first team, including Paul Cooper and Terry Butcher. Still only sixteen, but with no difficulty in being served because of my height, we descended upon the impossibly upmarket Butt's wine bar.

All I had ever drunk during my limited boozing career back home was Lorimer's Best Scotch, the cheapest draught beer in the pubs. This was not available in Suffolk, but I wasn't about to abandon the pretence that I was actually quite grown up, so I let someone buy me a lager; which I didn't like. I therefore graduated to wine, namely the infamous sweet plonk Liebfraumilch, which means 'beloved lady's milk' in German.

It wasn't beloved by me and rumours of how it could open the sluices at both ends of a man did not endear it any further. It was manky. As the only step down the wine list would probably have been Castrol GTX, I moved on to Southern Comfort and lemonade. This seemed OK, but by this stage I was becoming wary; not because of the alcohol intake, but because I had now spent about three quid and was thinking of the affordability for the rest of the week of my two slices of toast, tin of beans with cheese on top and brown sauce, washed down with blackcurrant and soda water.

We then trooped round to the First Floor Club in Tacket Street, one of Ipswich's two nightclubs (sadly the First Floor Club was mainly patronised by white people, the other club by black). We were given a concession pass for free admission any time we wanted, which was handy for someone on twenty-five quid a week. They didn't bother asking us for tiresome, irrelevant details, such as our dates of birth.

• • •

Most days began with a 25-minute walk from my digs to report for training by 9 a.m., along Norwich Road, past the Broomhill outdoor swimming pool (yes, Ipswich had a lido). Training was at Portman Road because there was no training ground as such. There was a pitch behind one of the stands, not far from the River Orwell (from which the writer Eric Blair took his pen name of George Orwell, fact fans).

We had to put out all the kits, clean the boots for the next day's training, then carry out a variety of menial tasks that were overseen by Trevor Kirton, who was the kit manager, stadium manager, club driver, chief bottle washer and whatever else had been lobbed in his general direction. Time permitting, we would have a go on the weights because we had to be on the pitch for 10 a.m.

The first six weeks of pre-season training were a shock to the system. It wasn't football training, it was circuit training. We rarely saw a ball. I was a fit young fellow and I still found it to be hell. My blisters were severely affected by blisters. What felt like infinite running was only interspersed with rigorous exercise and accompanied by what is known in the armed forces as 'beasting', although the SAS themselves would have been in no condition to go about the place storming embassies after a morning like that.

These sessions were horrible from their beginning, but they would end with 'five-four-three-two-one'. This entailed running on a 400m track at the police headquarters. We would be split into two groups; the first group would set off doing five laps and if any one of these laps took more than ninety seconds, a thorough hammering would ensue. My group would meanwhile be performing press-ups, sit-ups, squat thrusts and so on. When the first group came back and rested, we had to run five laps under the same rules, then the first group would do four laps before another swap with us, then three, two, one. The last lap had to be done in under a minute. There were variants of this, but a severe bollocking was a permanent feature.

It was home from home for me. But not for certain others who

were miserable with the constant berating as well as homesickness
– and packed it in. I don't know if apprentices still undergo a regi-
men of this nature. The Geneva Convention may have put paid to
it. But if you want to be a footballer…

• • •

Once that few weeks of pure barbarism had elapsed, we finally had
a few practice matches. The first team had a friendly coming up,
so the youth team was bibbed up and given a game against them.
I was marked by Terry Butcher himself, the Ipswich and England
captain (assuming Bryan Robson was injured, which he usually
was). Our full-back launched a high diagonal ball with Terry and
me beneath it. I was being nurtured as a physical centre-forward,
but I overdid it by several degrees when I walloped our leader in
the mush with the back of my arm as we jumped.

He was lying on the ground, his anger developing further by
the laughter that greeted the sight of the club's most senior professional being flattened by a sixteen-year-old trainee, who was now
receiving encouraging, high-spirited shouts of 'Give him it, son!'
and other ill-founded advice. Norman would have exploded with
pride had he been there.

Butch rose silently and ominously to his feet, without relent-
ing from the glare he was giving me. I swallowed hard. Those of
you familiar with the opening scene in *A Clockwork Orange* will
understand what that glare was like. The physical 'dual' became
notably more one-sided after that. For the remainder of that game
he kicked me so, so hard at every opportunity, leaving me with no
illusions as to who was boss. His retribution was carried out before
the full glare of the coaching staff, so I wondered nervously what
he had in store for me when the game was over and they weren't
looking.

As it turned out, nothing. It was simply not an issue, because if ever there was a man who relished the tougher side of football, then it was Terry Butcher. However, the consequences for me of the misguided ploat I had administered to him would be protracted, deep – and positive. He appreciated (if that's the right word) my physicality and remembered it when he became manager of Sunderland in 1993. He gave me the opportunity to join the club I loved most from complete obscurity. I hesitate to advocate to the apprentices of today the delivery of an elbow into the kisser of the England captain as a prudent career move, but it didn't do me any harm in the long term. The harm to my shins in the short term would prove to be worth it.

For that was my job. I was what is often described as a 'traditional English centre-forward', meaning that I would never allow a defender to take me lightly, even if I could not undo him with sublime skill. This meant clattering people. Preferably legally, but let's not be naive. It was and is sometimes done illegally too.

This might mean doing something that the referee couldn't see, or ever so slightly delaying a tackle so he couldn't be sure that it was deliberately late. I might be ready for the opposition to kick off the match, upon which they would invariably pass the ball to a full-back who would then release the ball down the line. I would go across the full-back with studs up, but I wouldn't kick him; he would kick me on the sole of my boot, meaning that the top of his foot would zestfully meet my studs. Painful – for him. Then as now, referees grant unofficial immunity to fouls in the very early stages of a game and it allowed me to make an immediate impact; a statement of intent. The philosophy was not unique to me. As the New Testament suggests, I did unto others as they would have done unto me.

But my game was not exclusively about mangling opponents. I was developing as a player and scoring a fair few goals; still gangly but developing and often playing against lads who were years older than me, which mattered greatly at the age I was. It was obviously a different level of football compared to playing for the school and town, scoring literally hundreds of goals with Clive Mendonca, almost the only striker I had encountered who was as good as me. Occasionally I would be struck by the old anxieties, but would disregard them in favour of just doing my best, giving it a whirl and learning all that I could about the professional game, which at Ipswich Town was a considerable amount.

•   •   •

Our last match before Christmas in my first year was away to Southend United on 21 December. We weren't allowed to play at Roots Hall, but we changed there and were minibussed to and from the pitch we did use. After the game, which we lost 2–0, Neil Emmerson, Martin Young and I were milling around outside Roots Hall. We were about to make our way back to the North East for Christmas and working out the walking route to the railway station when we heard a shout from behind.

'What are you waiting for, lads?' We turned round.

Oh my God – and it very nearly was.

Bobby Moore stood before us. 'Star struck' might be a hackneyed expression, but there is no better way to describe the moment. The man we had seen in all those famous, famous images from 1966 was addressing *us*. Our powers of speech were momentarily in retreat, but between us we managed to explain. He smiled.

'Come with me. I'll ring you a taxi.'

Mr Moore was in charge of Southend at the time. We followed him to his office where he rang the cab. While we were waiting for it he asked us about ourselves, what positions we played, where we were from, what we wanted out of life and football generally. He seemed to take a genuine interest. We answered him politely and eagerly, but our solitary collective thought was: '*It's Bobby Moore! It's Bobby Moore! It's Bobby Moore!...*' All too soon the taxi arrived and we said our thank yous and goodbyes. When it pulled away we sat in complete silence, still unable to comprehend what had just happened.

That was my sole and brief experience of the great man and it only reinforced the general opinion of him: that he was a true gentleman. All these years later I remain thrilled at the thought of that chance meeting.

• • •

Matches were usually played on a Saturday morning except for ties in the glamorously named Floodlit Cup which, as the name would suggest, were played during evenings. These fixtures were often against some of southern England's best youth teams such as Arsenal, Tottenham and Chelsea. A good many opponents would become very well known in football: Paul Merson and Kevin Campbell were playing for Arsenal, the Holdsworth twins David and Dean plus David James were at Watford. Gareth Hall was at Chelsea.

Another opponent who would achieve fame was an incorrigible gobshite called Neil Ruddock, who, for whatever reason, became known by the *nom de guerre* Razor Ruddock after the Canadian heavyweight boxer ... er ... Razor Ruddock.

Neil was one of those people who, to his credit, managed to locate a charisma in himself that no one else could ever find. A year older than me, he began his career at Millwall for whom he was marking me one evening when, oddly enough, we had something of a physical tussle; although his jaw was being exercised far more than any other part of his anatomy, boasting about how he would soon be off to Tottenham to earn a million pounds an hour, etcetera, etcetera. I was rather more laconic (everyone was) and replied by exchanging with him a succession of thumps. We were successfully irritating each other in the second half when a corner was awarded to Ipswich. During an aerial challenge when the corner was delivered, I took the opportunity to elbow him in the back of the head, which felt good. To me, anyway. But I fell down on my side when I landed. Retaliation came in the form of a full-blooded, far-from-surreptitious boot up the arse. I'd had the foresight to commit my crime away from the eyes of the officials. Evidently, such indemnity had not occurred to Neil.

He was instantly sent off, but as he marched furiously from the pitch he snarled at me: 'You might have ruined my fucking career.' Always at the ready with a pithy rejoinder, I told him to fuck off.

I really shouldn't have elbowed him. It wasn't pleasant but it was only a clout on the back of the head. It wasn't one of those retina-threatening jobs. The ensuing kick up the arse I can accept, but it was something of an overreaction to say that I had put his career in jeopardy; it can't have hurt *that* much.

He went on to have a very good career at Southampton, Spurs, Liverpool and other clubs, as well as winning an England cap. But latterly his calling has been for television. Apparently he has spread his wings into acting and, according to the International Movie Database, appears in a crime drama called *The Middle Man* – in which he has extended his range by playing a character called Razor who takes no shit from anybody. No way.

And just think, if I really had finished him as a footballer, the wider world would never have known the edification he provided when eating a wallaby's knackers or whatever he did on *I'm a Celebrity... Get Me Out of Here!* In recent years he has also been seen on *Celebrity Big Brother*, *Who's Doing the Dishes?* and *Can't Pay?*

We'll Take It Away, where he entertained the public by arguing in the street with High Court enforcement agents over a £3,000 debt to a company that had kennelled his dogs.

Who knows? He may even do *Flockstars* one day, or become the face of Liebfraumilch. It's what we all dreamed of when we played football in the streets as children, so I'm glad he was all right.

• • •

A year ahead of me when I arrived at Ipswich, and therefore a second year apprentice, was Dalian Atkinson; a fine striker for the club who also made a mark at Sheffield Wednesday, Real Sociedad, Fenerbahçe and Aston Villa. He is fondly remembered at Villa for his goal and performance in the 3–1 win against Manchester United in the 1994 League Cup final, as well as scoring one of the Premier League's best ever goals, against Wimbledon in 1992.

Dalian and I had a contretemps which I am hideously embarrassed about to this day, although at the time I was completely unaware that I had said anything that was even particularly offensive. In its own way it's an interesting little piece of social history, but it still curls my toes.

A few months into my apprenticeship, Dalian and I had a fight – a humdinger, proper fisticuffs. It had fomented in the dressing room but, as per an unwritten rule, was carried out in the drying room. It started because my job was to make sure the away dressing room at Portman Road where we apprentices changed for training was in an acceptable condition. Memories of what started the fight are now vague, but Dalian was probably preventing me from completing my chores by taking his time, titivating his hair and generally trying my patience. I lost my loaf and whacked him, whereupon the festivities commenced. We eventually wore ourselves out, our exertion heightened by the heat in there – it was like spending an afternoon at gas mark five – and we stopped.

When we had calmed down slightly he asked me pointedly: 'Why did you call me a black bastard?'

That was not what had instigated the fight, but was indeed what I had called him. Yet I was genuinely befuddled by his question and replied that he was black and was being a bastard – so why was he so offended? This was how unworldly I was. I had no concept of having been racist. It had to be explained to me that it was utterly unacceptable to call someone a black bastard, or indeed a black anything. It seemed peculiar to me then that had I called him a stupid bastard, a selfish bastard, or merely a bastard, then there would not have been an issue.

Usually there would be six or seven black lads (who were all furious at me that day) in the same changing room as me, including Dalian, Jason Dozzell and Michael Cole. Still my ignorance and naivety remained intact until that point.

There are reasons for this. One was that, unlike in Ipswich, a black face in Sunderland during the mid-1980s was a rarity. There had been one black lad in my year at school, but as he was not in my class and didn't play football, we had nothing to do with each other. When we played for Moorside, Clive Mendonca was known as Choc because of his skin colour. No one ever called him Clive and it never seemed to matter to him or anyone else. Perhaps it would if he was a teenager now. Gary Coatsworth was known as Cocoa. Because of my high cheekbones and matinee idol looks, I was known as Plug. None of these epithets, although hardly complimentary, was a source of controversy.

When I had hitherto exchanged insults with my peers it would be skinny bastard, fat bastard, lanky bastard, ginger bastard, big-nosed bastard, spotty bastard. Everyone was a bastard but prefixed with some or other accompanying physicality. I therefore failed to see why 'black bastard' was an insult that belonged in another universe.

Some people, bless 'em, still don't. My excuse was that I was an empty-headed sixteen-year-old and, as excuses go, I think it's a pretty damned good one. I also immediately learned the lesson. A racial slur is not 'only a joke' and does not compare with a fatty slur, a spotty slur or any of the other slurs in the previous paragraph (although they are all insults) and it is depressing anyone should still think otherwise. Race riots have occurred, but not, to the best of my knowledge, ginger riots. Nor was there ever a Double Chin Relations Act. No one was ever enslaved because of their big ears, prohibited from voting because they had a beer gut, or denied accommodation because they were a bit on the thin side.

It is unlikely that teenagers of today would repeat my mistake; or if they did it wouldn't be a mistake. The whole incident with Dalian was a real that-was-then-this-is-now moment (although racism from the terraces in the 1980s was appalling to us even then, and white players simply never had to endure what the black ones did) and I still cringe at the memory. I could have omitted the story, which has never been in the public domain until now, but this book is an honest account and I think the tale is worth relating. I have done so entirely at my own volition. Please don't think of me unkindly because of it; think unkindly of me for the shitty stuff I did deliberately. No more can I say or do in my own defence, although I could have simply *not* written the story. It happened. It can't unhappen.

Dalian and I became good friends. We lived in the same digs for a year and a half and would regularly knock around together, usually in the 'black' pubs of Ipswich. I am aware that the less forgiving readers might now be saying sarcastically to themselves: 'Oh yes. *Some of my best friends…*'

But I had been believed and, more importantly, forgiven. I had become significantly smarter and wiser after one solitary teenage punch-up.

I learned a great deal about life from Dalian. I looked up to him. Not because he was such a gifted footballer or because he was a year older than me; it was his enormous confidence and zest for life. He was considerably more street-wise than I. It was largely through him that I realised what a comparatively sheltered up-bringing I'd had. Before I could even drive, he owned a flash car; a 'Ferrari red' Alfa Romeo Alfasud. He later replaced it with a Talbot Sunbeam, a more modest-looking vehicle at first glance, but with a Lotus engine. It spewed oil but went like a missile.

He would be haring around in his car by around 4.30 p.m. and I would usually accompany him, often until the early hours. He didn't drink; blackcurrant and soda would be his usual tipple. Women loved him and so did everyone else. He really was a top lad, exuberant, charismatic and tremendous fun to be around. He was very much the main man on the social scene, while I was very much the sidekick. Eventually some of his colossal reserves of self-confidence trickled down to me. Not as much as I would have liked, but enough to improve my social standing. Suffice to say that when I left Ipswich, he was one of the people I missed most.

Football fans are probably aware that this story doesn't end well.

The last time I saw him was in 2004, or thereabouts, at a charity function in Sheffield where he is also fondly remembered as a strike partner of David Hirst at Wednesday. He was still outgoing, but by now the confidence seemed to be more of a front. Perhaps this was because we were both much older. I had heard some stories about him that saddened me, although that doesn't make them true.

On 15 August 2016 at 1.30 a.m., the police were called to his father Ernest's house in Telford, Shropshire, where there was an incident involving Dalian, who had recently undergone kidney dialysis treatment. He was subsequently tasered by police and went into cardiac arrest. Dalian Atkinson was pronounced dead in hospital at 3 a.m. He was forty-eight years old.

It's still difficult to believe.

• • •

The first year of my apprenticeship was really a matter of settling in. If I was really going to make a move and become a professional at Ipswich Town it would be in my second year, which I began with quite some gusto. I was turning into a man, had gained half a stone in weight (in a good way), become quicker, stronger and more confident. Best of all, I was banging in the goals; for more than one team as I had graduated to being a reserve team member as well as still playing for the youths. Finishing pre-season training for the second time, I was feeling more than content with life. I specifically remember being in the shower and singing a song at the top of my voice. ('The Way It Is' by Bruce Hornsby and the Range, as music historians will be demanding to know. Such was my overall confidence in life at that point, even the tricky middle eight was not a problem. Some of the other players would struggle with G major, but not me, and my pleasant light baritone was renowned throughout football.)

I remember that exalted feeling as though it was yesterday. I was loving my football, and weekends without a game were halcyon too; out with my mates for a drink or two of anything but Liebfraumilch, meeting girls (yes, girls) and generally having the fun I had seldom known in Sunderland. Most importantly, three months into my second year I was offered professional forms. My salary leapt up from £27.50 to £100 per week. I contemplated the purchase of a platinum Lamborghini, but was thwarted in this because I now had to pay the £40 digs money from my own salary. Besides, I couldn't drive. The rise also made me eligible to pay income tax and national insurance, so I ended up being about twelve quid a week better off (remember, I had an O Level in economics and was able to work these things out). Still, there was largesse to be had with an extra dozen big ones landing in your pocket every seven days in Ipswich in 1986. Spend, spend, spend, was the motif.

Life was about to get even better. I was receiving a massage in the treatment room before a 2 p.m. reserve game against Watford at Portman Road one Tuesday in October, when Bobby Ferguson wandered in and said: 'Good luck today, son. Keep yourself right. You're playing for the first team at Bradford on Saturday.'

He meant in the starting XI too, not on the bench. It was a concise and thrilling piece of news to give to a seventeen-year-old, and it was difficult to imagine how my life could have been any better at that exact moment – unless Catherine Zeta-Jones had been performing the massage.

You may now be expecting a 'but' and you are correct to do so. The delight I felt was profound, but it only had hours to live. In goal for Watford reserves was Steve Sherwood, a fine keeper. Regrettably for him he is probably best remembered for having the ball headed out of his hands and into the net during the 1984 FA Cup final by the misogynistic Everton striker, Andy Gray. I remember him with far more clarity for that 1986 reserve match.

About twenty minutes into the game, we were leading 1–0 after I had scored from a Gary Cole cross. The ball was played high to the edge of the Watford penalty area, where it bounced. I attempted to put myself between Steve and the ball, but he came out to collect it, nudged me downwards and broke my right ankle when he landed on it. It was a complete accident and it meant that I would never play in Ipswich's first team.

I felt the pain but ignored it at first and played on, because I did not want to think the worst; that my recently promised Football League debut might not happen after all. I had never broken a bone before. I plodded on for about another fifteen minutes before finally coming off. The swelling beneath my sock was extreme and I was examined at half-time before ice was applied to the wound.

Just as I thought my mood could not descend further, Bobby Ferguson came in to see me, took one look at my ankle and said: 'You fucking useless bastard!' Then he stormed out again. His bedside manner left a little to be desired.

I don't think badly of him for this. He was a tough, but genuinely nice bloke, as I discovered during my subsequent dealings with him, and truly, he had much to contend with at Ipswich Town.

Having been one of the best teams in Europe just five years earlier, the club was struggling. The previous season they had been relegated to the old Second Division. This season of 1986–87 would end with defeat to Charlton in the play-offs and Bobby's resignation. They had also lost several more important players since my arrival, including George Burley, Russell Osman, Eric Gates and Terry Butcher, who was sold to Rangers to recoup some of the outlay the club owed for a new stand. Having been forced to sell twenty-two players, eleven of whom were internationals, the squeeze was undoubtedly on Bobby, and my injury hadn't helped. He must have been hoping that some unknown youngster who had been scoring prolifically in the reserves was about to come to his aid. One ankle-breaking collision with a goalkeeper meant that this was not about to happen.

The out-of-form Mich d'Avray played at Bradford instead of me, and Ipswich won 4–3 in a game of many chances. Surely I would have scored one (Nigel Gleghorn hit a hat-trick). The main thing was that Ipswich took the three points, but the fact that the game I missed out on was such a free-scoring affair only added to the crushing disappointment.

My time in plaster followed by rehab totalled about ten weeks, but it wasn't until the back end of the season that I felt as fit as I had done before Steve Sherwood landed on me. Ferguson called me into his office and reassured me that I was still in his plans. I signed another year's contract, this time for £120 per week. All the other apprentices who had joined at the same time as me were released. The only one of them who would have a playing career was Steve McGavin, a diminutive striker whose clubs included Colchester United, Wycombe Wanderers and Birmingham City. Afterwards, he worked for Ipswich's academy.

Being retained towards the end of 1986–87 seemed like a big moment when it happened. But it wasn't. Following Bobby's resignation, John Duncan became manager; he was brought in from Chesterfield. Without ever having bothered to watch me play, he bought two forwards. They were David Lowe from Wigan Athletic, who was a success, and Neil Woods from Rangers, who wasn't. Their combined fee was £200,000, which was a significant amount and one that the manager had to justify by using the new players rather than taking a punt on a teenager. This put me even further adrift of the first team. Sound familiar? Matters were about to deteriorate further and I was to look back upon those days of nursing a broken ankle with something like nostalgia.

I was playing at centre-half for the reserves when I received a whack on the leg and felt my right knee go. It was a cartilage injury; a lateral meniscus tear, for those of you with an interest in either medicine or just blood and gore. I was back on the pitch within four weeks. Another three weeks passed before it happened again to the same knee. This time it was a tiny tear and it only took me ten days to return. About six weeks after that, it happened a third time and it was beginning to seem less coincidental. This was in February 1988 and drastic action was required.

Enter the famous Mr David Dandy, consultant orthopaedic surgeon of the renowned Addenbrooke's Hospital, sixty miles away in Cambridge; a man with an international reputation as a knee-sorter-outer. Eminent? He couldn't be eminenter. He was the author of *Arthroscopy of the Knee – A Diagnostic Colour Atlas*. It's one of those books that I have never quite got round to reading. But he is probably best known in football as the bloke who put Paul Gascoigne back together following his infamous, serious and wholly self-inflicted injury following a ludicrous lunge at Gary Charles during the 1991 FA Cup final. Mr Dandy carried out the work on my knee too.

While I was becoming *compos mentis* as the general anaesthetic wore off post-surgery, he told me that I was finished and that I could not play football again. As you will appreciate, this information did not immediately penetrate. I lay there for three or four hours during which time I concluded that his previous visit and dire prognosis had been an unpleasant dream (I was rendered even more woozy having been 'nil by mouth' for quite a while).

The Ipswich physiotherapist, David Bingham, came in and asked: 'Have you spoken to Mr Dandy?'

'He came in. At least I think he came in. I'm not sure if I was dreaming.'

David must have realised what had happened, because he looked directly at me and said: 'Oh, Lee. He's taken all the cartilage out. You can't play again.'

• • •

There didn't seem much point in arguing with Mr Dandy. He was one of the world's leading orthopaedic surgeons, whereas I could only manage a 'U' in my O Level biology. My departure from Ipswich Town FC was imminent.

John Duncan was horrible. He gave me no indication that he cared in the slightest and seemed to regard me as an inconvenience. The most consideration he showed was when he asked me if I had insurance. Aged nineteen, my life was over, or so it seemed. In exchange for this I was given £1,500 from the PFA and a month's salary from Ipswich. Even in 1988, this wasn't going to tide me over for long.

Duncan said dismissively: 'It's probably for the best. D'yer know any other trades?'

He barely made eye contact and his whole manner was one of nonchalance. I am aware that there wasn't a great deal he could have done for me, but the merest suggestion of sympathy would not have gone amiss. None was given. In 1990 this twat became the first ever Ipswich manager to be sacked. I guarantee I was less upset about this than you were – and you probably don't even remember him. Our paths would cross again and I would enjoy the meeting immensely.

I had a discussion with David Bingham and Brian Owen; unlike Duncan, he was kind and attentive. Brian suggested a programme for recuperation and said: 'Look, you can't play professionally but you might be able to play part-time – if you look after your knee.'

I had returned to Sunderland and begun to look for work when John Carruthers contacted me again. He'd had a chat with Blyth Spartans, the famous non-league club twenty-five miles away in Northumberland, who were interested. I agreed to play for them for their final few games of the season. But every time I played the knee swelled up and I had no option but to pack it all in.

Apologies in advance for the bad language, but sometimes only swearing will suffice. I was not downhearted, despondent, dejected or even melancholy.

Try fucking distraught.

CHAPTER 3

BELGIUM

I had little option but to return to the parental home and renew hostilities with Norman and Yvonne.

This was expectedly difficult, but at least I was now old enough to come and go as I pleased and this was exactly what I did, regularly lurching in at daft o'clock in the morning after a night out with the chaps (in my defence, cribbage evenings in Sunderland do occasionally get out of hand). I was accused, understandably but with nothing like originality, of 'treating the place like a hotel'. The compensation I received from Ipswich and the PFA was dwindling and it was time to get a job. I almost became a policeman.

We had a family friend, John Yearnshire, who was an officer in forensics for Northumbria Police. He loved football and photography, so when he wasn't capturing the best side of a corpse, he would take action pictures of kids' football games and hand out copies to grateful parents – free of charge too, because he did it purely for enjoyment. That was how we got to know him. His wife was (still is) Steph Yearnshire MBE, a senior officer who rose to be superintendent. Wheels were put in motion and I was given a date for an interview to join the ranks of the police. This was during the summer of 1988.

My knee was on the mend, so in the meantime I took up an offer to sign for Gateshead FC. My time there was brief but successful. That is to say, it was successful on the pitch.

I was promised £90 per game by the Gateshead manager Dave

Parnaby (father of the future Middlesbrough and Birmingham defender Stuart Parnaby), which was to be paid monthly. So my plan was to earn a few quid playing football while waiting to begin a completely new career as a copper. I began to visualise it too; no villain would rest easy when Howey of the Yard was on the case. What could possibly go wrong with this plan?

Kidney disease, that's what. During the close season and some weeks before I was to be interviewed by the police (in a good way), I was admitted to hospital after realising that I was pissing blood. First I was put in Sunderland General, where any reassurance I might have felt was expunged when the bloke in the next bed died during my first night there. I was petrified. I was then moved less than a mile away to a kidney ward in the Victorian non-splendour of another hospital, the Royal Infirmary. This was something of a misnomer because no one who was royal and infirm would have trusted their luck in that dump. The merely infirm had less say in the matter. It was demolished in 1996 with no lament.

I was in there for almost three weeks, during which time I lost weight quickly and quite dramatically. This was all the more alarming for someone who had been a fairly skinny specimen to begin with. I was also as yellow as custard. A doctor said he would run a few tests, with a view to possibly starting dialysis at the end of the first week if there was no sign of improvement. Oh boy, did I pray the night he told me that. Mercifully I began to mend. My condition, which was never properly diagnosed, began to improve of its own accord and dialysis was unnecessary.

My brother Steven was by then an apprentice at Newcastle and, in a seldom seen display of compassion, would come and visit me on his way home to Thorney Close and tell me how his career was progressing. I had no appetite and was admonished by the nurses for not eating properly. I evaded further censure with his help; he would eat my meals for me.

Guzzling a pile of sausage and mash on someone else's behalf does not perhaps put him among our foremost humanitarians, but I was grateful at the time.

• • •

I seemed to be as far away from being a footballer as ever, so I was extremely glad to be discharged and free to turn out for Gateshead, even in the unforgiving maelstrom of the Northern Premier League (they had been a Football League club until 1960 when they were, quite outrageously and grossly unfairly, voted out of the league under the nonsensical re-election system).

My teammates there included another ex-St Aidan's lad, Joe Olabode, and Simon Smith, who would play over 500 games in goal for the club. The captain was John Carver, who had not quite made the grade at Newcastle and Cardiff City, but was a pretty decent midfielder at this level, strong-willed and a leader on the pitch. Many years later, in 2015 to be precise, he managed Newcastle United to Premier League safety. Only just, but he succeeded where Alan Shearer failed in 2009 and Rafael Benitez in 2016.

Due to my skiving kidneys, when the 1988–89 season began I was thinner and weaker than I had been in years. Nevertheless, I was put up front where I played five or six times, scoring about the same number of goals. As I said, my time there was brief and successful. It was brief for a reason.

It was now mid-September. My interview for Northumbria Police was due and I was confident I would be accepted. I was due to be paid the £90 per game for Gateshead I had been promised, which was for expenses incurred rather than wages. I was claiming unemployment benefit, so I wouldn't have accepted wages, come what may. Heaven forfend. After Tuesday night training, money was being handed round the squad by Mr Parnaby and it was about an hour before he got to me, during which time I had mentally invested my few hundred quid on Guinness, kebabs and disreputable women.

Eventually, and looking decidedly sheepish, he handed me an envelope which contained exactly – a fiver. It was a nice crisp new fiver too, but that did not seem to me to be the most salient point. When a man has O Levels, not only in maths but also in economics, he can sometimes sense, almost instinctively, when he is being paid seventy-two times less money than has been agreed. This seemed like such an occasion.

A fiver was purportedly all that was left in the kitty and I was seriously pissed off. Mind you, the year was 1988 and in those days five pounds could buy you… almost bugger all, the same as now. There were still two players in the queue behind me who were given a fiver less than I had received, although this did not make me feel especially fortunate. I had played my last game for Gateshead.

• • •

The following day I received a phone call from a gentleman named Kenny Ellis, who had played for both Hartlepool and Darlington. He was now an agent for football clubs in Belgium, where he had also played. I didn't know him, but he knew my dad and was aware of me as a footballer. He was in the process of arranging for five lads to travel to Namur, a city in central Belgium on the River Meuse, for a trial. He asked if I would be interested. I would.

'Great. I'll pick you up at 6.30 tomorrow morning,' said an enthused Kenny. This was a problem, because this trip to the continent would coincide with my scheduled interview for Northumbria Police. What to do?

Something inside me resolved the dilemma by making me want to try my luck on the continent. Why not? You're only young once and all that. My police career would be put on hold, where it remains to this day. The North East's criminal underworld could hardly believe their good fortune.

Having made my apologies to the police, I headed for the airport that Thursday morning where I met the other trialists including Mickey Robinson, cousin of the Mickey Robinson I had been at school with. I also saw Danny Olson, the most absurdly self-confident person that Whitley Bay had ever produced and who was with me at Ipswich. We arrived in Namur a few hours later, found our digs and took part in the trial match the same evening.

The game was against Union Royale Namur in their home ground. We would nominally be an Éghezée XI; Éghezée being a village ten miles north of Namur. The trial was part of quite an ambitious project; it featured players trying their luck from various parts of Europe, Africa, Turkey and now the westernmost region of Thorney Close.

Danny had a superb game in midfield and did not need to remind everyone present of how well he was playing; but he did anyway. Each incisive pass he made was met with effusive self-praise such as 'Look at that pass, man, I'm fuckin' brilliant, I am' and 'I'm better than Zico, me'. He wasn't what you might call reticent. Those who could speak English were no less bewildered than those who couldn't.

I, on the other hand, barely touched the ball. Even then there was the distinctive continental pass, pass, pass, pass style of football which didn't quite suit a big English centre-forward who was waiting impatiently for a decent cross to be placed on his bonce. So the game passed me by somewhat. Yet in the bar afterwards I could see Kenny Ellis schmoozing, talking up my talents to local bigwigs, including a father and son called Louis and Stéphane Gemine.

Louis was a portly fellow who would have been fairly tall, had Nature made it possible for him to be rolled out like Plasticine. As it happened, he was a short-arse. However, for the benefit of those among you who may be unfamiliar with the Belgian business community of the late 1980s, he was also a wealthy and influential short-arse, the president of a nearby club called AS Hemptinne (*l'Alliance Sportive Hemptinne*) and owner of a local company called Hydrocar. I believe Louis is still head of the firm today, supplying asphalt, paving blocks and suchlike. He barely spoke any English and I spoke even less French, but Stéphane, slightly older than me, was fluent in both.

After a fairly tortuous translated conversation, it was agreed that AS Hemptinne, based in the village of Hemptinne twenty-five miles south-west of Namur, would take Danny and me for a three-month trial period, which would bring us to Christmas and the winter break (so beloved of football leagues virtually everywhere in Europe except Britain).

We were to be put in digs that would be paid for by the club and given wages of, I think, slightly under a couple of thousand Belgian francs per week, which worked out at approximately £180. Not a fantastic salary even then, but it must be said a considerable improvement upon the fiver that Gateshead had offered me. Despite having never heard of AS Hemptinne, Danny and I were excited by the prospect of a new life ahead of us, and agreed. We then headed back to the digs with Kenny to change clothes for a night/morning out to celebrate. In fact we stayed for several days while contracts were being sorted. Namur on that Friday 18 September, was a sight to see. The city centre was lined with tables and crammed with revellers. It was reminiscent of Sunderland on black-eye Friday, but without the black eyes.

Kenny knew all the best places but I soon realised that he was not a big drinker. He was way beyond that; in fact, he was an alcoholic. Indeed, the booze killed him in 1992 while he was still only in his mid-forties.

Instead of heading straight back to the North East, we flew to London in order to call in at the FA's headquarters at Lancaster Gate, where we could sort out our registration. Inevitably, this was followed by another big night on the razzle in the capital. I don't remember where we stayed or what it was called. What I can confirm is that it was a special kind of shit-hole. The image of Kenny, snoring on his back in his antiquated undies, is one that I retain with the utmost clarity. Believe me when I say that I wish it was otherwise.

●   ●   ●

I returned to Namur on the Monday. Training took place on Tuesdays and Thursdays with matches played on Sundays. My pay might not have taken very long to count, but I could hardly complain of being overworked. The light schedule was also very good news for my dodgy knee.

The Belgian football league pyramid had the first division or Pro League at the top, featuring the likes of Anderlecht and Club Brugge. Then there was a second division, with the third division – the Provincial League – split into the north and south of the country as had been the case in England until 1958. When we were promoted in 1990, AS Hemptinne went into the south league, although geographically we were slap bang in the middle of the country. Before then we were in the Southern Province or, to anglicise it, the Belgian Conference.

After attending to business in Blighty I was looking forward to living the high life in Belgium, mindful of what a fabulous Friday night out we had enjoyed when we first arrived. But my social life was dealt a double blow. First, Danny informed me that he had changed his mind, deciding that he wanted to stay in Whitley Bay with his other half. This left me alone in Namur, unable to speak a word of French and pondering whether I had done the right thing in duffing the police interview.

I slept on the matter and decided that for three months I may as well give it my best efforts and try to enjoy the experience. After all, things were still looking decidedly rosier than they had just a few weeks earlier when I had been lying in a hospital bed, wondering if my kidneys were about to drop out and relying on Steven's minimal better nature to eat my tea for me. As Francis Bacon said, to Norman Collier I believe, adversity is not without comforts and hopes.

However, none of this up-and-at-'em attitude could prepare me for my first sighting of AS Hemptinne's 'stadium' when I reported there for my first day of training. I had naively expected something similar to where I'd played the trial game in Namur where they had a decent little ground.

I have seen ramps on the backs of car ferries with a lower gradient than the Hemptinne pitch. It seemed to be the only piece of land within a 100-kilometre radius that was not absolutely level. It was back to the days of Gilley Law. There was one tiny stand at the side of the pitch. The changing rooms were behind one of the goals in a building that also housed the club bar. Beyond that, filling the entire space between eye and horizon was nothing except cow fields, cow fields and more cow fields. If the cows themselves had fancied a kick-about as a respite from eating grass and breaking wind, then they would have been playing on a better pitch than I was. It was seriously clarted. I had agreed terms with a definite lesser light.

Whatever the ground capacity might have been was neither here nor there as only around 500 people lived in Hemptinne anyway. The stand could hold about a fifth of the population, while everyone else could just congregate wherever they liked around the pitch. Unsurprisingly, there was no concern over 'crowd' congestion or hooliganism. The most serious safety risk for spectators was if any of them should step too far back from the pitch, as they might then absent-mindedly lean against the electric cattle wire and have 150 volts sent through their arse cheeks.

On the positive side, the Hemptinne squad comprised a really good set of lads. I was introduced to them and, apart from feeling slightly discomfited at being kissed on both cheeks by other men for the first time in my life, rubbed along with my new colleagues very well (for the benefit of the truly unworldly, it was the upper cheeks). A few of them spoke English, which was obviously useful on the training pitch, but also helpful in assuring me that none of my new teammates actually fancied me. The coach, Fernand Brabant, spoke English about as well as I spoke French, but apart from that, all was well on the playing side.

There was not a huge amount to do in my spare time. I had no access to the BBC and, to any meaningful degree, the world was still awaiting the advent of satellite television. My viewing was all but confined to Eurosport. There wasn't much point in watching the news in French or Dutch. And don't believe the hype you hear about Belgian soap operas either; they're not nearly as good as they're cracked up to be.

But there was always Friday night, something I had been keenly anticipating since that first session on the tiles with Kenny Ellis. This, alas, brings me to the second blow to my social life following Danny's volte-face over moving abroad. The swinging scene that I had informed my friends was rivalled only by 1920s Manhattan, was actually rather sedate. It turned out that my previous soirée had coincided with the weekend of the Wallonia Festival, an annual public holiday held on the third weekend of September to commemorate the Belgian Revolution – and a quite spectacular piss-up.

Downtown Namur on an *average* Friday night was virtually deserted, something that only became apparent when I hit the town in my best cheesecloth shirt and some liberally applied Old Spice (the classic masculine fragrance, the mark of a man). I tried to make the most of not so much a grim situation as a very dull one. I ambled out for a few drinks and reacquainted myself with a waitress I had met during my first trip there. We communicated as best we could. She didn't possess particularly voluminous English, but it still eclipsed my French. So it must have been a combination of the most exclusive aftershave on the market and sheer animal magnetism that made her want to come back to my hotel after she had clocked off for the evening.

It was there that we made love with an intensity that the poet Byron might have said was...

Well, we had a shag, anyway. An otherwise disappointing week had ended on a high, not to say with a bang.

• • •

After a friendly on the Thursday, my proper debut for AS Hemptinne was a 2–1 win over an opposition I have long since forgotten, but I do remember scoring both of our goals. Good goals they were too, one from each foot. The crowd went wild – or at least the gathering went wild.

I quite quickly became something of a local celebrity. It was novel for the natives to have an English footballer within their midst, incidentally the club's first professional, with the whole enterprise being bankrolled by Louis Gemine, whose factory was situated close by. My signing was a major part of his plans to make the club a bigger force than it had ever been before. In the bar after that first game I was apprised of the scheme by Stéphane. He also acted as an interpreter between myself and a local journalist who was keen to write a story about me. The Rolling Stones were unlikely to roll into Hemptinne any time soon; therefore I was the nearest person to the A-list that this particular hack would meet that day. He asked me some fairly prosaic questions about if and how I was enjoying Belgium, how I was fitting in at the club and the like. Then he dug deeper.

He asked: 'How are you finding the girls?' Saucy.

'Well, I've only just arrived,' I replied tactfully, as a gentleman never tells. Actually I had told all the lads, but I drew the line at giving details to the local media. Stéphane did it for me.

He blabbed: 'Lee likes the girls; especially one.'

Evidently something was lost in translation when the newspaper went to print. Stéphane's comment of 'especially one' had been published in French as 'a special one'. The girl I had the liaison with read the article and was soon knocking on the door of my hotel room, smiling warmly at me under the unfortunate misapprehension that she was the unnamed special one. I tried to let her down as gently as possible by explaining the situation as delicately as I could.

Then we shagged again and I sent her packing. *Merci, mademoiselle*, if you happen to be reading this.

Oh, come on. Don't look at me in that tone of voice. I was a fit and healthy nineteen-year-old bloke who was presented with an opportunity. Show me the man who, as a fit and healthy nineteen-year-old, would not have leapt (twice) with glorious abandon at this chance, then I will show you a liar; or as an outside bet, Mahatma Gandhi. Mine was not the behaviour expected of a *preux chevalier* from Thorney Close and I'm not proud of what I did, although describing myself as ashamed would be pushing it.

• • •

By the end of my three-month trial I had played eleven games for Hemptinne and scored in every single one of them, giving me sixteen goals in total; back to the scoring of my school days. Anyway, my efforts led to a renegotiated contract, my wages being increased to £280 per week and the club renting an apartment for me.

This wasn't the big time I had dreamed of a few years earlier when I should have been doing my biology homework, but still not too shabby for someone of my age at the turn of 1989. More so when I was only expected to take part in two training sessions and one match each week. Additionally, the fact that I had been informed only the previous year that I was finished as a footballer somehow made life seem all the better. Perhaps more importantly, my knee was bearing up.

At the risk of incurring the wrath of a Walloonian waitress scorned, I would still venture out for the occasional spot of socialising in Namur and would even attract some appreciative shouts across the street: 'Hey, grand Anglaise! Vien assis!' – or something. As I would later discover at Burnley, this type of moment is to be savoured.

My conversational French improved and I became acquainted with the essentials such as ordering a drink, please, thank you, hello, goodbye, yes, no, where are the bogs, you have beautiful eyes, my hovercraft is full of eels, etcetera. Even a tenuous grasp of the language is extremely useful on the football field. When learning any tongue in its native setting, it is usually the case that locals will teach you all of the dirty words first as they will never fail to find this hilarious. I was no exception and they just loved hearing the big Englishman behaving like a performing seal, trying to repeat whichever obscene vernacular they had just requested from me. I had no idea what I was saying, but it clearly was not the patois of civic occasions.

I was getting to know people and, although occasionally lonely, I was generally enjoying a perfectly splendid experience. I was a bit of a barfly at the time, something that was possible for a young footballer then, but certainly not now. It was definitely a bucket of fun and my extracurricular activities did not hamper my football.

One irritation that ground into me on the pitch was a cocky little winger we had called David Culot. David (pronounced *Daveeeed*) was a tricky wee player, but he had the aggravating habit of cutting back with the ball to unnecessarily beat a defender two or three times, while the striker was waiting in the penalty area for a cross that could easily have been delivered, but wasn't. A winger delivering a bad cross is quite forgivable. A winger deciding not to deliver the cross at all is another matter entirely. One particular day, this tendency of his got completely out of control, so I attempted to calmly rectify the situation by threatening him with physical violence.

He was chopping back to a quite infuriating degree, oblivious to my shouts of: '*Traversez la ballon, David, traversez la ballon!*' (good eh?).

This had no effect whatsoever, so I switched to some very primitive English.

'I'll fucking kill you. You little *bastard!*' and other eloquently phrased suggestions.

No matter what language I used, be it English, French or foul, it made no difference. When he had chopped back for the third time in the second half, to add to the umpteen other occasions in the first, it finished off my temper and I decided that my only remaining course of action was to chase him down and politely stave his face in. In the middle of a game, I ran after him with the express intention of eating his spleen, turning momentarily into the Basil Fawlty of the Belgian Provincial League.

At last, sensing that I may perhaps have been piqued, he wailed a panicky: '*Mon dieu! Mon dieu!*'

'I'll *mon dieu* you! You little twat!' I responded cleverly.

Remarkably, he seemed to have no idea what this meant. Dieu

Himself would have been no help to David if I had actually managed to catch him. Eventually things calmed down a bit and an indignant winger was substituted (for some reason), his departure accompanied by well-intentioned advice from me, such as: 'Fuck you! Get off!'

There was a peculiar atmosphere after the game, perhaps palliated by victory and me scoring again (although not by meeting the end of a David cross). I chatted to Stéphane Gemine who told me that the referee had taken no action, possibly because he didn't have a clue what was going on. The ref's only query on the whole affair was: 'What does "fuck" mean, because the big Englishman seems to say it a lot?'

It was usually Stéphane who would give me a lift for the 25-mile journey from Hemptinne back to my place in Namur. However, after this particular game he apologised, saying that he was unable to drive me back but it was OK because one of the lads was going my way in his car. Using your skill and judgement, can you guess which of the lads he was referring to?

I sat in the back of the car with David and his wife in the front. Perhaps not surprisingly, there was barely a word of conversation. My, what an awfully long twenty-five miles that was. When they finally dropped me off I thanked them and said a conciliatory 'Ah, David'.

He was still nettled and responded with yet another '*Mon dieu*', this time muttered and followed by some other sulky sounds that may have included a '*Zut alors!*' or two, but were for the most part just indistinguishable French noises. For the first time in a while I thought of Steven.

David continued to be one of life's irritants after that. But he did start to cross the ball more often.

• • •

At the end of the 1988–89 season, we narrowly missed out on promotion. But on a personal note, I was the league's top scorer, the *Major Buteur* with twenty-nine goals (I still have the trophy). I was the star of the team and the proverbial big fish in a small, small, Low Countries pond. Hardly anyone outside a minute section of central Belgium had heard of me, but I was having a jollier time than most professional footballers – in any country.

My success was reflected in my salary, which was now up to about £300 per week. I sent much of it home to my parents, who banked it for me. As the club was still paying for my accommodation and utilities (they had put me in a better apartment too), I didn't actually need a great deal of cash, so my savings accumulated steadily. I only really spent money on socialising and phone calls.

Mobile phones were virtually non-existent, so I would make a weekly call from a payphone to assure Yvonne and Norman that I was still breathing and in one piece. It was still the quickest way to get the all-important football results, although my dad would also send me the fabulous *Football Echo*, which I would read until the ink became dislodged. It contained every result and fixture from the European Cup down to schools and pub leagues. Being away from home makes you disproportionately interested in how the The Dun Cow got on against The Hastings Hill in the Cowies Five-a-side League. Like all the Saturday 'pinks', Sunderland's *Football Echo* has now sadly gone. The last one rolled off the press in December 2013.

• • •

We signed just a couple of players from somewhere in northern Belgium, one of whom was big Frank Beys, a good midfielder. Otherwise we started 1989–90 with the same squad as the previous season.

Life was good and it improved further when we signed a centre-half I knew and liked who had been on the books at Newcastle, Paul Watson. Paul had learned French at school, so linguistically he became my wingman and, as he was Glaswegian, was arguably more adept at French than English. My reliance on him slowed down my learning of the language, such as it was. I didn't see all that much of him socially as he had his wife with him, but he was a fine bloke and a fine footballer who later played back in Scotland and around the north-east of England.

Despite too frequently falling back on Paul to translate, my conversational French was improving (conversation being almost exclusively about football) and I continued to be heartily greeted in the street by strangers in Namur. Life was good and my social life was more than agreeable. Occasionally it was fabulous.

It may have been me who inadvertently started it off, but players from all the local clubs, not just AS Hemptinne, would gather at the same café/bar in Namur after Sunday matches and remain ensconced there until the small hours. It became the social hub for all the footballers in the area. If someone had a birthday they would have to buy a cake and drinks for everyone else in the bar. Tequila and whichever spirits were to hand were lobbed into a punchbowl along with the occasional lump of fruit. We were professional athletes, after all. These evenings served to encourage bonhomie between players of different clubs, not to mention cordial international relations. Truly I was the Ban Ki-moon of Namur, although it would be remiss of me not to mention that the main objective of these evenings was to get completely shit-faced.

Another of my teammates, Daniel Clamot, was there each week no matter where we had been playing. He was in his late twenties and married with kids, but still he would often end the evening literally crying. This would involve him saying his goodbyes, leaving and then returning about an hour later because he couldn't remember where he had parked his car. The remaining squad members would help him find the errant vehicle, decant him into it and leave him. I hope he didn't drive it. If he did, at least the roads were straight.

I was only involved in one regrettable incident and it happened in April 1990. I had become best of friends with our right-back, Daniel Demaerschalk, and not only because his parents ran the *Renaissance*, the only pub in Hemptinne. I was invited to his cousin's wedding in Namur. This was held on a Saturday night, so I was under strict instruction to show professional restraint as we had an important game the next day: a top-of-the-table fixture against RUW Ciney (*boo!*), a team based twenty-eight miles east of Hemptinne who were second to us by just a couple of points.

The wedding was a genuinely pleasant occasion. My plan was to have one drink. But among the other guests were several fans who each bought me a beer. I found myself becoming deeply embroiled in football talk. Every time I turned round another beer had been planted at my elbow which I then had to politely drink. It's worth remembering too that this was Belgian beer and not the horse's piss that we have delivered to pubs in steel tanks in the UK that takes anything up to two hours to brew. The upshot was that by midnight I did not know if I was in Wallonia, Estonia or Catatonia. It was about then that I had this ingenious idea of having some more beer, as by that stage I simply didn't care.

Daniel was doing his military service, which he had to attend the following morning and therefore had to make sure he had a disciplined, temperate evening (although so did I, supposedly). He said he would look after me. However, his vigilance seemed mainly to take the form of laughing and pointing at how completely bollocksed I was. He thought of a plan, such as it was, that he would shovel me into his car (by then it was 2 a.m.), take me back to his place and drop me back at my apartment (later) in the morning on his way to military service. Stéphane would then pick me up as normal to take me to the game. This faultlessly cunning plan was to ensure that no one would realise that I had been completely blotto in the early hours of that morning.

At 6 a.m., I was woken by Daniel after what felt like three minutes' sleep. Did I want anything to eat? The answer to that was an emphatic 'no', but he insisted. I mused that he was probably correct to advise me to eat something, but he came back with a huge slab of gateau – a fucking cream cake.

I was hardly an authority on nutrition, but even I knew that this was not the ideal start to the day. However, in the absence of muesli, yoghurt, orange juice or indeed anything that might actually be beneficial to one's health, I forced the cream cake down. I was aware that it wasn't a breakfast that enjoyed the approval of dieticians, or even my mother, but I was still too drunk to argue. In other circumstances, I might have enjoyed it.

I was in my own bed for a couple of hours before I awoke for the second time that day, upon which I had about a gallon of coffee before Stéphane arrived at 11.30 a.m., ninety minutes before kick-off and with me still momentously hungover. I hoped he wouldn't think that I looked like a bag of shit, because I certainly felt like one.

'Good morning, Lee. *Mon dieu!* You look like a bag of shit!' were his first words.

'I'm OK,' I replied defensively, yet perhaps not convincingly. We had gone a few miles along the motorway in Stéphane's Mercedes when I had to abandon even this feeble pretence.

'Stop the car! Stop the car!' I yelped.

This he did, allowing me to leap from the passenger seat and introduce my breakfast to the hard shoulder of the N951. Reason leads me to conclude that my mouth was the only orifice on vomiting duties, but at the time it felt as though I was puking from my nose, eyes and ears too. I gave myself a wipe and returned to the car where I was met Stéphane's curious gaze.

'Was that coffee and cream cake?'

'Mind your own business.'

Twenty minutes later I gave a repeat performance. Stéphane was quicker to hit the brakes this time, fearful that my second Technicolor yawn of the day should land on his upholstery. We eventually arrived at the ground with my head feeling as though it contained an extremely busy blacksmith. It was a pleasant spring day, but it felt to me like an afternoon in Death Valley and a downpour would have been a treat. I didn't get one. All I could do was keep telling myself that I would be all right. If you're going to lie to yourself, make it a whopper, I say.

We kicked off, with me gamely attempting to give an impression of fitness and vitality when in reality I could barely move. When the offside flag was raised against me for the seventeenth time in the first half alone because I was incapable of getting back onside, even the least perspicacious onlookers realised that I was not perhaps in peak bodily condition. Playing with only ten-and-a-bit men, we commendably kept it to 0–0 at half-time and, as you will readily believe, I hadn't really played well. I was glad to retreat to the changing room and drink a bucket or two of water.

Fernand Brabant was going ballistic. I didn't understand the words he was using in their most literal sense, but the tone of his shouting did not sound particularly complimentary. I could barely hear him anyway with the continued clangour between my ears. I cadged a couple of headache tablets from the physio and traipsed dizzily back on to the pitch for the second half. Remarkably, I had not been substituted. Ten minutes later we were awarded a penalty.

I was the designated penalty taker and was not about to relinquish the opportunity of a goal merely because most of Belgium appeared to be spinning around me, so I picked up the ball to indicate this. I still retained the burning desire to score, which overpowered the issue of how patently stupid it was for anyone to take a penalty in that condition. There were at least a couple of thousand supporters there (our results had bolstered attendances) and there seemed to be a collective mutter among the crowd indicating that they thought it was a stupid idea too. Undeterred by the enormous potential for a red face, as opposed to the green one I was still wearing, I bent over to place the ball on the spot. The Ciney goalkeeper was gyrating in an attempt to put me off, although there was really no need.

When I stood up I immediately felt sick again and for the third time that day evacuated my stomach, leaving a stringy puddle of vomit about eighteen inches from the ball. What a crowd-pleaser I was. The eighteen-yard box began to resemble Picasso's palette.

In the fullness of time, the fans have probably forgotten this game, save for the bit when the barely sentient Hemptinne centre-forward emptied his guts in the opposition penalty area. Perhaps I should have aimed my puke at the ball; it would have discouraged the keeper from putting his hands on it. Incapable of attempting anything even remotely scientific, I decided to just smash it as hard as a man with a Duvel-related illness possibly could. I duly did this – and completely miskicked.

The ball flew into the top corner, reminiscent of the penalties that Matthew Le Tissier used to hammer home at the Dell, the crucial difference being that Le Tissier would do so on purpose. My penalty would be the only goal of the game.

The fact that I had scored and the delight of the crowd did not prevent my substitution. My number was finally held up and I was off. Unless injured, it is customary for a substituted player to sit in the dugout and watch the remainder of the game. I amended this convention slightly by having a lie-down on a row of half-a-dozen or so empty seats behind the dugout and gulping fresh air. It was my final act in an all-round classy display.

There were celebrations at the final whistle and the air was jubilant in the bar afterwards. Most of the team were enjoying a beer or two. I decided not to have a drink myself; that sort of thing doesn't help a man's game, you know. Stéphane came over to me and I could see his scowling father behind him. Louis Gemine's mood had not been emolliated by our victory and his face resembled a litre of cold piss. There was no question of fibbing about having a touch of indigestion. Quite apart from stinking of booze, everyone at the club knew I had been to the wedding. Louis was not amused and thought I had been a disgrace (as indeed I had been). Stéphane told me that if I had missed the penalty I would have been sacked on the literal spot.

This was not my finest hour. It was a stupid and extremely unprofessional thing to have done. I got away with it, but I was not proud. Ensuring you aren't rat-arsed within twelve hours of a game isn't asking for much of your highest-paid player.

• • •

Such unhealthy diversions notwithstanding, I did undertake additional fitness training of my own accord. Off-field shenanigans did not mean that I wasn't serious about my career, and the Ciney incident was an uncharacteristic one-off. My right knee was settling down too, although I never had it examined. There was no pain and no restriction. It was mended but bent because the tendons at the back had healed tight. I could get my fist under it when it was supposed to be stretched flat on the ground, whereas my left knee was normal. I should have done better rehab after leaving Ipswich. This was my fault and I would pay for it years later. It felt OK then, however, so I left it alone.

Extra training helped. The second season was more successful than the first. Most importantly we were promoted and again, on a personal level, I rattled in a good number of goals. These included a hat-trick on 29 April 1990 against Marchienne. I found out at a reunion in 2015 that their side featured Thierry Hazard, father of Eden Hazard (regrettably that's how old I am). Eden must have been conceived at about the time of the game (though not at exactly that time, I hasten to add). I was still the star of our little show. There was another 4–2 win against Marchienne during which Paul and I both scored, although he was sent off.

A sign of Hemptinne's burgeoning ambition under Louis Gemine was that they even found money to invest in the creation of a pitch that was actually flat. Consultants with a laser level machine, not to mention a few packets of grass seed, were brought in. What had been a piece of land that looked like it might yield a lorry load of King Edward potatoes became a first-class pitch. Whichever team's captain won the toss before the match now had to elect to kick towards a specified geographical direction, rather than just 'downhill, please'. State-of-the-art or what? The rest of the ground remained a shambles, but one step at a time. Louis meant business. His long-term plan, however unlikely, was to be in the top flight and play against the leading Belgian clubs.

Our promotion began to attract media interest and a national television company came to interview Paul and me. It was unprecedented for a village club like AS Hemptinne to have professionals from Scotland and England among their playing staff. To unnecessarily emphasise the point that Paul really was Scottish, they made him wear a kilt and stroll around the winding lanes of the town. I don't know if Paul actually owned the kilt or whether the crew had come prepared, but there was certainly one handy. Bagpipes, haggis and bottles of Irn-Bru were rather more difficult to procure; otherwise I suspect they would have been added to the cliché.

Later that day, we sat before the television in Paul's flat to watch our new slice of fame. I am obliged to admit that, most unfortunately, I spoke English in an attempted French accent. I have no idea why I did this.

I suppose it was subconscious mimicking, a quite preposterous attempt to make myself more easily understood. But I sounded like a character from one of the less plausible scenes in *'Allo 'Allo!* – pointing out that *eet ees gerrrayt to score a gerl* and other such gibberish. I had done a Steve McClaren about twenty years before Steve McClaren. At least my pre-internet interview has been zapped for all eternity (at least I hope it has; Paul Watson might still have a video), the same can't be said for poor old Schteev's burbling in Holland. I cringed more than most at the McClaren interview. Believe it or not, it's easily done and I knew exactly how.

Despite making a holy arse of myself on television, life abroad was going as swimmingly as ever. This was not to last.

•   •   •

I spent the summer of 1990 at home watching Gascoigne, Lineker and Butcher in the World Cup. There was also fantastic news for Sunderland when they managed probably the most fortuitous promotion to the top flight that anyone can remember. They finished sixth in the old Second Division then beat Newcastle in the play-off semi-final. This was despite the best efforts of the Newcastle fans who invaded the St James' Park pitch in an unsuccessful and highly embarrassing attempt to have the second leg abandoned with the tie at 2–0 to the Mackems.

Sunderland were then hopelessly bad throughout a 1–0 final defeat to Swindon Town at Wembley, but made it to the First Division anyway after Swindon admitted to making illegal payments to players. My brother was most dischuffed and by now could not go running to our mother to rectify the situation.

I travelled to the final on a minibus with a load of mates. Our designated driver, Mark Wilson (known for no reason whatsoever as Jim), got lost, having taken a left turn on the A1 (also for no reason whatsoever). In London, we slept for a while in deckchairs in St James's Park which we 'forgot' to pay for, then headed to the stadium. Ah, memories. Like so many trips away to watch Sunderland, it was a great weekend spoiled only by the football.

While all of this was going on, Louis Gemine continued to invest in AS Hemptinne, which included the replacement of Fernand Brabant as coach. Poor old Fernand had done nothing wrong but was sacked anyway; dispensed with to make way for one Roland Docquier from the Belgian second division. Docquier rolled in (almost literally; he was no stranger to pastry) before the start of my third season. He was supposed to be a respected figure, but the fact that he was routinely referred to by the players with the less than reverential soubriquet of 'Fat Bastard' (which we thought used up about as much wit as he deserved) would seem to belie this. He was a perfectly loathsome individual and would have rubbed along quite nicely with John Duncan.

Docquier brought new players with him too, which had to be done if Hemptinne were to make further strides. The atmosphere around the club palled. The locals did not warm to the newbies, seeing them as mercenaries. Comparatively speaking, I was a big earner. But my salary had been raised incrementally as the club achieved more and I had put away all those goals. Also, I had only come to the country in the first place because I loved playing football and was taking up the one chance I had been offered to do so professionally. The new players were only semi-professional while I was full-time, but they were being lassoed from many miles around and paid decent money, whereas I lived locally and had become something of an honorary Namurian while still bringing a dash of Thorney Close glamour to the area.

Post-match, there was little socialising or interaction between the more recent intake and the rest of us. A drink and a slice or two of flan with the supporters was the norm (although I could never eat after a game), but the new lads tended to leave almost immediately for home. I had no problem with them personally. They were polite enough and weren't there to socialise. Besides, why shouldn't they play for money? However, there was a disconnection because the fans felt that they detracted from the all-in-it-together family atmosphere as local players were being shoved to one side. Docquier was a first-class wanker, but for all his unpleasantness he was under pressure and did what he could to improve the team. It was why he was there.

President Gemine's ambitions were about to be yanked backwards, and so were mine.

• • •

We made an indifferent-at-best start to the 1990–91 season. We knew the opposition would be better, but failed to create as many chances as we had hoped, and I wasn't scoring with my usual regularity. Before many games had passed, I was dropped in favour of a huge bloke called Mathieu Crowels, who was actually a centre-half. He was years older than me, in his late twenties, 6ft 4in. with blond hair and matching moustache. At first I thought he could not have been more German if he had trained in lederhosen and drank his Lucozade from a musical beer stein. However, he was actually from the easternmost part of Belgium, on the border with the Rhineland.

A common and lazy perception of Teutonic people is that they lack a sense of humour. But with Mathieu it was actually true. I suppose he was a decent enough fellow and my opinion was perhaps clouded by him keeping me out of the team, but he genuinely was a blank-faced dullard. Like my cod French accent, he too could have featured in an episode of 'Allo 'Allo! I don't resort to such crude national stereotypes lightly – it's just that it happens to be true in this instance. Anyway, it isn't just us Brits who reduce other nationalities to cardboard cut-outs. Hadn't the Belgians been blasé about making Paul wander round the streets in a kilt because he happened to be Scottish?

I wasn't completely out of the scene, but did not feature in the side anything like as much as I had hoped, playing well in some matches and not so well in others. I needed a run in the starting XI and, even though the team as a whole was generally performing quite badly, Docquier wouldn't let me have one. Things had deteriorated for me and the whole of the club in a short period of time. Then they got worse.

I was brought on as a substitute during a home game and was desperate to show what I could do. The score was 1–1 when the ball was crossed into the opposition penalty area. One of the new players was shaping up to attempt a volley; something I was not about to allow him to do. I was adamant that I would get my bonce on the ball before it reached his foot. I virtually ran through him on my way to battering the ball against the post with my head. Not only had neither of us scored, I had injured his leg and cracked my own collarbone. My popularity at this point was at its nadir; beneath even the aftermath of Puke-gate the previous season. It hadn't helped my cause or the atmosphere at the club – and I was in limbo.

As I would not therefore be playing for a few weeks, I asked if I could go home for a while, and they agreed. I returned to training afterwards and was no nearer to making the team. It was October. Following another substitute appearance that lasted all of three minutes, Docquier more or less told me, in that effortlessly charmless way of his, that he didn't rate me. I was by now only slightly less miserable than during my time in Sunderland Royal Infirmary and went to speak with Stéphane to ask for some more time off. To steal from a far superior writer, I could see that, if not actually disgruntled, he was far from being gruntled. But I wasn't playing anyway so he reluctantly agreed and off I went, with the proviso that I paid for my own travel.

I was allowed three official visits home each year with the air fare paid for by the club. This was before the birth of EasyJet, and flights then between the UK and Belgium cost hundreds of pounds. This meant buses and ferries for me; Namur to Brussels, Brussels to Paris, Paris to Calais, Calais to Dover, Dover to London, London to the centre of Sunderland then aboard the 123 bus to Thorney Close. Michael Palin wouldn't have made *that* journey, but I had to. It took about eighteen hours.

The bus back to London was cancelled due to snow, so I was delayed by a day. I was supposed to report for training in Hemptinne at 7 p.m. on the Thursday, but could not arrive there any earlier than late that evening. When I arrived back at my apartment there was already a letter waiting for me on the doormat. It was short and typed in French with a translation. I had been sacked in two languages with immediate effect. It mentioned me missing training, but also the leave I had taken – as agreed.

It seemed to me then as it seems to me now: extremely harsh. I was top earner at the club but was not playing and my abiding suspicion is that they were keen to eject me for that reason. At the 2015 reunion, Stéphane confirmed to me that it was his father's decision to give me the heave-ho. Louis was a successful businessman and there aren't many of them who earned their money without making a decision or two like this.

I was twenty-one years old and as green as Kermit's arse. I

should have made some attempt to apologise, however difficult, and inveigle myself back on to the subs' bench at least. But I told my parents over the phone what had happened and they suggested that I return home on another journey at my own expense. The voyage from Namur to Brussels, Brussels to Paris, Paris to Calais, Calais to Dover, Dover to London, London to the centre of Sunderland then aboard the 123 bus to Thorney Close was arduous enough without the additional impediment of carrying everything I owned.

Never mind. A glorious career at BT was about to commence.

CHAPTER 4

BIG BREAK

Once again, I was back with the folks in Thorney Close where, I regret to say, I treated the place like a hotel. Yvonne may have alluded to this at some stage.

My original plan back in England was to sort myself out with a team and earn a few quid, only to find that this was simply not allowed. AS Hemptinne held my registration, which meant that, as a footballer at least, they effectively owned me and the fact that they did not pay me a penny as soon as I was dismissed had no bearing on this. Again naively, I had assumed that I was able to play for another club as soon as I had been given my cards. Wrong. Then I thought that once my contract had elapsed at the end of the 1990–91 season, I would be eligible then. Wrong again.

I just wanted to play football. Bayern Munich might have been nice, but I would have settled in the interim for anyone who could top that fiver-a-month I had been on at Gateshead. Further investigation and discussions with the FA and PFA revealed that I was, to use the legal parlance – fucked. As I recall, Louis Gemine wanted something like £10,000 to release me, which no one was waving around; certainly not me. This meant he had me tied up more or less indefinitely. Just to reiterate, I had been sacked by Hemptinne who immediately ceased to pay me anything, my contract had run down, but it was within their power to stop me from playing for anyone else. I was not a unique case. I would not be playing for anyone because this was four years before the world would hear of Jean-Marc Bosman.

Younger readers may appreciate a short history lesson. The old farts can skip this bit.

Jean-Marc Bosman was an obscure midfielder who would transform the lives of footballers across Europe. He was Belgian and joined RFC Liège from their much bigger neighbours Standard Liège in 1988 – the same year that I joined Hemptinne. Despite being a small club, RFC Liège were in the Belgian first division and Bosman would only play three league games for them. When his contract ran out he wanted to move to Dunkerque in France, but Liège held his registration and – perfectly within the rules – demanded a transfer fee for a player they didn't want and who was not contracted to them. As he was stuck at a Belgian club, the symmetry with my own situation was noticeable; at least by me.

Today all this sounds incredible, but back then it was accepted practice. Bosman took his case to the European Court of Justice, claiming that this interfered with his right as an EU citizen to freedom of movement. In December 1995 the court ruled in his favour. Since then, it has not been possible for clubs to demand transfer fees for out-of-contract players joining other clubs within the EU, and the number of EU citizens in a single team is unlimited (well, you can only have eleven, but you know what I mean). It seems unlikely that the 2016 Brexit vote will see a return to the old rules in the UK.

Too late for me, up shit-creek in 1991, this completely transformed footballers' employment. Before Bosman, players wanted to be transferred for big money as they received a portion of the fee. To be told by your club you could leave on a free transfer was a dent to the ego before 1995. Players today will happily see out their contract and leave on a free transfer because the signing-on fee at their next club could be – and often is – enormous.

Jean-Marc Bosman is one of the single biggest causes of Premier League footballers now being so incredibly well paid and having such power. But the zillionaires he helped to create have done little to thank him. He lost his money, ended up on benefits and descended into alcoholism. In 2013 he was jailed for twelve months for a drunken assault.

•   •   •

Barred from playing before all that, I ended up taking a job at BT at the instigation of my then girlfriend, who would eventually become my wife. I had saved enough money from my years in Belgium to put down a deposit on a house in Nookside in Sunderland. It was a two-bedroom semi, the sort of mansion that you would expect for £36,000, and it ensured that I was away from Norman and Yvonne.

Entry to the company would require five O Levels, so I dazzled them with my qualifications in English language, maths and economics, as well as two others that I lied about, before I was placed in the post room at Swan House, a plug-ugly office block at the Newcastle end of the Tyne Bridge. Until recently, the company had been called British Telecom, but then the wackier element took over and the name was changed to BT.

My job at that place would not have put undue strain on an idiot. I read the letters, designated where they needed to go to by giving them a reference number and dropped them into trolleys, which were then shoved around the building by others who would lob mail at whomever it was for. That was about it. My duties would not take long and when they were done, the rest of the day was mine to play keepie-uppie back in the mail room. Obviously we couldn't do that every single working day. No, sir. Sometimes we played cricket instead. We made a parcel tape ball and someone provided a bat. My batting average was 31.67; quite respectable.

One of the other menial tasks I would carry out during my meteoric rise in the world of office clerking, in between prolonged periods of arsing about, was to enter the flexi-time for various other staff members into the work sheets. A few of the staff were old friends of mine from school. They tended to clock up a few extra hours between them when I did this.

Years later, the football writer for the *Sunderland Echo*, Geoff Storey, would write match reports including regular descriptions of me as 'the gangling BT engineer'. This was quite an exaggeration. To this day I have yet to scale a telegraph pole and would imagine that it takes years to become a qualified BT engineer, whereas a monkey could have done my job. I also took exception to 'gangling' – I hadn't gangled in years by the time Mr Storey was writing about me.

Actually, to conclude that a monkey could have done it is not technically correct, but only because certain Health & Safety Executive approved codes of practice prohibit other primates from entering the workplace. The job paid the bills, but wasn't at all challenging; and why it required five O Levels to play cricket and post letters I would never know. But that was the requirement and eventually I was asked to provide my exam certificates.

This was a worry because someone had recently been given the bullet for lying about his qualifications, which was precisely what I had done. I couldn't possibly pass two more O Levels before the end of the week, but I could attain the certificates. Forgeries of course, courtesy of a friend who worked for Edward Thompson's, the printers. I awarded myself English literature and history, laminated them and thereby wriggled out of the problem. I decided against a PhD in forensic psychology as that may have aroused suspicion.

• • •

All good fun, but I missed football terribly and was doing all I could to get back to it. At BT there was a fax machine – at that time the last word in communications technology – and every day at 9 a.m. I would fax the FA in London to ask when I would be released by Hemptinne. In October 1991, after exactly 364 days of limbo, some sense prevailed and I was indeed released and free to play non-contractual football. This meant that I was still unable to play professionally for a salary, but could receive expenses – hopefully plenty of them.

I knew Kenny Mitchell, who was from Sunderland, but a former Newcastle player. He was managing Seaham Red Star, and I began pre-season training with them to get back into condition. I wasn't allowed to play for them, even in friendlies, until I was freed. As soon as possible I signed the forms and would be paid £60 expenses per game.

So desperate was I to play football that I signed for another team to play on Sundays. This was Plains Farm Working Men's Club for a ten-pint signing-on fee and £25 per game (they matched my terms). I was in a league that was a far cry from the glamour and mystique of Highbury, Anfield or even Roker Park. It was even a far cry from playing in the middle of cow fields in Hemptinne. But it was football of a variety known to men with allotments as 'proper football'. In the technical arena of Belgian football I was revered as the most aggressive centre-forward that teammates and opposition alike had ever seen. In the Sunderland Sunday League, I was just one of many.

My first competitive game back was for Plains Farm against Lakeside; a derby match (*ooooh*) and a reminder of what Sunday league football was all about. Lakeside's centre-forward was a tough nut called Craggsy. He was being marked by my mate Keithy 'Robbo' Robinson, who wasn't the meekest of blokes either, and there was much mutual antipathy and niggling.

We defended a corner and I was on the edge of our penalty area. The ball was cleared and I was on to it, breaking away with not much ahead to stop me. I passed the last defender but was curious as to why the goalkeeper was not even looking at me.

It was because he could not avert his eyes from the scene at the other end of the pitch, which if filmed could have been inserted seamlessly into *Reservoir Dogs*. Robbo was on top of Mr Craggs, developing their relationship by repeatedly punching him in the face. Even I was shocked. Such a spirited disagreement in today's Premier League would result in headlines of 'Football's Shame' and the like, as well as a ten-match ban for one or both players. The referee in 1991, Charlie Tye, also took a dim view.

The protagonists were dragged apart, the tip of Craggy's nose by now within the vicinity of his left ear. Standing in a puddle of warm blood, Charlie summoned them both before passing sentence.

He firmly pronounced: 'Now that's *it!* Shake hands and I want to know nowt more about it.'

My jaw went south. Evidently Charlie considered this to be a sufficiently punitive measure and continued with the rest of the game.

It felt great to be back.

Plains Farm was one of the better sides and the broad standard of the league was still fairly high. Aside from Robbo, other useful players included Steve Golightly, the Callaghan brothers, John Gamble, Kenny Mitchell, Kevin Todd and a few others. This wasn't the Champions League, but trust me when I say that these men knew what they were doing on a football pitch. Plains Farm had won the FA Sunday Cup final at the Hawthorns in 1990, a feat they repeated in 2014 at Ewood Park, so the standard remains high even in the current era.

Violence was endemic. I have a graphic memory of a particular punch in the ear I received from an opponent. I was getting the better of him and he was frustrated, although ear-punching was the sort of thing that this bloke would have categorised as recreation.

It was best not to take such things personally in this routinely vicious environment, and the £25 per game I was receiving was well earned. Remarkably, we were all insured, so it seems unlikely that there were many actuaries among the spectators.

• • •

At the end of the 1991–92 season, I moved from Seaham Red Star and up a couple of divisions to Bishop Auckland in the Northern Premier League. I was called by Bishop's manager, Harry Dunn, as was another Plains Farm stalwart, John Gamble, and we agreed to join. Another friend, Kevin Todd, formerly of Newcastle and Darlington, was already there. They gave me £100 per game, which, along with my BT salary and money from Plains Farm on Sundays, saw that I wasn't badly off. I started well on the pitch too. One of the first games was a 5–1 win at Worksop in Nottinghamshire where I scored four.

It is virtually impossible to make a reasonable comparison of the standard of football I was involved with in Belgium to that at Bishop Auckland. Technically Belgium was well in advance, but there was the physical exertion and the more than occasional brutality of the Northern Premier League to consider, which would have curled hair in Wallonia. Had tackles that were considered the norm in County Durham been seen at Hemptinne, the ensuing red cards would have left a five-a-side game at best. I suppose it was symptomatic of the differences between English and continental football at any level. When I played in the Northern Premier League I was still in my early twenties and up against blokes in their thirties; literally battle-scarred men, who had played hundreds of games at a decent level, that I would have to match for aggression. No weakness or fear could be displayed, not least when you felt weak or fearful. I was a bit of a name in that league and was therefore subjected to even worse, so I knew what I had to do. And as for the Sunderland Sunday League…

•   •   •

Apart from playing twice a week myself, I was as football-obsessed as I had been as a child and watched Sunderland as often as possible. In 1992 they reached the FA Cup final. The run included a 2–1 victory over Chelsea at an electrified Roker Park thanks to a sensational headed winner from Gordon Armstrong. I was also at Hillsborough to see Norwich City beaten 1–0 in the semi-final by a much simpler header from John Byrne (who scored in every round except the final). From a neutral perspective, the semi-final wasn't much of a game, but there were no neutrals in Sunderland and the place went bananas.

I couldn't get a ticket for Wembley, where the opposition was Liverpool, so I went to a cup final barbecue instead and became extremely overwrought about the game, as I always have done with Sunderland. Sick with excitement and anxiety, not to mention spare ribs, I had to leave the barbecue as soon as the game had finished to have a lie-down.

Happily it was the Sunderland team who were given the winners' medals. Less happily this was done by mistake. They had to go and swap with Liverpool, who had been given the runners-up gongs. John Byrne squandered a decent chance in the first half, which finished goalless. The second half was far more predictable and Liverpool won 2–0. Still, it's far better than being dumped on your arse in the third round.

As an aside, the way that FA Cup final tickets are distributed was – and still is – a disgrace. The 1992 final had an attendance of slightly below 80,000, with the two clubs involved being given around half of the allocation. This is a bad joke. Surely that figure should be at least 75 per cent. The idea is that all of the counties which encompass the FA are rewarded for the sterling work that they do throughout the year by being offered first refusal on cup final tickets. But the fans are the financial and emotional backbone of the game and not many businesses would treat their paying customers so shoddily. The reality is that most of the people who end up attending the final are fans of the two participating teams, who have bagged a ticket either through good connections or, more likely, being ripped off by 'ticketing agencies', which is another term for touts and glorified spivs.

Anyway, rant over – except to say that twenty-two years later I was overjoyed to get tickets for my son and myself to see Sunderland in the League Cup final against Manchester City in the new Wembley Stadium. This was courtesy of a good friend and neighbour Trevor Alderson (owner of a racehorse called Roker Park). So I got there in the end, even if it was 3–1 to City.

• • •

I was doing pretty well at both Bishop Auckland and Plains Farm. Training was Tuesdays and Thursdays for Bishop's. They didn't bother with highfalutin ideas like training at Plains Farm, although they did expect you to drink in the club after the game. In that regard they ran a tight ship. You had to be in the club post-match anyway to collect your £25 and I suspect they deliberately made us wait for the cash, safe in the knowledge that we would fill the time by drinking, and then have a couple more once we were paid. By the time you left the club, at least half of your £25 would be gone. They were paying us with money that we would immediately give back. Of course, we could have used temperance, prudence and restraint – it's just a pity that we didn't.

It wasn't notably genteel at Bishop Auckland either and this occasionally applied to the supporters too. After one home game against opposition I don't recall, but it could have been anyone, there was an almighty ruckus in the bar at Kingsway (Bishop's old ground), the highlight of which was a beer barrel being hurled by a visiting supporter into a group of home supporters, who failed to appreciate the gesture. I did not witness the combat myself but was told about it later, including a description of how my dad had knocked someone unconscious. This astonished me, although when I say 'astonished' I am clearly lying.

• • •

Socially acceptable violence and all, life was rumbling along quite reasonably. Again, it wasn't the football career to fulfil my wilder childhood ambitions, but I had a steady job in the Arsing About Department at BT, I was playing a great deal of footy for a significant secondary income, I had a girlfriend and I owned a house. Yet things were about to become a great deal more exciting. In February of 1993 there came a pivotal moment in my life. At first it seemed incidental, but the personal repercussions would be huge.

Malcolm Crosby was sacked as manager of Sunderland.

Malcolm was appointed on a caretaker basis in December 1991 following the dismissal of Denis Smith. Smith had taken the club from the post-McMenemy despair of the Third Division and all the way back to the top flight. However, immediate relegation back to the Second Division followed, as did a poor start in 1991–92. With the club in seventeenth place, Smith was dismissed and replaced by Crosby, the first team coach and a Sunderland fan.

This was initially temporary, but Malcolm was given the job full-time after a flying start in the league and, more memorably, because he took Sunderland to the FA Cup final. The consensus is that Malcolm was a lovely man who is respected to this day as a coach, but not cut out for management. Sunderland may have reached Wembley, but they finished the season seventh from bottom (ahead of Grimsby on goal difference and Newcastle by a point) and in hindsight he was appointed on sentiment, which rarely works out in football.

Nevertheless, his sacking was cruelly timed. Sunderland were due to play away to Tranmere Rovers on 30 January, but the match was postponed because of the weather. Three days later he was fired and it looked as though the decision had been made on the back of a pools panel home win. Bad news for Mr Crosby, fantastic news for me, and what's more, I knew it.

Various names were lobbed around by the media as Malcolm's replacement, including Bryan Robson, Phil Neal, Joe Jordan and Neil Warnock. But the Sunderland chairman, Bob Murray, was not a man renowned for imagination and the job went to someone who was handily already at the club as a player: Terry Butcher.

Butch had had an unsuccessful fourteen months as player-manager at Coventry City, culminating in the sack in January 1992. Malcolm Crosby then offered him the opportunity to resurrect his playing career at Sunderland before the start of the 1992–93 season.

Not only did Terry Butcher replace Malcolm, he also brought with him some familiar faces from my Ipswich days. Bobby Ferguson was his assistant and John Carruthers would be his scout. I was out and about with my old mates when Butch's appointment was announced: Eddie Harrison, Vincent Marriner, Gary Clark and others who might buy this book if I mention their names. I confidently told Eddie that I would soon be playing for Sunderland.

'*Au contraire*,' replied Eddie dismissively but not unreasonably. Or it was words to that effect. It may have been 'Fuck off'.

But I knew that if I couldn't get in under these circumstances, then I never would. It all came about after a fixture for Bishop Auckland. It was a dour 1–1 draw at Durham City in the first qualifying round of the FA Cup at New Ferens Park in Belmont. I didn't play with any distinction. John Carruthers was there and engaged me in some small talk after the game. I hadn't exactly dazzled him, but he agreed to come and watch the replay ten days later.

In the meantime there were invitations from other fronts. I was asked to train and trial at Doncaster Rovers. I travelled down with Norman and played in a game against Garforth Town that was farcical due to high winds that had overturned lorries on the A19. We played anyway. For obvious reasons it was a true game of two halves. The 110-mile car journey home took four-and-a-half hours.

The replay against Durham City went extremely well. We won 5–2 and I scored a hat-trick. On the back of this John Carruthers got me a trial game at, of all places, Ipswich Town, who were then competing in the inaugural season of the newly formed Premier League. He had a foot in the camps of both Sunderland and Ipswich. A reserve match between Ipswich and Charlton Athletic had been arranged somewhere in London and I was to play up front alongside Paul Goddard, a former England international and quite a prolific goal scorer for West Ham among others, but now at the veteran stage.

Ipswich won 1–0 and I scored the best goal of my entire life. Bollocks to false modesty; it was a fucking worldy.

Twenty minutes into the game I took the ball down on the left wing, just inside our half. I laid it inside to Paul, who played it back to me, upon which I smashed the ball into the top corner from about thirty-five yards. As the less original commentators say, it rocketed into the net. Mike Salmon in the Charlton goal had no chance. Their team was coached by Keith Peacock (father of the Chelsea player Gavin) and years later he told my dad that I had scored one of the best goals he had ever clapped eyes on. As I said, false modesty my arse.

Unfortunately I had to limp off with fifteen minutes remaining due to a twisted ankle. I had done enough to impress the Ipswich staff who said they would advise the club's manager, John Lyall, to sign me. They wanted me to come down the following week to train and speak with Mr Lyall.

My reply was: 'I can't come down next week, because I want to play for Sunderland against Newcastle at Roker Park next week.'

• • •

It would only be a reserve game, but it meant everything to me. Ipswich understood completely and were very gracious about it, telling me to keep in touch and to let them know how it went. It would go wonderfully well.

The game took place on Wednesday 10 February 1993 (things had moved very quickly). Before almost 2,000 spectators, Sunderland won 4–0 and I scored the first goal, with Stephen Brodie, Brian Mooney and Craig Russell providing the last three. Others in the side included Richard Ord, Gary Bennett, Anton Rogan and Ian Sampson. But Newcastle didn't put out a load of mugs either. Their line-up featured Alan Nielson, Mark Stimson, Kevin Brock, Andy Hunt, Alan Thompson, Steve Watson, Bjørn Kristensen and Tommy Wright in goal. Kristensen was marking me and I took quite some pleasure in smashing him all over the pitch (nothing personal). He was sold to Portsmouth soon afterwards.

The crowd was delighted. It may only have been a reserve game, but Sunderland and Newcastle want to beat each other at any level of football, as well as any level of rowing, darts, tossing the caber, Ker-plunk, custard eating…

However, at the full-time whistle I was not quite as joyous as you might imagine. My ankle hadn't fully recovered from the Ipswich game and was strapped up. It became worse when I landed awkwardly after a header and I had to be replaced by Warren Hawke.

I was alone in the dressing room, wondering if I had played well enough, or if my chance had gone.

This was paranoia on my part. Terry Butcher came down to see me and said that I should return to Roker Park the next day and bring a decent pen. That seemingly ill-conceived wallop I had given him as a sixteen-year-old had finally benefitted me and I was going to sign for Sunderland Association Football Club.

I was dizzy with the thrill of it all (and took specific satisfaction from telling Eddie Harrison that he was wrong). I would be contracted up to the summer of 1996 for £500 per week; modest even in those days and not significantly better than my combined wages from BT, Bishop Auckland and Plains Farm. But that definitely wasn't an issue. I was not about to haggle; in fact Butch was lucky to get his hand back. It was all I had ever wanted. The fact that it was a three-year agreement meant he was serious too. The length of contract was presumably to make Sunderland a more attractive proposition than Ipswich, but I would have signed for six months if that was all they had offered.

My trial at Roker was common knowledge at Bishop Auckland and Plains Farm and I left both clubs on excellent terms, with good wishes and compliments ringing in my ears. Harry Dunn immediately picked up the phone to offer me his congratulations. Other verbal bouquets came from the lads at both teams (albeit they were usually accompanied by requests for match tickets). There was also good news for AS Hemptinne, because to clear up the issue of my registration, Sunderland gave them around £6,000. Louis Gemine must have been wobbling with glee at this unexpected windfall a year and a half after my departure, although he never wrote to say as much.

BT would have to manage without me. My understanding is that the company is still in existence today.

• • •

My personal joy was unalloyed, but similar elation was not prevalent at Sunderland AFC as a whole. The FA Cup final had only been nine months earlier, but it may as well have been ten years. On the day I signed we were sitting less than proudly in seventeenth place and had been long eliminated from the cups. Only Don Goodman offered much of a goal threat.

Matters were compounded for the fans by the concurrent success of Newcastle. The Magpies had been on their knees in 1991–92 when they took a punt on Kevin Keegan as manager at the back end of the season. This was a quite desperate move as he had zero managerial experience. Yet it worked. By merely turning up he almost doubled their attendances overnight. Their last home gate before he came was 15,663 and would surely have dropped further. Their first game after his arrival was watched by 29,263. Life and fervour was restored to the club and would prove crucial. They survived on spirit, narrowly but successfully averting relegation. Then they made shrewd investments, including the acquisitions of Andy Cole from Bristol City, Barry Venison from Liverpool, Rob Lee from Charlton – and Paul Bracewell from Sunderland (which was a further kick in the collective knackers of Wearside). Newcastle United appeared to win the 1992–93 First Division without breaking a sweat and their glide into the Premier League was rammed down the throats of everyone else in the North East, not least by Tyne Tees Television.

In the heart of their defence throughout all of this was one Steve Howey.

Back on the Wear there was more hope than expectation at the signing of another Howey from Bishop Auckland. Dragging a bloke from the sixth tier of English football to the second might have seemed like an act of desperation to the fans (indeed, Sunderland's season would very nearly end in disaster). This made it prudent not to publicise the fact that I had also been playing even further down the football pyramid for Plains Farm Working Men's Club as recently as a fortnight before signing at Roker (my trial game for Ipswich was four days after my last match for Plains Farm).

I was too happy to be downtrodden by these wider issues and just wanted to stride on to a pitch and do my utmost for Sunderland. Partly because of my ankle, this would not happen for a while. But I soon felt like part of the squad. I *was* part of the squad and also within sniffing distance of the substitutes' bench (pardon the expression; I have never sniffed a substitutes' bench in my life). This would do for now and I was soon playing again for the reserves, which was in itself a lovely novelty.

•   •   •

As part of the squad's preparation for the big one, away to Newcastle on Sunday 25 April, we spent some time away at Turnberry, the posh golf resort in Ayrshire (modestly renamed the Trump Turnberry in 2014 after its bashful new owner). Terry had also arranged for us to watch his beloved Rangers play against CSKA Moscow in the Champions League at Ibrox (they were eliminated). I enjoyed the trip for the most part, but it was the first time I ever saw animosity between the players and the coaching staff. Established pros like Don Goodman, Gary Owers, Gordon Armstrong and Anton Rogan didn't like Butcher, but could not get on with Bobby Ferguson in particular. I found this awkward because Bobby had been good to me.

I was in the squad for the Newcastle game, but still didn't make the subs' bench (my best realistic hope). I was, however, in the changing room and it was quite extraordinary.

The derby was played on a waterlogged pitch during a day of torrential rain. It is widely suspected that live television coverage played a part in its non-postponement. The Sunderland team was getting changed and wondering where on earth their player-manager could be when he appeared about thirty-five minutes before kick-off. Quite the lad for a grand gesture, his head had been shaved down to the wood. For some reason he seemed to think this was inspirational and the stuff of leaders, rather than what it really was – bonkers.

He bellowed: 'We're fucking commandoes! I've had this haircut because I'm a commando and you're all going to be fucking commandoes too. We're gonna parachute in, get the victory, then fuck off out! *NO SURRENDER!*'

Despite looking at this precise moment like someone who was quite deranged, Butch was actually an intelligent man and knew exactly what he was saying. He was aware that several of the lads were Catholic – I was one of them – but must have thought that he would fire them up by striking a few nerves with a massively loaded two-word phrase. There were some very experienced professionals in that changing room, including England internationals Peter Davenport and Mick Harford, who was the same age as Terry. Everyone just stared at Butch in silence. It was truly bewildering.

Butch's first touch of the game raised eyebrows even higher. Under no challenge whatsoever, a man who had played in three World Cups showed zero composure when he received the ball. He had wound himself up so much that he just smashed it with all his might, much as Peter Kay would do later in a beer commercial. No one could be sure if the ball was still within the United Kingdom and the home fans were pissing themselves laughing. My heart sank and so did Sunderland. Newcastle won 1–0 and the narrow scoreline was the only good thing about it.

· · ·

During my years playing in Belgium, Bishop Auckland and Plains Farm, not to mention singlehandedly upholding the share price of BT, my brother had made accelerating progress at Newcastle United.

Steven made his debut as a seventeen-year-old in a First Division game as substitute at Manchester United on the final game of the 1988–89 season. Newcastle were already relegated and Jim Smith, their manager (known as the Bald Eagle, so presumably he had just been the Eagle when he was younger), thought he might as well try a youngster or two. Still matey with the flesh and blood at that time, I travelled to Old Trafford with Norman and a load of Mags to support Steven (if not the Mags), who played up front with Tony Lormor.

This was a big moment in Howey history. Newcastle's starting line-up featured David McCreery, Kenny Sansom, John Anderson and Glenn Roeder. Opponents included Bryan Robson, Brian McClair, Mike Duxbury, Steve Bruce, Mark Hughes and Lee Sharpe. McClair and Robson scored in a 2–0 home win, but what a start to a teenager's first team career before 30,000 fans. It was a good atmosphere with no animosity from the Newcastle supporters, who were resigned to their fate. Incidentally, Manchester United finished the season in eleventh place – between Millwall and Wimbledon.

Howey minor did not feature at all in Newcastle's first team the following season, which ended with that defeat to Sunderland in the play-offs. But he made a handful of appearances in 1990–91, thirteen starts and eight sub appearances in 1991–92, before playing in almost every game of 1992–93 as they steamrollered their way to promotion under Keegan.

Steven had always been a midfielder, and an excellent one at that. He could dribble and score goals with both feet. In fact, he was exceptional. Between the ages of about fifteen and seventeen he had a rapid growth spurt and this newly acquired height led someone at St James' Park to believe that he should be a centre-forward, which he had never been. These were more primitive times in football.

Then came the more perceptive Kevin Keegan, who was fantastic for Steven. He watched him in training and decided he was better suited to centre-half. You probably know the rest. His career took off; he spent the majority of it in the Premier League and played for England too.

My £500 per week at Sunderland was supplemented with a win bonus of around £400. Not bad, except that it wasn't supplemented too often because we weren't winning many and I wasn't exactly the first name on the team sheet. Steven went from struggling along financially to a salary of four grand a week as Newcastle's resurrection rolled spectacularly on. This was a massive wage for a 21-year-old outside the top flight, and a Howey on £200,000 a year was a novel concept.

Money may have played a part, but it was the idolatry more than the salary he was receiving that meant we ceased to occupy the same planet. He was socialising with some very famous footballers, while I continued to knock around with the same lads I had known since childhood (although it should be said that I still do and will never regret this). From then on, the Howey brothers, having never been especially close, would only drift further apart.

For the time being we were cordial enough, even if my half of our increasingly rare conversations was to say that I hoped he would play well during a 4–0 defeat. I meant this too. He was my brother, but I was a Sunderland fan, so this seemed to strike a reasonable balance. I wished him well, but not his team.

He played for Newcastle the day Terry Butcher shaved his head. Our interaction was confined to a polite nod before the game. We were both in match mode, even if I wasn't going to play. Our parents were there and I think we all had a drink afterwards. Matters at this stage were not irreparable.

• • •

Six days after the derby, on the beautifully sunny Saturday of 1 May 1993, came the moment I had been waiting for all my life. I played for Sunderland.

It was a huge game for the club too. I was named as substitute and my chances of making it onto the pitch would surely be increased if the game was going well. In the event, it could hardly have gone any better.

The opposition was Portsmouth, who were top of the table, at that stage above even Newcastle, who had two games in hand. By 3 p.m., Pompey supporters had filled the Roker End, having arrived in their thousands to witness the formality of an away win, giving full throat to the never-irritating-at-all 'Pompey Chimes'. It was their second last game of the season and they needed four more points to ensure promotion. It was about to go horribly wrong for them.

In the thirty-fifth minute, they were reduced to ten men when Guy Butters stopped a certain Gordon Armstrong goal with his hands. Don Goodman battered in the penalty. Early in the second half, Don put away another penalty. Eventually it was 4–1 with Pompey down to nine players after Paul Walsh had also walked. It was a stroll for Sunderland. Gordon did get a goal in the end and even Martin Gray scored (his only ever Sunderland goal).

With a few minutes of the game remaining and the result beyond doubt, I was told to get stripped. This was it. I was about to play before the largest crowd of my professional career to date. Yet, partly because it was 4–1, I wasn't nervous. I was gagging to be on that pitch. I was brought on in place of Shaun Cunnington, given an encouraging roar from a happy crowd and from that moment, whatever happened in the rest of my life, I could say I had played for Sunderland.

Playing for the team you love is an emotion that few people get to have. I was only on the pitch for a few minutes and barely touched the ball. At twenty-four I was also something of an elderly debutant and had taken an extremely unorthodox route to reach this point. But none of that mattered and I felt a pride I had never previously known. Proud as a peacock with a new conservatory. I got to applaud the fans at the final whistle, wave at people and generally do all the things I had seen footballers do and always wanted to try myself. It did not seem real. The next day, Manchester United became the first ever winners of the new Premier League, but I can't believe they felt any happier than I did that weekend. Mr McAuliffe, are you watching?

I had done it.

• • •

Pompey failed to be promoted. They were edged out by West Ham before losing to Leicester City in the play-offs. Portsmouth and the Hammers both finished on eighty-eight points, but there was a six-goal difference, West Ham having beaten Sunderland 6–0 earlier in the season.

They must have loved Sunderland in Portsmouth in 1993.

• • •

Portsmouth would be my only first team appearance of the season. Three days later we were at Tranmere for our penultimate game. I sat behind the visitors' dugout for this fixture, which had been rearranged after the infamous pools panel defeat that preceded the sacking of Malcolm Crosby. Tranmere Rovers were in a play-off spot and expected to win. They did: 2–1. But we played reasonably well. Brian Atkinson gave us the lead, before Dave Martindale and Pat Nevin took it away. Kevin Ball was sent off for Sunderland – if you can imagine such a thing.

This left us seventh from bottom with one game remaining that we needed to win to guarantee our safety. Bristol Rovers were already down and it was any two from seven for the other relegation places. The final game was at Notts County, themselves one of the seven. They started the game a point behind Sunderland, who never started the game at all.

There was nothing in our performance to suggest that we were fighting for football survival and at half-time it was 3–0 to County. Our supporters had sold out their allocation and were justifiably furious. When fans of the same team are fighting each other, then you know a club is in trouble. The atmosphere in the dressing room was poisonous too, but not in the way I expected. Let's go back a few years (screen goes wobbly)…

I'd had personal experience of Terry Butcher as a genuine leader of men and, when required, an absolute animal. He was a fearless footballer. Playing for Ipswich in a 2–0 defeat to Chelsea at Portman Road in November 1985, he had been given a torrid time by the gifted but obnoxious David Speedie. Butch's bad mood was distended by some awful decisions from the officials and he went to remonstrate after the final whistle, only to find the referee's door locked. I was an apprentice hanging around and witnessed him put his considerable foot straight through it. The poor ref must have felt like he was in *The Shining*.

Terry played for England in a World Cup qualifier against Sweden in Stockholm in 1989; a goalless draw remembered more for a mad-eyed, grinning Butcher finishing the game with an understitched head injury, his white shirt turned crimson with his own blood (believe it or not some photographs exist to prove this little-known tale).

Returning now to 1993, those memories of him were still very vivid and everyone had seen his more recent antics before the Newcastle game, when he might have appeared unhinged, but was at least passionate. When the half-time whistle blew at Meadow

Lane I suspected he was about to rip a few heads off, possibly literally, for an appalling forty-five minutes of football. At that moment it was something that I, as a Sunderland fan, would have enjoyed watching. Instead our leader sat in complete silence, his face like that of a haemorrhoid-stricken pallbearer. His head was in his hands. It was hard to comprehend that this was the same head that had so famously and copiously bled in Sweden. Five minutes passed. Ten minutes passed. Not a word; Butcher continued to sit in silence. It was like a party at the clap clinic.

Eventually, Gary Owers stood up and screamed: '*Are you going to fucking say something or what?*'

This instigated a heated argument between virtually everyone in the room; a morass of foul language and acrimony. Fingers were pointed, blame was allocated, but no responsibility was accepted for the fiasco. At least it was a bit of zeal, but it wasn't good. In this frame of mind they had to trot out for the second half and attempt to score four goals. Guess what happened next.

Well, what do you think happened? This isn't *Roy of the Rovers*.

There was a slight improvement and Kevin Ball, possibly the only Sunderland player who wasn't pure shite that day, scored. We lost 3–1. The most important thing is that we survived; John Cairns from BBC Radio Newcastle kept us up to date with the other scores. Cambridge United and Brentford both lost and we finished one point and one place above the relegation zone. The fans were placated by this, but it was more relief than appreciation and could not disguise the fact that a poor season had ended shamefully. That performance is remembered today by any Sunderland supporter present as one of the all-time worst, and we only stayed out of football's third tier because two comparatively tiny clubs had lost. In all their travails since, Sunderland have never sunk so low.

Perhaps I should have been happy that the worst was averted, that I was not involved and was therefore untainted by the performance. But as I helped to fetch and carry a few things after the game, I was fuming. I was no stranger to playing badly myself, but there is a wealth of difference between merely playing badly and playing without spirit – and the Notts County display was all but spiritless. The mood deteriorated further when an irate Sunderland fan managed to board the team bus. It was me.

I could no longer contain my anguish and erupted, informing them in nothing like a casual manner: 'You're all a fucking *disgrace!* Those fans have paid money to come here and *that's* what you've given them! They're so upset that they're fighting each other...'

I was roaring with frustration but was eventually calmed down, if not appeased. This was part of a realisation that players and fans are not necessarily of one mind. It's difficult to understand sometimes that even when professional footballers are representing a club, it still isn't usually 'their' team. It's a job, and if they are offered a better job, they'll take it.

Terry Butcher would never play again.

CHAPTER 5

MAKING A MARK

In the summer of 1993 I went on holiday somewhere or other in the sun. I don't remember where. When I returned it was to the worst pre-season training I would ever endure.

No one could fathom what Mr Butcher was thinking. We were told to report to the Silksworth Sports Complex and, as had happened when I was an apprentice at Ipswich, we didn't see a ball for five weeks. But in terms of physical torment it was way in excess of even that. With the first team and reserve squads, as well as some of the youths, there were about thirty-five of us at the start of training. After a week this was down to about a dozen. It was that bad.

Twenty-odd players had been injured or made ill by this horrendous regime. I had correctly envisaged something beyond the training at Bishop Auckland (bit of exercise and a kick-about) and Plains Farm (nowt), but this was far beyond anything I had expected.

We would run up and down the side of the artificial ski slope which, being a ski slope, is on the steep side. Then we would have shuttle runs around the bowl in which the adjacent running track was sunk. Run, jump, run, sprint, press-ups, run, squat-thrusts, run back up the ski slope, more shuttle runs, jump, run, sprint, run, run... Numerous cones would be placed at the top and bottom of the bowl which designated where we were to run up to, then down to, up then down, up then down ... It was fearsome and imbued with all the fun and gaiety of kidney stones. I could imagine Daley

Thompson thinking better of it and popping into the Sportsman's Arms for a few jars and a game of pool instead.

As a treat we were allowed the occasional deep breath and a banana; otherwise it was uniformly awful. My legs were crying out with calf strains, thigh strains and other ailments that will inevitably be caused by such a programme. It did the squad no favours in terms of either injuries or *esprit de corps*. It did even less for the popularity of the manager.

We were taken to the University of Stirling for a training camp in another well-intentioned but ultimately futile team-building exercise. We did spot the occasional ball on this trip, but it was mainly more running.

In fairness we were allowed a couple of beers in Scotland and it was during such a respite that Alec Chamberlain, our goalkeeper newly signed from Luton Town, spoke to his mate Phil Gray over the phone. Phil was still at Luton and Sunderland had put in a bid for him. He signed the next day. He was a skilful player, a Northern Ireland international and his £800,000 fee was a significant outlay. His price meant that he was almost guaranteed to play because Butch would have to justify the expense. Phil, or Tippy as he was known, was a striker too. As long as he stayed fit by not being involved in road accidents (more on that soon), he was in the team. Ah, bollocks.

Phil's signing was dispiriting for me. He improved the squad, but I wanted to play, dammit. I would just have to do my best. In the meantime the atmosphere among the first team squad seemed to fester more and more by the day. It was coaching staff and playing staff, us and them, them and us – when the whole club and not just the players was supposed to be a team.

I found this very awkward because I shared some of the misgivings of the lads. But Terry Butcher and Bobby Ferguson (who had left in May) had done a great deal for me. I also liked Ian Atkins, who was someone else I knew from my Ipswich days (he was also a former Sunderland player and a good one too). I had known Butcher as a player and been in his company socially a few times too. As a manager you have to step away from the players in certain respects, but a wall went up, which is not quite the same thing. I completely understood the displeasure of the lads because I was being tortured by the military training as much as anyone.

The summer of 1993 saw Gary Bennett's testimonial game and, thanks to Terry's relationship with his counterpart at Glasgow Rangers, Walter Smith, Benno struck gold. A match against Rangers on the evening of Wednesday 28 July was arranged and 21,862, a near sell-out, turned up at Roker to watch it. The 8,000 Rangers fans arrived in town and duly lived up to the image of Scottish football supporters on a day out. They were mainly drunk and largely, but not entirely, good-natured. There was a particularly nasty incident when a Sunderland supporter was slashed across the face in the city centre.

We had a training session on the morning of the game and were told what the starting XI would be, with Phil Gray and Don Goodman up front. As expected, I wasn't in the team but still hoped for a run-out from the bench at some stage. I travelled to Roker Park in the evening by car with my parents. On and around the Wearmouth Bridge there were bodies everywhere for us to negotiate; hordes of pissed-up people in blue football shirts, lolloping around and singing jaunty songs about burning Catholics, incarcerating the Pope, the Potato Famine – that sort of thing.

When I arrived, I was told that Phil was injured and I would be starting. As a fan of both Sunderland and Celtic I was hugely excited and, better still, I wasn't even beset with nerves. I hadn't been given enough time to become nervous. It all just happened in an instant. I had a good game too, but best of all was scoring in front of the Fulwell End.

With the score at 0–0 in the first half, I laid the ball to Gordon

Armstrong, who played it forward to Benno on the edge of the Rangers penalty area. Benno nudged it to me to run on to and I dinked it with the outside of my right foot and past Ally Maxwell in goal. Testimonial or not, the roar was something I will never forget and I really felt like I had arrived. I had scored for Sunderland.

Regrettably, the match ended 3–1 to Rangers, which was hardly surprising, really. Their side included Mark Hateley, who scored twice, Steven Pressley, Oleksiy Mykhaylychenko (I cut and pasted his name there), Ian Ferguson, Stuart McCall and John Brown, who was given a hard time by me. Ha. Ally McCoist, Gary Stevens, Gordon Durie and Richard Gough were left out. Rangers really were the business in those days and the gap between the top side in Scotland and their English equivalent was considerably narrower then. We had acquitted ourselves well. At full-time, Brian Atkinson said: 'Fucking hell, big man. They'll want to sign you after that.' He meant Rangers.

Shame we lost, but it was one of the good days. Never let them go.

• • •

As the next part of our programme of pre-season games, we could have gone to Blackpool and taken in an afternoon of fresh air and fun on the Pleasure Beach. But we decided instead to travel to Belfast during the peak of violent sectarianism. The IRA was in particularly ruthless and murderous form; earlier in the year they had bombed Warrington and London. So the trip provided some levity amid the ongoing fitness sessions.

The preponderance of Union flags and Red Hands painted onto the gable ends led me to assume that it was Butch who had decided which areas of Belfast we would be playing in. It was a truly intimidating experience and heavily armed soldiers wandering around the two stadiums we played in was not a sight I was used to. We played Ards and Glentoran and won both fixtures, although I remember nothing more about them. Following the games we could have held a triumphal march through the streets; after all, it was our right – but we decided against it.

Ian Murtagh, a North East football reporter, accompanied us. One highlight of the tour was persuading Gareth Cronin, a trainee from Cork, to call him on his mobile phone, claim to be from the IRA and say that they knew who and where he was, what he'd been writing, etc. Correctly, Mr Murtagh was almost, but not entirely convinced that he was the subject of a tasteless practical joke and tried to play it down. But he still couldn't completely dispel the facial expression that can only be worn by a man who is concerned for the future of his kneecaps. What terrorism-related larks we were having (we did let him know, eventually).

'The Troubles' is a euphemism that makes paramilitary murder and thuggery sound like an elderly lady describing her irritable bowel. Fear and intimidation permeated. Let's not forget that it was literally a war zone. We had armed guards to accompany us to the games and roads were blockaded to facilitate us. Even Eddie Harrison's stag night wasn't this bad. Alec Chamberlain and I went to some or other bar in Belfast during a free evening, a respectable-looking establishment and fairly busy. We naively attributed the stares we were attracting to our strange accents and striking good looks.

We ordered a drink and the barmaid began to make friendly chat, asking where we were from, what had brought us to Belfast and so forth. We didn't realise that she wasn't just making small talk, or that we were in a nationalist bar. When we explained that we were Sunderland footballers the relief on her face was apparent – even to us. Then we discovered how perilously close we had been to a thoroughly good hiding. Our short hair and obvious Englishness had erroneously suggested to the locals that we were squaddies. A number of large gentlemen had been called upon to rearrange our body parts in the manner of their choosing and they were on their way round.

Matters had been clarified by the time they arrived and they were quite happy to chat with us about football. They were pacified further when I told them I had scored against Rangers. Although affable, they were blankly open about what their intentions had been when they thought we were members of the British Army. Alec and I took leave of that bar thinking that a match at each of the remaining branches of Butlin's would be quite adequate for the next pre-season tour.

The next day, Phil Gray, a Belfast boy, gave us a guided tour of certain sections of the city. Nothing we had seen on television could quite prepare us.

• • •

When we returned to Sunderland, nothing had changed. There were the same old arguments.

Our final pre-season game was another testimonial on 8 August, this time at Middlesbrough for their midfielder Gary Hamilton, who had been forced into retirement through injury. This was largely forgettable, but we won 2–1 and I came off the bench to score the winner.

When I arrived at training the following day, Martin Gray bounded over to me and asked: 'Have you heard about the lads? They've had a car crash.' He was referring to four of the five players we had bought over the summer.

Alec Chamberlain had arrived free (because of a clerical error at Luton Town). Bob Murray, the Sunderland chairman, then found £2 million for Butcher to invest in the squad. The money was spent on Phil Gray, centre-back Andy Melville from Oxford United, with midfielders Ian Rodgerson and Derek Ferguson (older brother of

Barry Ferguson) from Birmingham City and Hearts respectively. These four had all squeezed into Ferguson's Vauxhall Astra after the Middlesbrough match.

Derek was at the wheel when he abandoned established custom by entering a roundabout on Dame Dorothy Street in an anti-clockwise direction. Unfortunately, a woman in a Ford Granada had come onto the roundabout in a clockwise direction, which was more traditional. Phil, who was in the passenger seat and not wearing his seat belt, ended the incident with his head through the windscreen and glass in his eye. Ian sustained a dislocated shoulder and Andy had whiplash. The woman also incurred whiplash, her son suffered bruising and shock and her mother fractured several ribs.

Of the seven people involved, only Derek was unscathed, but he was later fined and banned from driving for a year. Being a footballer occasionally bags you free entry into a nightclub, but judges tend to be less easily impressed than bouncers.

Sunderland had made a calamitous start to the season six days before it had even begun. However, my chances of playing had improved significantly with one wrong turn of a steering wheel. I was sorry for the lads in the crash, not forgetting the people in the Granada. But when opportunity knocks…

With Phil unavailable I knew I would start the first game of the 1993–94 season against Derby County at the old Baseball Ground. This would be my first start in a Football League game. Again, this was hugely exciting because it was more important than any friendly. I trained hard as usual, working with special attention to set-pieces. Throughout the week I was telling myself all the right things – that everything would be fine and the nerves would dissipate. I just wanted to get onto the pitch. I felt ready.

On a sunny 14 August we arrived at the stadium where there were a couple of telegrams (yes telegrams) waiting for me. They were from well-wishers including Neil Emmerson, my old mate from Ipswich. Another was from my Auntie Margaret and Uncle Colin in Australia. This was all very lovely and I realised how massive the fixture was for everyone, not just me. More so than on my brief debut as a sub against Portsmouth in May, this was it. I only hoped I wouldn't let anyone down.

But I did.

We all did.

I used all of the breathing exercises and attempts at mental fortitude, went through the same pre-match routine as always, including all the silly superstitions that footballers tend to have; I felt compelled to put on socks, shin pads and boots right before left for no rational reason whatsoever. Then it was on to the pitch for the warm-up, which in those days was little more than kicking a few balls around (it wouldn't become any more scientific at Sunderland until Peter Reid arrived), trying to absorb the opening day atmosphere in that iconic old ground. None of it worked. My legs felt increasingly heavy and by the time we kicked off I was like a dachshund on Bonfire Night, beset with anxiety.

I continued to tell myself: 'Once that whistle blows I'll be fine. I'll be fine. I'll be fine...' It was all wishful thinking. The problem was that I cared too much.

All my aggression was gone. I could barely lift my feet and was hyperventilating at times. Marking me that day was Craig Short, who dominated me. He took full advantage of my nerves and totally negated my presence. It wasn't just his assured performance, it was the occasion. Short was a fine, not to say expensive centre-back, but confronted by a striker temporarily unable to run, jump, hold up the ball or even breathe properly, there were lesser defenders who would have coped.

It was no consolation to me that everyone else connected to Sunderland was suffering too. Chamberlain, Ferguson and Melville were also having dreadful first starts for the club. We were a goal down after ten minutes when Mark Pembridge scored a penalty. Marco Gabbiadini is to this day a Sunderland favourite, but he scored Derby's second on forty minutes, with Pembridge's second arriving five minutes later. A half-time deficit of three, then; but could it be turned round with Terry Butcher putting his attuned, managerial mind to the problem?

Nah.

I was replaced by Lee Power, then on loan from Norwich City (he later became the owner of Swindon Town), but it was deck-chairs-on-the-Titanic stuff and the final score was 5–0. It was a fucking disaster. The worst thing was that having stayed up the previous season by a point, we already looked like strugglers and this performance was every bit as horrific as the one at Notts County – and this time I had been part of it.

The atmosphere at the club became even worse after that. Three days after Derby County, we came through a League Cup first round, first leg at home to Chester City, two leagues below us, by three goals to one. But we were trailing at half-time and the atmosphere at Roker during the break was toxic. Training was niggly too, with Derek Ferguson in particular wanting to fight everyone. Fight me, by all means – just don't offer me a lift.

• • •

A home game with Wolves on 18 September stands out. In keeping with the period it was for all the wrong reasons. We actually played quite well, but somehow contrived to lose. Wolves took an early lead when Alec Chamberlain attempted a clearance, only to boot the ball against the midriff of Mike Small. The ball then trundled into the net for the only goal that Small would ever score for Wolves. It was that sort of day.

We dominated the game, but nothing went right. Don Goodman had a goal harshly disallowed. At that point you could have bottled the frustration in Roker Park and sold it to science. The general mood was reddened further by the behaviour of the Wolves midfielder Geoff Thomas.

Thomas had made his name at Crystal Palace, where he captained the side in their 1990 FA Cup final defeat. He was hardworking and extremely aggressive rather than tough, and that's about it. Graham Taylor gave him nine inexplicable England caps, thereby fuelling the belief held by some that if London-based players can part their hair and learn the national anthem, then they can play for England too. No one liked to play against Thomas, but not because of any guile he possessed. Most people's abiding memory of Geoff's international career is his thoroughly entertaining miss against France in 1992 when, spaciously unmarked and with only the keeper to beat, his 'lob' failed to rise more than eighteen inches from the turf before rolling slowly wide of the post by a matter of about forty-five feet. The French goalie is probably still giggling.

Unlike most players, he seemed to be completely unaware of his own limitations. When he signed for Wolves after Palace's relegation in 1993, he seemed to imagine that his past glories made him the star of Division One, as it was then called. I base this opinion on personal observation. However, he was presumably one of the league's bigger earners and certainly one of its better-known names.

I watched most of the Sunderland–Wolves game that day from the dugout, seething at Thomas's display of persistent nastiness and provocation. He deliberately left his foot in for virtually every challenge, constantly harangued the referee David Allison to book people, mouthed off at opponents and incited the home supporters. I decided that if I got my chance then I would let him know that I was on the pitch.

Despite all of Geoff's twattery, Sunderland continued to dominate and always looked likely at least to draw until – well obviously – he scored a second for Wolves completely against the run of play in the eighty-eighth minute. At this point, he and Mark Rankine thought it would be terribly funny to antagonise the crowd further. A couple of minutes earlier I had replaced Gary Owers.

My two main aims were first to score and second, if the opportunity arose, to do unto Geoff Thomas as he had been doing to others all afternoon; not necessarily to damage him but to leave him in no doubt that I was representing current public opinion. Hurt rather than injure. The ball bounced around in our left-back area with him somewhere around the middle of our half while I was in the centre circle just inside the same half. I anticipated that the ball would break to somewhere near the two of us. It did. I'm not sure whether it was a bad touch by him or if the pass wasn't great. Either way, the ball was equidistant between us and we both went for it at full pelt.

All I was thinking was that I would omit nothing in my effort to win that ball. I used my whole body weight to go for it and was a couple of inches from the floor with both feet aimed at the ball. I had matched him for nastiness. I won the ball; one foot went into the middle of it, my other foot skimmed over the top of it and hit him just below the knee, leaving him spinning and ululating, like a Janis Joplin LP. In these days of legions of cameras at games there would have been more of an outcry and probably a six-match ban. In 1993, I was merely booked.

There was certainly no sympathy from any of his victims in red and white. The Roker crowd, who would normally give a sporting round of applause when an injured player from either side was stretchered off, did no such thing. I felt as much remorse as he would have done had the positions been reversed. In fact I was glad. However, he was out for a long time, which was not my intention.

In 2007 Geoff Thomas wrote a book, *Riding Through the Storm*, which was part football memoir, but mainly the story of his Herculean effort two years earlier to ride all twenty-one stages and 2,200 miles of the Tour de France route to raise £150,000 for Leukaemia Research (now Bloodwise). Today he aims to eventually raise £1 million and is to be applauded for this. He was diagnosed with the disease himself in 2003, but happily he overcame it. I'm a cycling fan myself and read the book with interest. I can recommend it too. It's well-written, inspiring and certainly a superior read to most books by ex-footballers (although that isn't difficult).

There is a very odd passage about our little dalliance though. His version of the incident itself pretty much corresponds with mine. However, his recollection of attempted vengeance is at considerable variance. He says:

> The following season, as part of my rehabilitation, I came on as a substitute at Sunderland but I had a different agenda to the rest of the team. I wanted revenge on Howey for the tackle that could have ended my career. My chance came at a corner...
>
> I tried to throw an elbow in Lee's face when the corner was swung in but I missed him by a mile and ended up getting in a ruck with their striker on the ground. The referee thought I stamped on him, even though I didn't, and he sent me off.

So by Geoff's own account there was to be no revenge, but at least he got a good anecdote out of it. Sadly I am not in a position to verify it.

The records show that we were both unused substitutes in the corresponding fixture at Roker the following season; a 1–1 draw. He didn't play at Molineux either (although I had another eventful game there that I shall return to). Neither did he play in the reserve game, a 5–0 win for us in which I scored a hat-trick.

The game he refers to was actually two years later, when he did indeed come on as a substitute and was dismissed by David Allison (again) towards the end of what was a Sunderland victory. I played the whole ninety minutes and have no memory of him trying his luck with me. Nor was the incident from a corner; it was in the middle of their half, close to our right touchline by the Main Stand. Television showed that his red card was for a blatant stamp on Phil Gray and at no point in the incident was Geoff 'on the ground', although Phil was, thus enabling Geoff to stamp on him.

Geoff's written denial of the stamp on Phil is frankly laughable. Furthermore, I don't even appear in the footage of the incident, not even in the ensuing fracas. I was never interested in the posturing bravado of 'handbags': only proper violence (and beneath the cover of the tunnel is the place for that). But let's be generous. The memory plays tricks after all these years and he may not have had as much time to carry out the same assiduous research for his book as I have done for mine (I had to; you don't think I have instant recall of every fact and figure you've read, do you?).

I have never met him socially and bear him no ill-will. Quite the reverse, having read his book, and I hope he feels the same about me. But there were repercussions. The Wolves fans never forgave me and later made threats on my life. Bloody drama queens.

To be continued.

• • •

Three weeks later came one of the most wonderful highs that a footballer can experience: my first goal in the Football League.

By early October I had been confined to the bench at best in the aftermath of the knock-kneed debacle at the Baseball Ground. However, as I watched a youth game at Roker Park, Butch wandered over and gave me some much-needed good news. Phil Gray was suspended and I was to make my second league start, this time at home against Birmingham City. We were seventeenth in the league and had won just two of our first eight matches; pretty poor fare for Sunderland in that division. My personal confidence had been restored by some good performances in the reserves, and here was another opportunity. It would be a very good idea to make the most of it.

It was essential I should walk onto the Roker Park pitch in a better frame of mind than at the Baseball Ground. Indeed, I was unlikely to be in a worse one. My first priority was not to dwell upon how disastrous the Derby County game had been, which was difficult.

The Birmingham game was on Saturday 9 October 1993 and as the 3 p.m. kick-off approached, my legs began to feel heavy again. The anxiety had returned, but it wasn't as bad. Maybe a little anxiety is no bad thing. Even Pelé must have felt anxious on occasions (come to think of it, he made some commercials for erectile dysfunction treatment). The home crowd made a difference because they were as desperate as we were and wanted everyone in red and white stripes to play well. The roars of encouragement were a huge help. More importantly, for my personal confidence, we played well. With half an hour gone, the great moment came.

Derek Ferguson played the ball out to our right-back John Kay, who broke down the wing and played the ball to my feet a little way from the right-hand corner of Birmingham's penalty area. Initially I had my back to goal, so I let the ball run through my legs which allowed me to turn and face the defender, Richard Dryden. I jinked inside to make some space for a shot, then curled the ball about fifteen yards with my left foot into the far corner of the net. 'Past a despairing Kevin Miller in the Birmingham goal', as all the best tabloids would have it.

In the words of Aristotle: Get the fuck in.

The tension had palpably and immediately left me. I went to the corner of the Roker End where the daft lads would congregate to celebrate with them (you can never celebrate with daft lads enough). So this was what it was like; my first *real* goal for the club I loved.

Scoring against Rangers was a terrific feeling, but this was better. It was an important goal in a vital fixture; we really needed the points. I would have been barely less elated had my first Sunderland goal ricocheted into the net off my arse while I fastened my boot-laces. As it happened, my first Sunderland goal was a pretty good one. I had done what every fan would love to do: score for the team he supports. The remainder of the game breezed by. I linked up well with Don Goodman and also played my first full ninety minutes. The final score was 1–0. Three points. The fans were happy, the other players were happy, Terry Butcher was happy. I was euphoric.

I might not have dislodged Eric Cantona from the back pages, but from that moment on I felt as though I was a professional foot-baller at this great club on merit. I had established my presence and dispelled a few personal issues, not least from Derby, with a single kick. The only minor quibble with our performance was that we ought to have won more comfortably. But looking at it from a wholly selfish perspective, the chances we missed meant that I had scored the winner. It was an enormous buzz. There were little diagrams in the newspaper, which I still have, of how the goal had been worked and all the other ephemera that I revelled in.

I looked at the *Football Echo* and the Sunday papers where they all said: 'Sunderland 1 (Howey 31) – Birmingham City 0.'

The results service on the BBC's Ceefax also said: 'Sunderland 1 (Howey 31) – Birmingham City 0.'

Still, you couldn't be too sure, so a glance at ITV's The Oracle was necessary to confirm: 'Sunderland 1 (Howey 31) – Birmingham City 0' (some of you may need to ask your dads about Ceefax and The Oracle).

Further confirmation could be garnered by walking into any pub in Sunderland – or a few in Birmingham. Then there was the local television news for anyone who hadn't been at the game to witness the event in the flesh.

What is better still, even now, is that when a goal is entered into the record books it is done so unalterably and indelibly. There will never be circumstances under which the annotated result of that game, 9 October 1993, will read anything other than 'Sunderland 1 (Howey 31) – Birmingham City 0'.

Today, I can burn down an orphanage, steal marmalade from Harrods then throw up over the Queen and the record books will still state: 'Sunderland 1 (Howey 31) – Birmingham City 0', even if I have to read the record books in a prison library.

I think I have made my point. Decades after the event, it's still a wonderful thing and I would recommend it to anyone.

• • •

On more than one occasion, I have been asked: 'What does it feel like to score a goal?' Well let's get something out of the way before we go any further: No, it isn't better than sex.

Beyond that, it depends upon the context of the goal. I have already said that my goal against Birmingham felt bigger and better than the one against Rangers. But it didn't just *feel* bigger and better, it *was* bigger and better, because it was more important. Later that season I pulled one back at Kenilworth Road; a scruffy goal after an awful mistake by Trevor Peake. But what makes that goal less fondly recalled is not its scruffiness; it's the fact that it was late in the game and Luton Town were already 2–0 up. A consolation. To be honest, I don't remember it; I am relying on the word of someone else (although the record shows that I did score in a 2–1 defeat). I was fortunate enough to rattle in a few winners in my time, of varying quality. But ultimately a winning fluke feels better than scoring the goal of your life in a defeat, especially at the final whistle.

In essence, the emotions of the player scoring the goal are not hugely different for him than for his teammates or the fans. Think of a goal your team once scored that made you go even more doolally than normal; temporarily deranged. The late derby winner, the one that won a semi-final or averted relegation. Well the player scoring the goal felt pretty much the same as you did. When your team bangs one in you say: 'We've scored', not 'They've scored' or 'He's scored'. When your lads net, it's a communal pleasure rather than a vicarious one. A vicarious pleasure is when you see someone win a large amount of money on a game show and you feel pleased *for* them rather than *with* them, and because of this your feeling of wellbeing is fleeting. The glowing feeling occasioned by a goal can last for a lifetime.

There is an extra frisson when you personally have put the ball into the net, but not much. In April 2015, I was in the Stadium of Light to witness Jermain Defoe score the greatest goal I have ever seen in a North East derby. It had everything. It was a stunning, dipping volley from twenty-two yards, the only goal of the game, a psychological hammer-blow because it was literally the last kick of the first half, the match was crucial to both clubs and, above all, it was in a fixture between Sunderland and Newcastle. I was just a fan that day, but I can truthfully say that Defoe's goal sent me into greater delirium than any I had scored myself. Such was the magnitude and importance of this strike that his reaction (he was in tears) was one of a man who, despite having scored on hundreds of occasions, including in a World Cup, was not used to such an event. As I said: context.

The short answer therefore to the question of how it feels to score a goal is as follows:

You already know.

• • •

Regrettably, the Birmingham game is not best remembered on Wearside for its only goal. I wish it were otherwise. Talked about forevermore was the horrendous injury to John Kay. Every Sunderland supporter above a certain age knows the story. Here it is for the rest of you.

With a minute of the first half remaining, thirteen minutes after the goal, John went into a tackle deep within Birmingham territory with a cheerful and characteristic disregard for his own safety – which broke his right leg in two places. There are leg breaks and then there are leg breaks; and this one was a pearler. When he looked down at his injuries in hospital later that day, his right leg appeared to have one more knee than normal.

In the more immediate aftermath, he stood up and attempted to play on, but soon abandoned the idea (well, you would) and was carried from the pitch to tumultuous applause. Whether or not he was our best player, he was almost certainly the most popular among the fans. Accepted medical procedure in football these days is to place an oxygen mask over the patient's face then quickly and efficiently transport him to the nearest hospital. John was simply lobbed on to a stretcher which he 'rowed' back to the tunnel, similar to the closing credits of *Hawaii Five-O*, sitting up and waving to the admiring crowd as he went.

He wasn't the luckiest player. In 1992 he played in every single game of Sunderland's FA Cup run, until missing the final through injury.

John Kay is worthy of a further mention because any story you may have heard about him is probably true, particularly the stories that don't sound at all plausible. He was like a character waiting for an author. To use the correct terminology, he was off his bonce. As daft as six dogs. This applied even more when he had sipped a medium sherry or two. We would occasionally find him asleep on a roundabout, but this was subject to the availability of the roof of a bus shelter, which he preferred. This was not a good thing, but at least he seemed to have no trouble sleeping.

When we went away on pre-season jollies, he would arrive for the journey in shorts, trainers, a T-shirt, a neck wallet for his money and with his passport in his back pocket. That was about it, except that he would also wear a cap beneath which he kept a bar of soap. This was actually a clever bit of lunacy, because he knew there was a fair to middling chance of him nodding off on a beach and being unable to return to the hotel, so he would just wander into the sea to conduct his morning ablutions. Cleanliness is next to godliness.

In football terms he was one of the greatest bargains that Sunderland ever had. Although a County Durham lad, he began his career at Arsenal. He was recruited to Roker Park in the summer of 1987 by Denis Smith, bought from Wimbledon for six marbles and a catapult – or £22,500 if you insist on properly audited figures. Sunderland had just been relegated to the old Third Division and were all but skint. Another £80,000 spent on Marco Gabbiadini was considered to be quite a gamble. But John played all the way back to the top flight under Smith and would make over 200 appearances for the club. What more could anyone want for £22,500?

His instinct on the pitch, some might say his modus operandi, was to 'get in there'. He was, to say the least, a tough lad. He loved a tackle and never went in to deliberately hurt anyone, but didn't mind if he did. This meant that he was often underrated, because he was actually one hell of a full-back and not just an assassin. Still, if the opposition's left-winger annoyed him or worse still (for the winger), fouled him, he would not let it go or allow anyone to calm him down. Retribution would follow.

But as Geoff Thomas could attest, those who live by the sword and all that. Rowing that stretcher down the Roker Park tunnel was his last action for Sunderland. He never played in the first team again, but it can't be said that he didn't try hard enough to get back.

As part of his rehab he was sent to the George Washington Hotel on the outskirts of Sunderland, where there was a swimming pool. Swimming is excellent exercise for someone with a leg injury, but only if the injured party can actually swim, and John couldn't doggy-paddle the length of himself. While at the George Washington myself one day with a lesser ailment, I witnessed how undaunted he was by his inability to swim as he set about having a go anyway.

His initial success in the pool consisted solely of not drowning. But when I returned a couple of months later with another niggle, there was John, doing length after length after length, surging through the water like a Polaris missile. There was as much dedication as daftness with John. He would work religiously on his rehab all day, every day. Sadly, his hard work would never earn him a return to the first team, but he did play another 115 games in the Football League, mainly for Scarborough.

• • •

The Birmingham result was only a temporary reprieve, both for me and for the club as a whole. I was soon back in the reserves. Had Phil Gray been faster, he could have been a real top-end player. But even without pace he still wasn't going to be omitted from the starting line-up for long. He was too good, not to say too expensive for such a fate. His strike partner, Don Goodman, was even more expensive. In fact Don was then the club's record signing at £900,000. He scored goals too. As a man who had recently plied his trade with Plains Farm Working Men's Club, I was in no position to grumble about this. That doesn't mean it wasn't frustrating, however.

Terry Butcher made ever more curious decisions. In the never to be remembered League Cup first round, second leg against Chester City at the Deva Stadium (a goalless draw), he introduced me at half-time and played me in right-midfield. If anyone reading this can explain why he did this, then please drop me a line because to this day I don't have the faintest idea. I hadn't played down the right since I was an eleven-year-old at St Cuthbert's, so the possibility of Butch having watched me play there before was a remote one. I was glad to be in the team, even if it was all very perplexing – and much to the annoyance of the lads who really were right-midfielders. This was the only time I would play in that position in my whole professional career. I'd had doubts about Terry Butcher's managerial abilities from the beginning; doubts that became increasingly augmented by incidents like this. But what was I supposed to say?

Chester were the better side that night, but we nudged through and had the pleasure of beating Leeds United in the next round, winning 4–2 on aggregate. This was a rare highlight in Terry's stint as Sunderland manager. Younger readers may be surprised to discover that Leeds were then one of the best sides in the country and had been champions of England only a year earlier. They featured Gary Kelly, Gordon Strachan, Gary McAllister, Gary Speed, John Lukic and Rod Wallace, but we still beat them. Twice. It was 2–1 both home and away and Sunderland have always loved to beat Leeds. Phil and Don both scored in each leg and both were excellent throughout the tie. It was a great night at Elland Road, followed three days later by the victory over Birmingham. Alas, this was to be a fleeting respite.

Whenever I felt that the atmosphere between Terry Butcher and the senior pros could not become any more fractious, I would be proved wrong the following day. The most noticeable mutual contempt was between him and the pair who were the heartbeat of the team, Gary Owers and Gordon Armstrong. Both had been at the club since they were kids and had played in hundreds of games. The antipathy would commence without any obvious reason. It's true that some people just don't get on and nothing will alter the situation, but I suspect that Terry was trying to assert his authority by letting such established figures know who was boss. I don't know why he would have thought this was necessary. Gary and Gordon were good blokes, not arrogant or conceited, or in need of being taken down a peg or two. They were Sunderland fans as well as players who knew that things were not right and so would voice their opinions.

I don't suppose that Terry telling Gary and Gordon, along with Anton Rogan, Tim Carter, Tony Smith and Peter Davenport, that they should talk to their agents because he wanted rid of them, did an awful lot to effect more chumminess. Nevertheless, Owers and Armstrong were both regular starters under Butcher. It seems odd that he simultaneously wanted shot of the two but didn't think there was anyone better in his squad.

Whenever the players were chatting socially, talk would invariably turn to extreme dissatisfaction with the manager. When that happens, there can only be one outcome. Something has to give and you can't get rid of a squad of footballers with anything like the ease you can dispose of a manager.

Mick Buxton was added to the coaching staff, I think by Bob Murray over the head of Terry Butcher, although I am sketchy on the details. Mick was an odd character, but he did have a decent CV. Another Sunderland native, his playing career at Burnley had been heavily chequered by injury. However, as a manager in the 1980s he won two promotions at Huddersfield and had also been in charge at Scunthorpe United. Butch must have recognised the threat as soon as Mick appeared, hanging over him like a chubby sword of Damocles.

Mick was not quite the lad for madcap antics; in fact he was dour and introspective. We would train while he wandered alone around an adjacent field in his flat cap, like a poet waiting for inspiration to descend. Pity he never found any, because we needed some inspiration ourselves. Had we not been informed of who he was, someone would have given him a quid and said: 'Get yourself a cup of tea somewhere nice and warm, mate.'

Training continued joylessly and relentlessly. We turned up at Roker Park one day to find that we couldn't use the pitch because of snow. So instead of a practice session, Ian Atkins sent us for, you've guessed it, a long run. I suppose any alternative might have placed us in danger of enjoying ourselves. A seven-mile route was planned from the stadium to the Charlie Hurley Centre (our training ground), back along Seaburn and ending at the famous Bungalow Cafe by Roker Beach (it overlooks the North Sea and has the best view of any eating establishment in England; try it). The cafe is atop a cliff and a further piece of running from there, down a long bank to the beach and then back again, was instructed upon completion of the initial seven miles – and to be done twenty times.

I was among the front runners along with the younger, fitter members of the squad: Micky Gray, Martin Smith, Martin Gray, Craig Russell. The less youthful and not so keen soon began to lag behind. We finished the course and were about to amble back to the ground to do some weight training (a comparative treat), when we were told in no uncertain terms by Terry Butcher to repeat the entire course, including the twenty bank runs at its end. I was one of the more compliant members of the squad, but even I was furious. Still, as I had only a few months earlier been serving my sentence at BT, I did as I was told. At this point I was unaware of Butch's reason for ordering us to repeat the exercise.

It transpired that a heinous deception had taken place and he had unearthed it. Phil Gray, Don Goodman, Derek Ferguson and Andy Melville had cheated. Dressed in training kit, they had no money on their persons, but being a footballer opens doors. In this case it was the doors of the number 27 bus which dropped them off, free of charge, a couple of hundred yards from the Bungalow Cafe, which they then had the audacity to sprint.

Gary Bennett was appalled by this. A man of his professional standing, in his testimonial season too, was not about to abase himself by using public transport to avoid physical exertion. The very thought was an abhorrence to him. Instead, he and Tony Norman managed to persuade a passing fan in Whitburn to give them a lift in his Austin Maestro. Buses? How plebeian. Benno was dismayed at the lack of panache that his colleagues had shown.

Alas for everyone, including those of us who had been mug enough to carry out instructions properly, some greasy sneak, perhaps a scandalised fellow bus passenger, had informed the authorities, who failed to see any humour in the incident. Neither did I, at first.

•   •   •

The next day we were told to run from Roker Park to the Charlie Hurley Centre, where the pitches were usable following a thaw. By this time rumours were rife that the manager would be sacked. This was soon confirmed and there were some undisguisedly jubilant footballers in that changing room. I estimate that of the seventeen or so players present, about ten of them were openly chuffed. Ian Atkins was also shown the door.

The dismissal was carried out quite cack-handedly. Butch arrived at the ground and was ambushed by the media, who had heard the rumours. Essentially they knew before he did. Apparently the deed was not carried out by Bob Murray himself. He had stood down as chairman and was replaced by another director, chartered accountant John Featherstone; although this seemed somewhat academic as Bob was still the majority shareholder and therefore remained the real boss.

I did not share in the training ground merriment at the news. Terry Butcher and I went back a few years. I take no pleasure in someone losing their job. Aside from that, he gave me the biggest break of my career by signing me for the club I worshipped and I looked on him as a friend. I also got on well with Ian. There was another issue for me; the possibility of not featuring in the plans of a new manager.

But all that was on a personal level. On a professional level the board had made the correct decision. It still pains me to say it, but the club was only going one way under Terry, who was sacked when he was statistically Sunderland's worst ever manager, winning ten of his thirty-eight league games in charge – and not in the top flight either. We had lost ten league games in the 1993–94 season when he left and it was still only November. Two and a half years later when we had been promoted under Peter Reid, Terry himself admitted: 'Sunderland have never looked back since I left.'

The poisonous atmosphere was largely caused by Terry's single biggest failing: man management. The biggest shock to me, having witnessed first-hand what he was like as a player, was that he didn't command respect. Tactical and transfer failings happen to all managers at some stage, but respect was the one thing everyone thought would not be a problem. Perhaps if he had retired as a player immediately upon becoming manager it might have been better, but he had that brief and mainly awful stint as player-manager. How do you berate someone else's performance when your own has been even worse? This was also a surprise because he was undoubtedly a fantastic centre-half in his day, which had not been so long ago. He joined Sunderland only two years after starring in England's second-best ever World Cup.

As a person, I won't hear a bad word about Terry Butcher. He is a gentleman; a top bloke. But as José Mourinho would discover in 2015, when a manager at any club is disliked by the senior pros, then he won't be around for much longer. They have always wielded that power. Two years after Terry left Sunderland came the Bosman case, which resulted in these players wielding even more. A squad tends to be close-knit. As well as being colleagues and a team, they don't spend many days apart. They play, train, travel and take holidays together. My roomies and confidants in 1993–94 were Ian Sampson and Martin Gray. I spent more time with them than I did with my fiancée, and I knew more about them. So if a manager upsets one or two of his players, there's a reasonable chance he could upset them all.

CHAPTER 6

THERE'S A SONG ABOUT ME, YOU KNOW

The board at Sunderland had appointed Malcolm Crosby, as he was already at the club when Denis Smith was sacked. It didn't work out.

They then appointed Terry Butcher, as he was already at the club when Malcolm Crosby was sacked. I think we have established that that didn't work out either.

In late November 1993, they then appointed Mick Buxton, as he was already at the club when Terry Butcher was sacked. Read on to see what dividends were reaped by doing exactly the same thing three times in the space of two years. You may be surprised, although I doubt it.

I mentioned earlier that when he was a coach, Mick would wander around the nearby fields in his flat cap during training sessions, contemplating the clouds and pondering the buttercups like a Tetley Tea man on a bank holiday. Yet as soon as he became manager... he was exactly the same. When he wasn't away with the fairies, he was a very old-school type of boss.

He recruited Trevor Hartley as chief coach. Trevor had been around as a manager and coach, having been employed by Bournemouth, Tottenham and the Malaysian national team. We never quite saw eye-to-eye. This was not in a heated toe-to-toe sort of way; he was intelligent and quite jolly. It's just that his methods were not as helpful as he seemed to think. He would give talks that were infused with inspirational quotes from Mahatma Gandhi, Abraham Lincoln and other towering historical figures. He may as well have quoted Rod Hull and Emu for all the good it did, because the players just sat there exchanging curious glances, wondering what in God's name any of this had to do with football.

I felt Trevor was too clever for his own good. He didn't see much merit in big old-fashioned centre-forwards either, which was even less helpful to my career than the thoughts of Alexander the Great or whoever the hell he dragged into it.

However, it can't be denied that matters improved for the club. Mick's first game in charge was a 3–2 defeat at home to Nottingham Forest, with a rising Stan Collymore scoring twice for the visitors (he scored a pile of goals against Sunderland in his career), but it was a marked improvement. Forest were one of the better sides and also had Stuart Pearce, Scott Gemmill, Steve Stone and Colin Cooper in their line-up. They would finish the season in second place. The general murmur was that we may have lost as expected, but would have been walloped by Forest had Terry Butcher still been around. Harsh and unprovable, but probably true.

The next two games were 1–0 wins over Portsmouth and Derby County (who had beaten us 5–0 on the first day, for those of you who weren't paying attention). Of the twenty-eight remaining league games after Forest, we would lose only eight and rise from third bottom to twelfth. This was hardly epoch-making stuff and no one is likely to ever bother making documentaries about Sunderland's 1993–94 season. But it was a distinct and welcome improvement. We had gone from being a poor team to a mediocre one. Hurrah for us. The fossilised expression is that Mick 'steadied the ship'. It would do for now.

It was exactly the same squad of players; so how much of this improvement was down to Mick Buxton? And what were his team-talks like? Well, think of George C. Scott in the opening scene of the film *Patton*, sometimes subtitled *Lust For Glory*. General

Patton's raw, charismatic persona and steely, mesmerising oration are such that his troops will do *anything*, down to their last breath, to ensure victory on the field of battle.

Now expunge George C. Scott from your minds, because Mick Buxton was nothing like that. His team-talks were so monotonous that no one ever really listened. The sounds leaving his lips were like static interference. He may as well have been discussing quantitative easing, in Dutch. The main reason for the improved results was the collective spring in the step of the senior pros, which was in turn attributable to their vast preference for Mick over Terry Butcher. They had a vast preference for virtually anyone over Terry Butcher.

When people say that footballers 'aren't playing for the manager' they are not referring to a conscious decision. No one had made a deliberate choice to *not* give their best under Terry. The problem is that when life is generally pretty miserable, your best is not as good as it would otherwise be. This is especially true in sport. As a professional footballer, if your manager can successfully cajole you into feeling more confident, then that extra 5 or 10 per cent it gives you (if we can quantify such a thing) makes a huge difference. Butch had somehow managed to achieve the opposite. It's the same in all walks of life. Some people need an arm round the shoulder while others need a kick up the behind, and a good leader will know which approach to adopt with whom. Mick wasn't a wizard of man management either, but as he didn't arouse strong feelings either way, the players were happier and this was reflected in his earlier results.

Training was about as basic as it gets. Mick favoured 'pattern of play' whereby we would line up against the youths, or sometimes against no one. It was to teach us where he wanted the ball to go and the positions he wanted us to take. Yet even against imaginary opposition there was still tackling, because Kevin Ball was involved. There would have been tackling during a Buckaroo tournament if Kevin Ball had been involved.

• • •

Sunderland's improvement after Terry Butcher's departure is perhaps summed up by our two games against Middlesbrough that season. We had been a bit of a shambles for the game at Ayresome Park under Butch in October and were duly pasted.

Sunderland AFC historians may remember that game for the debut of our winger Jamie Lawrence, who had recently been released from a four-year prison sentence for robbing a bank (for his home debut against Luton Town three days later, Sunderland's DJ played *Jailhouse Rock* before the kick-off; nice touch, that). When we played Boro at Roker on 16 January 1994, we were very different opposition. We had won our previous two games and only lost one out of eight since the Forest game. Confidence had gradually returned. We had limped up to sixteenth position in Division One by now, with Middlesbrough three places ahead in their pre-Bryan Robson, spending spree years. These were not heady times for either club.

A stone's throw from the North Sea, Roker Park was a famously cold stadium, although in the summer, temperatures could surge all the way up to tepid. This day was spectacularly cold. There was a light scattering of snow on the pitch and the air was bitter around the ears. Not unusually, I was on the bench at the start of the game. I ran up and down the touchline to warm up in the most literal sense, not just to stretch the muscles a bit, hoping as always to be given some time on the pitch. I would be given all of the second forty-five minutes which, injuries aside, is as much time as a substitute can realistically hope for.

The respective stadiums of the two clubs were (and still are) about thirty miles or a half-hour drive apart. This proximity means that most adult Sunderland supporters will know several Middlesbrough counterparts personally and vice versa. The fixture has an element of local rivalry, but it's the Middlesbrough fans who feel it more intensely. They are stuck geographically between Sunderland and Leeds United, who are similarly uninterested in Boro. The nearest club to Middlesbrough is Hartlepool United, whom they have never met in a league fixture.

Sunderland and Newcastle fans don't feel too badly about facing their Teesside work colleagues in the aftermath of a defeat to Boro. Middlesbrough attract about as much emotion from the Mackems and Geordies as do Fulham, Doncaster Rovers, Bournemouth, Stoke City, Gillingham or any other random opposition obstructing the acquisition of three points.

Actually that's a little unfair. As both player and fan I wanted to do well against them. There is a slight edge to Sunderland v. Middlesbrough; but not much of a one from a Wearside perspective and largely down to the efforts of the North East media. Many Sunderland supporters were pleased for Boro when they won the League Cup and reached the UEFA Cup final in the 2000s.

I'll put it another way. When Newcastle were thumped at home by Sunderland in 2013, some of their fans were so furious that they rioted in their own city and one of them was infamously imprisoned for punching a police horse. When the black and whites were relegated from the Premier League in 2016, the red and whites staged the expected gloat-athon. But some expressed regret that there would be 'no derby match' the following season, even though Sunderland would play Middlesbrough three months later. It was a them-or-us relegation in 2016 and, while Wearside whooped as Tyneside wailed, neither party seemed to care or even notice that Middlesbrough had been promoted.

When the 2016–17 fixture lists were released, the media were keen to pretend that Sunderland–Middlesbrough was a 'derby' (partly perhaps because their first meeting would be televised). It was simply *not* a derby. Only one club provides derby opposition for Sunderland, and we all know which one. It's only a derby if it *feels* like one. You can *feel* a Tyne–Wear derby through your feet from a many-mile radius. This is regardless of which league or competition the fixture is part of. Fans of both clubs worry about its outcome to the point of ulcers and other illnesses, and this occurs days before they actually enter the stadium.

But back to Sunday 16 January 1994. The game was broadcast live by Tyne Tees Television. Sky Sports had been on the scene for a couple of years by then and, regardless of anyone's opinion of Sky and Rupert Murdoch, their state-of-the-art, umpteen-camera football coverage had instantly made that of Tyne Tees look little better than something John Logie Baird might have whipped up.

The first forty-five minutes was toothless and forgettable, with neither side playing well. To address this I was told at half-time that I would be replacing the injured Gordon Armstrong. Great – for me, if not Gordon. The substitution worked too. Ten minutes into the half I jabbed the ball forward to Craig Russell who, not for the first time, got ahead of the defence and was upended by Nicky Mohan just inside the box. Penalty in front of the Fulwell End. Phil Gray. Down the middle. One–nil.

Four minutes later we were awarded a corner. The skilful Martin Smith delivered a left-foot in-swinger. I stood in the 'D' and, with nothing owed to scientific thought, decided to simply attack the ball wherever in the air it might travel. With the added advantage of poor marking, I trotted up to meet the ball with my head and battered it towards the goal. Other than ensuring it was on target I hadn't aimed for anywhere specific, so it might have gone straight into the arms of Stephen Pears. It didn't. The header entered the net from eight yards out, although it would have done so from eighteen. It was actually quite central but the power beat the keeper. This wasn't anything we had worked on in training, merely a piece of improvisation that went right. Ha!

The Tyne Tees summariser that day was Chris Waddle, then a Sheffield Wednesday player. He spoke of my goal in complimentary terms ('He's timed his run perfect and you can't stop them') and I was introduced to him after the game. Apart from that, I can honestly say that the presence of television cameras added nothing to the occasion for me. I had scored the winner against our 'local rivals' in front of the Fulwell End, absorbed the noise and watched the excited crowd surge forward as they still did in those days of standing spectators. I also enjoyed the final whistle in a way that only a victory can bring.

That sort of mutual joy between player and fan is not improved upon because the telly is in town. I like to think that the supporters were by now thinking that, at the very least, the six grand given to AS Hemptinne to secure my signature had been worth it.

In true Sunderland fashion, we allowed Steve Vickers to pull one back, which meant the final fifteen minutes were more interesting than we would have liked. But we squeaked home 2–1, and deserved to. However, my day wasn't over. I was drugs tested.

Before I reached the dressing room I was taken to one side and told that, along with Kevin Ball, I was one of the two Sunderland players who had been randomly selected. Jamie Pollock was one of the two Middlesbrough players. The testing team weren't wearing hi-vis jackets with the words 'Drugs Bloke' emblazoned across the back, but we were left with no uncertainty as to who they were. Until we had each provided 200ml (a third of a pint) of urine we would not be allowed to leave the ground. This isn't easy when you have just left the pitch dehydrated; in fact we thought they were taking the piss (it's faintly possible that the Drugs Blokes had heard this joke before).

I drank some water. I also used to like a cup of tea after a game. I still couldn't manage it. I had to be watched in the shower, which was not an entirely comfortable experience, but they had to make sure that no one else could provide a sample for me. What a job they had. I explained that it was customary to have a few pints after a match. That was fine. They weren't interested in whether or not there was alcohol in my sample; it wouldn't mask anything illegal. Drugs Bloke had to stand in my company while I drank a few cans with my family and gave several interviews. Eventually I was ready to leak.

But ooh. You know when someone's watching you, you struggle to go. So it took me about another quarter of an hour to deliver. Bally wasn't much of a boozer and had played ninety minutes, so he was struggling even more. An hour or so after the game he was still about 193ml short. He would be there for some time.

Apart from traces of Vaux's Scorpion Dry lager in my sample (perhaps more than a trace, now I think of it) we were both clean, as were the two Middlesbrough lads. It was a minor inconvenience rather than a problem. The same would not have been said of another member of Sunderland's squad had the Drugs Blokes ever pulled *his* name from the hat. I won't identify him. I won't even say whether he was on the pitch, sitting on the bench, in the stand or watching the game in the pub that day. I don't believe he was ever drug-tested in his career and he will have been mightily relieved at this, because illegal substances would have been found. And not of the performance-enhancing variety either.

● ● ●

The Middlesbrough game might not have been a derby, but the whole day is chiselled into my memory. This is partly because it was the first time I ever heard *the song*. Anyone who remembers me playing for Sunderland – and quite a few who don't – will know exactly what I mean by *the song*.

I was warming up behind the linesman and in front of the Main Stand when the chant was struck up. I was accustomed to hearing the opinions of the crowd: 'Get on there and batter them, Lee', 'Give us a hat-trick' or 'Sit down, man, Howey. You're shite!' and similar witticisms. It was generally good fun. On this particular day, they came up with something different. It was sung to the tune from the commercials for Direct Line Insurance, a sort of cavalry charge jingle.

Lee Howey! Lee Howey! Lee Howey! Your brother is a cunt!

I caught the use of my name but didn't hear *the song* properly at first. Brian Atkinson, who was warming up alongside me, evidently did, because he was greatly amused. It wasn't exactly 'Figaro's Aria' and was a terribly easy 'song' to learn. So when an encore was delivered it was with more volume and spirit as other sections of the ground began to join in.

Lee Howey! Lee Howey! Lee Howey! Your brother is a cunt!

It seems unlikely that any consideration was given to whether or not I was offended by this musical imputation of the good name of my only sibling. Football crowds tend not to be overly sensitive. They needn't have worried (not that they did). Even though *the song* isn't clever, witty or melodious and relies on an extremely offensive word for its impact, I thought it was very funny. Perhaps it's funny *because* it isn't clever, witty or melodious and relies on an extremely offensive word for its impact. It's the joy of obscene language. Of course swearing isn't 'necessary'. This is part of its appeal. Herbaceous borders and Chanel Number 5 aren't 'necessary' and no one disapproves of *them*, because they make life ever so slightly better.

To the best of my knowledge *the song* has never been performed by Aled Jones at Christmas, but it was an instant and ongoing hit on Wearside. It can be heard regularly in the Stadium of Light to this day; often chanted by people too young to possibly remember me playing. After the Middlesbrough match it was aired every time I warmed up as substitute – and I was substitute an awful lot at Sunderland (seventy-nine times in total, which is the ninth highest of all time; of the eight ahead of me on the list, seven are goalkeepers and the other is Paul Thirlwell). *The song* was almost a fixture of Roker Park in the mid-1990s. In essence, it's really an anti-Newcastle song and not about me as such. Yet it makes me feel strangely proud. It reminds people that I was there and this book would be incomplete if I didn't mention it.

Years later, a Sunderland fanzine, *A Love Supreme*, printed T-shirts with the 'lyrics' on the front, minus the last five words for decency's sake. They asked me to model it and I agreed to this after they submitted to my exorbitant demand of a free sample. I wear it every time Sunderland play Newcastle. The first occasion was the 3–0 away victory for Sunderland in 2013; the first of six consecutive wins over the Mags and the horse-punching day. It's my favourite T-shirt. Ever.

The song refuses to die and has a longevity that is rare for a football chant. It will probably be around when I'm not. When I attend Sunderland games these days, especially away from home, I zip up, wear a baseball cap and attempt to keep a low profile. But it only takes one person to recognise me and they're off: *Lee Howey! Lee Howey! Lee Howey!*

I don't suppose our mother gives wholehearted approval to *the song*, with its blunt and offensive reference to her younger child, but it has never offended me. Any time I am questioned about the oft-repeated, foul-mouthed choral abuse of my brother, my answer is always the same.

'Well he is.'

• • •

Later in the year, Steven joined me on my stag night in Edinburgh, where I refrained from singing *the song*. We were still rubbing along reasonably well, even if we weren't together too often. A jolly time was being had when my attention was taken by stitching on his head. He had clearly just had his ears pinned back. Looking now at 'before' and 'after' pictures, you can see how prominent his lugs had been.

Photographs where he *doesn't* appear to have a pair of Pyrex saucers clamped onto the sides his melon fall into the 'after' category.

It could have been vanity, or it may have been applied physics to benefit his game as the drag coefficient was slowing him down; either way, he had decided to go under the knife. He must have been embarrassed by this because when I asked him his reasons for the op he explained it to Eddie Harrison and me with a story about consulting a medical professional for something far more serious and career-threatening, and that while he was in there he told them they may as well perform the pin-back too. Things turned out to be not quite as they sounded.

Guinness played a part in me accepting the tale. I have no wish to elaborate on exactly what was said, but I was shocked and traumatised by it. Matters were deteriorating further.

• • •

Sunderland had a brief yet eventful FA Cup run. We drew Carlisle United at home in the third round; a team two leagues below us and a formality on paper. But as they say, the game is played on grass and not paper.

Despite their being fifteenth in Division Three at this point, we were only sixteenth in Division One and the Carlisle supporters could smell blood; perhaps literally, as there was quite some unpleasantness around Roker Park during their big day out. Derek Ferguson gave us the lead with a shot that bounced four times before crossing the line; the only goal he would ever score for Sunderland. But Darren Edmondson equalised ten minutes from time, and this was the minimum that Carlisle deserved. It was a bad afternoon for us, although I was at least personally untainted by it as I hadn't featured.

The replay came at Brunton Park ten days later and this time I started because Don Goodman was injured. Between the two cup games, we had won at Oxford, and only two days earlier there had been my own personal glory against Middlesbrough. But this upturn in results did not lessen the importance of the replay. Confidence remained fragile and defeat to the archetypal plucky minnows could have set us back to the despondency levels experienced under Terry Butcher. This was a fraught fixture for Mick Buxton in particular and it would be an extremely arduous evening in Cumbria for everyone who wanted the best for Sunderland. Carlisle were rightly buoyant after their performance at Roker. The game was a sell-out and we were being spoken of as underdogs.

The Brunton Park pitch, famously under six feet of water in 2015, was not exactly in pristine condition in January 1994 either. Before the kick-off, we didn't know whether to warm up or pick cabbages. The game itself was almost as much of a slog for our large following as it was for the players. It was goalless after ninety minutes when we were given the usual exhilarating rhetoric from Mr Buxton. None of your *carpe diem* and all that. It was like being geed up by Sooty. Whatever Mick said – and as usual no one was listening – the toneless noises leaving his lips were drowned out in my mind by a single pervading thought. Namely: 'Christ. Don't let it go to penalties.'

Joy came eventually and was hard-earned. The game went remorselessly into extra time and the 101st minute, when we were awarded a corner. As against Middlesbrough, Martin Smith raised his right arm (for no reason at all) then delivered another of his left-foot in-swingers. This one bounced tamely off a Carlisle head and plopped onto the saturated six-yard line to be jabbed home before the visiting supporters by a player who was having a very good couple of days: me. It is widely considered to be one of the greatest goals in the history of the FA Cup.

The previous sentence is of course complete bollocks. It was an unremarkable goal and all it achieved ultimately was a 2–1 defeat at Wimbledon in the next round. Wimbledon would finish the season sixth in the Premier League, so losing there would not be demoralising or embarrassing. But the same would certainly not have been said if we had cocked it up at Carlisle. The aesthetic value of that goal was irrelevant; it was the only one in the game and essential in maintaining morale among a side that couldn't afford to be any less confident. The goal can be seen today on YouTube (go on, look it up, you know you want to) and what is most remarkable about it is the reaction of the Sunderland supporters who had become increasingly tense about the tie – as had we.

Usually, scoring in the cup against 'lowly' opposition is unlikely to elicit much more than an appreciative cheer. But when the ball hit the net that night our fans went potty. I ran over to them to celebrate, but soon abandoned the idea when I saw how they were rather dangerously surging forward. Some of them ran onto the pitch. This outpouring was not because they thought we were about to open a new and glorious chapter in the club's history, or even win at Wimbledon. It was sheer relief, both when we scored and when the final whistle blew.

The relief was not because we had won; it was because we hadn't lost. There had been nothing of note to celebrate for a couple of seasons and on the night we beat Carlisle, Newcastle sat third in the Premier League and had been declared (by their good selves) as 'everyone's second favourite team'. Our fans (who could emphatically confirm that this was not necessarily the case) didn't need further humiliation from their black-and-white colleagues at work because we had failed against a team from the fourth tier in a cup tie. To sum up that dark January evening at Brunton Park then: 'Phew.'

None of these wider considerations were in my thoughts at the time. I was just delighted to have won and scored another winner for Sunderland. I remember nothing of the rest of that game, although the records show that Kevin Ball was shown a yellow card – if you can imagine such a thing.

• • •

We travelled to Wimbledon for the next round. All the stories you have heard about Wimbledon from this period are true. They called themselves the Crazy Gang. As we all know, anyone referring to themselves as 'crazy' is to be generally avoided. The same goes for other adjectives such as 'zany', 'mad', 'bonkers', 'nutty' and similar.

Despite all this, Wimbledon did not finish regularly in lofty top-flight positions simply by employing violence and the hoofed ball forward. They had good players too and on this occasion they included Hans Segers, John Scales, Laurie Sanchez, Robbie Earl, John Fashanu, Dean Holdsworth and Warren Barton.

This was during their time at Selhurst Park. By necessity, the visiting team would have to pass the home dressing room there as they walked along the narrow corridor. The Wimbledon door was always purposely left wide open and they would have a ghetto blaster turned up to eleven, thumping out loud, bass-heavy music while they lifted weights and snarled at us as we filed past. It was supposed to be menacing and, for reasons I will never understand, some of their opponents had actually been intimidated by this buffoonery.

Then again, perhaps they weren't trying to intimidate us at all. It could be that they had watched a few too many crap films; or they may have been overcompensating for something else. Whatever the reason, it didn't matter. We were not the cowering type and our response was a collective rolling of the eyes. When your home is Sunderland, meeting people who fancy themselves as hard cases makes a change from meeting people who really are hard cases.

During the first half Richard Ord received a cut to the head, which he shrugged off to defend a corner. John Fashanu strolled over and rubbed his hand on Ordy's wound, then licked his palm before declaring: 'I love white man's blood.' Weirdo.

This was, to say the least, unusual behaviour on the field of play.

Ordy was from the mining village of Murton, where vampirism and human sacrifice are not especially frowned upon. Nevertheless, consuming another chap's blood was still a surprise on a football pitch in the 1990s. It's probably the same now. Ordy was more befuddled than anything else. We were all annoyed and, similar to the Geoff Thomas incident, I was sitting on the bench, grinding my teeth and hoping for an opportunity for vengeance. I came on in place of Ordy late in the game, by which time Kevin Ball had beaten me to it – if you can imagine such a thing.

Kevin was not only fearless, he was one of the toughest players I ever saw and also physically very strong. It wasn't just mouth and mythology, as with certain other players with the same, but less deserved reputation.

By 1994 he had been at Sunderland for four years and become club captain as well as an adopted Mackem. Today he is adopted even more, if that's possible. During away games in London he would often be subjected to derogatory chants of: 'You dirty northern bastard!' This was most unfair and somewhat misinformed. He was actually from Hastings in East Sussex, site of the famous battle (appropriately enough) and was therefore more of a southerner than any Londoner.

The verbal pounding he received from opposition supporters was something that affected him deeply. He only wanted to try his best and was actually a very sensitive man and easily wounded. He once confided to me that he would weep copiously into his pillow at the 'dirty northern bastard' jibes. It gnawed at his soul.

Nah, only kidding. He didn't give a shit. In fact he loved it.

Anyway, Fashanu and Kevin jumped together for a header immediately in front of me in the dugout. They collided and both ended up lying on the ground, with Fashanu, who knew martial arts and about pressure points, on top and giving Bally little digs that the officials couldn't see. The elbow-loving striker would regret this later. About half a second later.

Kevin Ball got hold of John Fashanu and flipped him over like a mushroom omelette. Fash was now pinned to the pitch, unable to move and clearly frightened as Kevin was now in a position to do what he wanted to him until they were separated. Bally's stare was enough to achieve this. Now to us, this was a run-of-the-mill incident that we saw every day in training, but the Wimbledon players were startled and abandoned their campaign of 'intimidation', for the afternoon at least.

But we lost the game 2–1 and were out of the FA Cup. Kevin's little vignette aside, it was a disappointing first trip to Wimbledon for me. My second one three years later would be ten times worse.

•   •   •

There was still animosity on our training pitch. There always is. Derek Ferguson was still keen to fight anyone, particularly our right-back Dariusz Kubicki, who joined in March on loan from Aston Villa.

My own circumstances were not radically altered either. I was still a bit-part player, pleased whenever I was in the first team. Having previously been in charge of the reserves, Mick knew that I would never shirk whichever side I was in and that I was a good trainer too. Exactly as at school, I just loved playing football. Mick appreciated this more when he saw the sulky-chops faces of certain others who found themselves in the reserves. Acutely aware that I was not the star of the league, or even the club, and keen to earn another contract when this one ran out, the prudent course for me was to do as I was told.

Besides, if you don't train as you should then you aren't trying properly and won't get anywhere. Norman had instilled this into me a long time beforehand. Still, I just loved playing football at any level. School, Ipswich as an apprentice, Belgium, Bishop Auckland, Plains Farm Club, eventually the Premier League; my attitude never changed. Why would anyone not love playing the greatest game on earth – and being paid for it? Even if I was ping-ponging between the reserves and the bench and not making anything like as many first-team starts as I had hoped, I was still doing a job that literally millions of people would envy: people like me when I had been arsing about at BT in the recent past.

But there was still worry, worry, worry. I frequently felt the old anxieties, which meant that I couldn't feel my legs and was further disquieted by a rather injury-prone period of my career. My knee, which had not been straight for some years now, still caused occasional pain, and Steve Smelt, our physio, would give me anti-inflammatory tablets. I took four a day with the usual recommendation being that this should be carried out for a few weeks. I would do so for almost a decade. The long-term effects are bad, the main problem being that when the pain was masked I became less aware of the damage being done to the knee. Don't knock pain; it's there for a reason.

I don't blame anyone. This sort of thing was accepted procedure. I remember playing with a broken toe. I was injected with cortisone and told to put my boots back on and get out there. It was the same with twisted ankles; you were strapped up tightly and shoved back onto the pitch. None of this was considered remarkable and it happened to most players at some stage. Again, I never objected. I was still too grateful for being a professional footballer to object.

Play with a niggle? Too right. Strap me up. Long-term effects? What are those? I want to play for Sunderland.

In November 2014 I was given a new knee. Much of my back is new too.

●   ●   ●

In February 1994, we played a goalless draw at Charlton, then jointly managed by Steve Gritt and Alan Curbishley. In the twenty-seventh minute, I went in hard, very hard, on their captain Alan

McLeary. Again, I was fully committed to winning the ball and had little regard for anything else. Alan needed eight stitches in his calf and missed Charlton's next two games. I received a yellow card, but Mr Gritt was furious and passed his outrage to the press. To be fair to Mick Buxton, he defended me equally robustly, with the mandatory 'not that sort of player' statement.

I barely featured in the last third of 1993–94. Phil Gray and Don Goodman were well-established strikers and I now had the emerging Craig Russell to contend with. The season petered harmlessly out. We managed forty-eight points from twenty-nine games under Mick during the rise to twelfth. Although this blaze of mediocrity was of minimal interest to the wider football world, it was a modest and welcome accomplishment on Wearside.

For the second year running, the final game of the season was in Nottingham. But this time it was a jolly day out at Forest, who had already been promoted. We came back from two goals down (Collymore again) to draw a meaningless, but entertaining game. Don Goodman and Craig Russell scored late on and the poisonous atmosphere at Notts County twelve months earlier was just an unpleasant memory. Pre-match entertainment for the Sunderland fans was sitting in The Aviary pub and watching compatriots jumping fully clothed from the Trent Bridge into the river below. If you can't be good, be safe; or in this case, neither.

Thus ended my first full season at Sunderland; a big one for me, but for everyone else connected to the club it was a campaign of virtual nothingness with neither danger nor any real achievement.

It was a zillion times better than a job at BT.

The club and the fans were desperate for someone to arrive who could transform one of England's biggest and finest clubs from its comatose condition into one that would, ideally, force its way into the new and much hyped Premier League.

They would only have to wait another eleven months.

CHAPTER 7

PUNCH-UPS, MY GOAL OF THE CENTURY AND KLINSMANN

Two weeks after the Forest game, the squad was in the USA for an official-unofficial trip. To explain, we would usually go to Marbella and drink ourselves into oblivion in the name of 'bonding'. But the club told us that a game had been arranged in Florida and that our hosts would be paying. Bob Murray was never one to pass up such an inducement, so off we went. This was exciting for me, as I had never been to the country before.

We landed in Orlando and were ushered aboard a bus to make the four-hour journey to Naples, a small city on the south-west coast of Florida overlooking the Gulf of Mexico. The driver was instructed to stop at a five and dime (it didn't take us long to use the local patois) so we could load up with a few cans. This was not the greatest idea for two reasons: we were already suitably refreshed from the flight and there was no toilet on the bus. There was audible sloshing by the time we arrived in Naples.

Naples is one of the wealthiest cities in the USA and our hotel was an extremely high standard of dwelling, even posher than Thorney Close. My room was a super king-size. Including the bathroom it had more square footage than my entire house. I had it to myself too, although I'm not sure why. It was either a sort of wedding present because I was soon to be married, or it was because no one wanted to room with me as I had acquired a certain hedonistic reputation.

Andy Melville and Phil Gray weren't in the main section of the hotel. They were in a detached apartment where they took it upon themselves to be hosts to the rest of the squad. So we filled their bath with ice to keep the remaining cans from the bus journey cool and the party continued from there. As we had a game the following day, this was perhaps not the brightest idea either (very rarely did we have the brightest idea), although it was supposed to be a holiday too.

Our opposition the next evening was a Florida West Coast Select XI. Our hosts could not have been more accommodating and we were greeted by the son of the extremely wealthy president of the club who was footing the bill. The son was a nice enough fellow, but he seemed quite keen on himself and could hardly have been more American in appearance: tall, blond and with gleaming chompers. He would also be playing. The lads immediately decided that he was a figure of fun and encouraged me to do my level best to 'Fucking kick him, Lee. Go on. Kick him! Fucking whack him!' This wasn't terribly professional or nice. Nor was it within approved acceptance of hospitality. But we were still semi-bladdered. I started the game at centre-back because Melville pretended to be injured. Injured as a newt, was my theory.

The eighty-degree heat, humidity and booze made for an exceptionally sweaty evening. This was the most dehydrated I had been since Puke-gate in Belgium, although at least this time I was not the only one to disgrace himself. Under the circumstances, with me shambling around in an ungainly fashion, tongue lolloping from the side of my mouth, it was not surprising that Goldenballs in the Florida midfield was being made to look like the pinnacle of athleticism. The lads had only urged me to foul him for a lark, but it was beginning to look like the most viable option.

By approximately the seventieth minute, I was completely

knackered and he was about to prance past me again, when I presented him with a Claudio Gentile-style clattering. For the first time in the game, he had a hair out of place. The club president, having paid for our little excursion, seemed to think that my actions were somewhat undiplomatic and Anglo-American relations, as propounded at the time by John Major and Bill Clinton, were ever so slightly undermined. Not that my teammates seemed in any way perturbed; or if they were, they convincingly disguised their feelings by pissing themselves laughing while covering their own part in the incident with innocent cries of 'What are you doing, Lee?' and 'How could you?' all the while visibly sniggering when they were facing the other way. Bastards. Anyway, we won 4–0.

Afterwards we went to some complex for a pool party; something I had only ever encountered in films. My excitement was tempered somewhat when we were told that we wouldn't be allowed in the pool. I don't know why. Surely a pool party where use of the pool is prohibited is just a party. Still, there was a barbecue and we could have a few drinks. Just what the doctor ordered, if the doctor wanted to be struck off.

Not being allowed to take a dip became more frustrating the less thirsty we became. The point was reached where Reason was vanquished by Budweiser and we said: 'Fuck it. We're going in.' Martin Smith, Micky Gray, Phil Gray, a few others and I stripped down to our undies and did some bombing, ducking, pushing, shouting and everything that was banned on those signs you used to see in the swimming baths with the exceptions of 'smoking' and 'petting'. Before long, we were escorted from the pool and the disapproval was obvious, even to a load of infantile drunks like us.

It was disconcerting to be 'carded' when trying to enter a nightclub there and we had to carry our passports to prove our age. Fortunately, we had a sort of tour guide who escorted us around the local fleshpots. He would whisper something to the bouncers, who would then allow us in. I think our guide was from the Russian mafia, but he seemed a pleasant sort of lad.

• • •

I had now been at the club for well over a year and felt more than ever that I belonged. That said, I still kept a certain distance from the other players. We rubbed along very well, but I still didn't invite any of them to my wedding, stag night, or even the night do. The only other footballer at these events was Steven.

This was only partly because the wedding had been planned eighteen months beforehand. Most people don't socialise with their colleagues except at Christmas, when they're forced to. My colleagues were my friends, but not my best friends. It's the same now. I keep in touch with a few old players, namely Kevin Ball, Andy Melville and Richard Ord, as well as Steve Howard, Richard Hope and Dave Savage from my time at Northampton Town. I catch up with the others on the occasional golf day, but that's all, really.

• • •

If the post-season Florida trip was not the ambassadorial success that the club elders had hoped for, then the pre-season tour of Norway was a bad idea from the start. It was probably when things began to deteriorate again for the club and for Mick Buxton in particular. Everyone who went on that tour hated it.

I don't know who had the idea for the trip, or who organised it. I suspect it was someone who didn't have to be on it. It evidently wasn't anyone who owned an atlas. Norway is a thousand miles long and journeys to games were made by coach. Some journeys took twelve hours, which led to an outbreak of a condition known as 'numb-arse syndrome'. Accommodation was basic and located in the most desolate places imaginable. The travel, plus a lack of entertainment, led to extremely long bouts of boredom. A drink curfew was imposed too, just to ensure that everyone was quite massively pissed off. Still, it probably didn't cost much.

Remarkably, some supporters followed the team around the country for all five matches. They included, of course, the legendary Davey Dowell. It takes more than proximity to the Arctic Circle to curtail people like that. For one game, these supporters stayed at a guest house in a place near Trondheim called Hell. So there you have it: Sunderland fans will literally go to Hell to support their team.

Yet they almost certainly had a better time than the players. It was a wretched experience. The lack of quality opposition made it even less worthwhile. The final game was a 9–0 win over a side called Surnadal. What was the point of that? Never was a squad of players more pleased to return home from a pre-season tour.

But now for the good news. I wasn't there.

I stayed behind and trained with the reserves, run by Ian Ross. We played a few fixtures around the North East in pleasant summer weather, and I returned to fitness far quicker that I would have done chugging through the Norwegian countryside for half a day at a time on the back of a bus. You don't need to gallivant around the world to get match fit. When we all returned to the Charlie Hurley Centre for testing, I was as fit as anyone after non-gruelling journeys to Consett AFC, Crook Town or wherever it was that we went. No one was pining for the fjords.

I had been married in June. The reception was at the rather swish Ramside Hall in Durham, but the evening function was held in the Grindon Mill, an estate pub near my house (the pub has since been converted into a gym). It was around this time that football was being described as 'the new rock and roll', something that rather passed me by. This was the same day that Ray Houghton's goal for

Ireland beat Italy in New Jersey during the 1994 World Cup. I spent most of the evening watching it.

The reason for my omission from the Norway tour was that I had been on honeymoon in Kenya, during which I had gained eight or nine pounds in weight, which is quite a lot for a professional footballer. My flight back was delayed and I landed at Newcastle at 10 p.m. The next morning I reported for the start of pre-season training at 9 o'clock in something less than peak condition. I was plainly knackered, but hadn't expected to be lapped during the gentle jog we began with. The manager was furious and told me that I would not be going on the trip. This meant that, for now at least, I wasn't in the first team squad and I was most annoyed. Until I heard reports from Norway. It was the best 'punishment' I ever had.

•   •   •

There was more turbulence with my dear brother.

My wife and I decided to move to a bigger and better home. Nookside had been perfectly agreeable, but hardly big enough for an emerging superstar like myself, and we were looking for something a little more spacious. By happenstance, Steven wanted to move out of his home in Sunderland.

He lived in a new house in Silksworth and was keen to vacate it. This was not a reflection on the house or the area; it was more to do with him being a Newcastle United player living on Wearside. Most people he encountered were apparently pleased to see a local lad doing well, even if it was for an unloved rival club, but it was too much for a few to bear and he had to endure some unpleasant silliness, such as having his lawn painted red and white. It was hardly life-threatening stuff, but it wasn't nice and it was enough to drive him out to County Durham after about eighteen months in Silksworth.

I liked that house and was interested in buying it, but was put off when Steven told me that it was worth £122,000. This was expensive for the time in the North East. It was roomy, had four bedrooms, front and back gardens and a large garage. It was a 'well-appointed' dwelling and something similar could lighten you of a couple of million in other parts of the country in 2018. Regretfully, I began to look elsewhere.

But not for long. A week or two later I was peering into the window of a Halifax Estate Agents selling for Persimmons Homes when I saw the same property on offer – for £99,000. He had sold it to them as one of those 'we will buy your home to help you buy another Persimmons property' deals. So we bought it after all, just not from Steven.

This led to an interesting telephone conversation between siblings. I was still on a basic salary of £500 a week while he must have been on about twenty times that. I didn't think it unreasonable to ask him why he had attempted to wring another £23,000 that he didn't even need from his own brother. Despite having no acceptable defence for what he had done, he stuck to his unloaded guns.

'Well, that's what I thought it was worth.'

'Why was it on sale to everyone else for £99,000 then?'

The argument went nowhere. When someone knows they are in the wrong but won't admit it, further discussion becomes pointless. Yet we still remained friends even after this. Sort of. There are people in this world who just have to be accepted as they are.

Lee Howey! Lee Howey! Lee Howey....

• • •

I was more than ready for the 1994–95 season. A pity then that I was barely used in the first team. In spite of this, I was being worn to a frazzle and it was obvious why.

I mentioned earlier that Mick was old-school. He gave no credence to trendy modern concepts, such as a thing that sports scientists refer to as 'rest'.

I was a fringe player and therefore in both the first and reserve team squads. I had no problem with this in itself, but on an average week I would train on a Monday then do a tough double session on Tuesday with the first team. The first team would have Wednesday off, but I would be playing on the evening for the reserves. The reserves were off on Thursdays, but I would be training with the first team, running in the morning followed by pattern of play. I also trained on Fridays when I would be told whether or not I was required on the Saturday. I would have Sundays off, unless we had a game. On top of all this there was the travel to consider; I was sometimes not arriving home until two in the morning from a Wednesday reserve game, to be back for first team training seven hours later, which was at its most arduous on Thursdays and involved much running.

This exhaustion was a price I was prepared to pay, but it was horrible. The weariness this caused was adding to the old anxieties too. Had my grievance been made public, I would have doubtless been dismissed as a 'whinging footballer', followed by 'You don't hear (*insert noble profession*) complaining about their fifty-hour shifts'. The notion of a professional footballer being exhausted can, for some reason, be difficult for certain people to grasp.

Certain people included our manager. Mick was aware that I was doing much more training than anyone else at the club. Although as usual I did as I was told, I did challenge him on the matter one day because it was doing me, and by extension the team, no favours whatsoever. I had a feeling I would be wasting my time, but had a go anyway. I don't know why I bothered. He could not for the life of him see why anyone my age, twenty-five, would possibly require something as namby-pamby as a rest. Using his non-existent expertise on exercise and rest patterns, and with the air of someone who actually knew what he was talking about, he shared with me his 'theory' on fatigue. Excuse the spelling as it may well be wrong.

He said: '*Ptcha*! There's no such thing. Tiredness is all in your head.' Oh Lord.

I thanked him for dispensing this utter codswallop and went about my business; my business being even more training. He actually spoke at greater length on the subject, but that is all I remember of his rambling. As ever, his unswerving devotion to tedium ensured that I only heard a small percentage of what he said. He then meandered away round the fields in his flat cap again, looking as usual like a man in search of a lost pigeon.

•   •   •

I was an unused substitute for the opening game of 1994–95, which was a goalless draw at Bristol City. For Sunderland and for me personally, this was almost a microcosm of how the season would develop. We would finish it with eighteen draws, the most in English football. Six of them were goalless. I wouldn't step on the pitch until 15 October, as a late substitute against Burnley; again a 0–0 and another thriller.

This blizzard of non-events may be inducing you to nod off now, so I shall tell you about a rare good day that I had in 1994–95. It came at home to Bristol City (who would be relegated) a week before Christmas. It was my first start of the season. Don Goodman had left for Wolves and Phil Gray was injured. Luckily Mick remembered that I was still there.

It had been a turgid encounter with the score at its customary 0–0. The early stages of the second period were no more swashbuckling, despite the usual spellbinding half-time team-talk from Mick. The fans were discussing their favourite novels and how it was quite mild for the time of year, when we attacked the goal at the Fulwell End in the fifty-fourth minute. It may have been the first attack by either side. There was a scramble in City's six-yard box, which culminated in a six-inch pile-driver off my studs. The crowd had no chance of knowing for sure who had scored, as if they cared, but the PA announcer bellowed out my name, much to the chagrin of Craig Russell, who thought the goal was his. Well, it wasn't. The record shows that I scored it and always will, so he can bugger off; and it was his own fault anyway for having shorter legs than me.

Twenty minutes later, the day improved further. Gordon Armstrong had a long-range effort and it was dreadful. Left to make its own way in life, that shot would have gone for a throw-in. It was wildly inaccurate but had the virtue of being firmly struck. The ball hurtled towards me on the edge of the penalty area. I put my shin to it and then watched it ping past the keeper, Keith Welch. Quality goals my arse. As long as they go in. That said, it wasn't a complete fluke; I wasn't trying to miss.

The final score was 2–0. As we had won only one of our previous eight matches and were sliding down the league, the three points were more than useful.

It was a good victory and wonderful for me personally to score twice. But it was a terrible game. Perhaps more significant than the result was that it was Gary Owers' 330th and final game for Sunderland.

The team was shuffled around; Dariusz Kubicki was moved from right-back to left-back, with Gary moving to right-back and Derek Ferguson replacing Gary in midfield, while a disgruntled Richard Ord was dropped from left-back and from the team altogether to make way for Dariusz. Have you got all that?

The idea was to prove to Joe Jordan, Bristol City's manager, that Gary could play at right-back, as indeed he could (they already knew about him as a midfielder). Money changed hands and within a week Gary had signed for City with Martin Scott moving in the other direction. I was sad to see Gary leave, but this, along with moving Kevin Ball into midfield, was one of Mick Buxton's shrewder moves. Martin was the 'genuine article' as a left-back and would be at Sunderland until he was forced out of the game by injury in 1999.

• • •

Gary's departure left a void that needed to be filled: urgently. He had been organising the Christmas party.

Yuletide socialising for the pros and youth players over eighteen tended to be a combination of industrial quantities of drink, a similarly large amount of food and some strippers. Obviously, it wasn't as sophisticated as that every year, but we always tried.

The custom was that we would have the next day off, but Mick Buxton guillotined that idea, as it might have enabled fun. We usually went somewhere in Sunderland city centre, but for the Wednesday before Christmas of 1994, Mr Owers, in conjunction with a Geordie called Derek, had arranged for a meal and entertainment downstairs in a Chinatown restaurant in Newcastle. Derek was someone with contacts throughout the area who could provide pretty much anything: seats at the opera, crockery, three-piece suits, turquoise paint, kryptonite – you name it. For the entertainment we were desperately keen to have plate spinners or a harmonica player; perhaps even someone who could produce budgerigars from his sleeves. In the end we had to settle for more strippers, although the disappointment in the room was barely noticeable.

That morning I took a phone call at home from Gary Owers. He had just signed for Bristol City and wouldn't be attending the festivities. But he still didn't want to let the lads down and so entrusted me to take over the necessary arrangements with Derek. My wife was listening to my half of the conversation and heard the word 'strippers' at least four times. I toyed briefly with the idea of pretending I had been discussing plans to redecorate the dining room, but thought better of it, what with her not being an idiot. She rolled her eyes with menacing disapproval, before stomping off to do anything other than give me a goodbye kiss.

The plan, if it could be called that, was to have the meal and a couple of drinks before the ladies we had hired demonstrated their art. The younger members of our party were made to go on stage and 'assist', which they did with an aplomb best left undescribed on the printed page. This was early in the evening before a couple of minibuses arrived to take us back to Sunderland. Alec Chamberlain and Derek Ferguson went to St James' Park to watch Newcastle lose to Manchester City in the League Cup. It was far from sold out, so Derek procured the tickets quite easily. Kevin Ball, Phil Gray and Andy Melville among others stayed to have a few jars in Newcastle. The rest of us returned to Sunderland.

Not long after they had entered this particular bar, one of Tyneside's less evolved bouncers recognised an opportunity to make a name for himself as something other than a cretin. His ambition would go unrealised. This oaf locked the door and proceeded to provoke Phil for not even the slightest reason. Phil was never one to back down and the argument became more heated. The bouncer was left flummoxed by Phil's superior vocabulary, especially the longer and more complex enunciations such as 'fuck off'. Kevin's efforts at peaceful mediation were rewarded with a punch in the face from this near-human and a small scuffle ensued.

Actually, a large scuffle ensued. The police arrived and several arrests were made, including those of Kevin and Phil. Word got back to us through our swanky new mobile phones (they had been around for a couple of years and by then were down to the size of prize cucumbers). We found out later that much of this bouncer's time was taken up with telling apocryphal tales of how many Sunderland players he had filled in during the course of that evening and throughout his career as a whole. Someone from Wearside later went to discuss the matter with the gentleman and my understanding is that it went considerably beyond a ticking off. I am pleased for my own sake to have no more details on the matter.

In the meantime we all had to report for training the next

morning. Most of us were hungover. Bally arrived late, having been released from custody, and his left eye looked like a rotten plum. Mick Buxton had not expected us to spend our Christmas night out brass rubbing in Durham Cathedral, but this was a bit much and he was justifiably annoyed. He attempted a severe verbal dressing down which failed in its desired effect because his bollockings were like his team-talks: no one listened. Regardless of this, arguments and recriminations commenced among ourselves.

'It was your fault.'

'Don't blame me.'

'It was your idea to go to Newcastle.'

'But it was your idea to go in that pub.'

'I said there would be trouble.'

This went on for some time until we decided where culpability for the whole contretemps did truly lie: it was all the fault of Gary Owers.

In time-honoured workplace tradition, the blame was allocated to the one person who wasn't there to defend himself. It served him right for allowing himself to be sold.

Oh, Gary. What were you thinking of? Bristol City should have fined you a week's wages for that episode. Disgraceful.

• • •

We were due to play away to Swindon on 2 January. But the game, which never seemed likely to go ahead, was postponed at 9 a.m. due to snow. We had stayed the night in a Wiltshire hotel and were told that we could still have a training session after breakfast. The journey home was further delayed because the bus was knackered. It was eventually started, but with no electrics, so we couldn't even listen to the radio. To combat the boredom, it was suggested that we should (surprise, surprise) have a few snifters while we travelled and make a little party of it; not a Roman orgy, just a little party. Our next game was days away, so what harm would it do?

But, never a man to be mistaken for a ray of sunshine, Mick Buxton turned down the suggestion like a bedspread. Perhaps the Christmas night out escapade still rankled. Or maybe he decided it was better to be disliked than simply disregarded. Whatever, he decreed that only soft drinks were to be imbibed which, in the absence of electricity, did not even include tea or coffee. Water only. We could also have a game of travel chess if we behaved ourselves, so long as it didn't get too raucous. This bore all the hallmarks of a weak man trying to appear strong and it was not appreciated. We weren't after a day of unfettered debauchery, merely some levity to make a wasted twelve-hour road trip more tolerable. But that was Mick. He didn't understand and there was no joy in the man. Boozing was not all we were interested in, but he had needlessly made everyone as miserable as he was.

• • •

For the second successive year, we drew Carlisle United at home in the FA Cup third round. For the second successive year we drew 1–1 and for the second successive year we won the replay. The mathematical odds of this happening are precisely... best left to someone who can be bothered to work out that sort of thing. For the third successive year we drew Premier League opposition in the fourth round.

We would play Tottenham Hotspur at Roker Park on Sunday 29 January 1995. This was a big deal on Wearside. Despite the misgivings that fans of Sunderland AFC may have about the club today, they have become accustomed to celebrated opposition at the Stadium of Light. In 1994–95 only one of the previous ten seasons had been spent in the top flight; so the visit of Tottenham and their accompanying Sheringham, Barmby, Popescu, Mabbutt and who-have-you was an occasion to be savoured. There would be the added novelty of live television too and this time it was national. *Match of the Day* would be broadcast from Roker on BBC1, with the suave Des Lynam, the coolly analytical Alan Hansen and the cheating Jimmy Hill.

Everyone at Sunderland, not least the fans, was greatly looking forward to the game because it was a welcome respite from yet another season of struggle. On the day of the Spurs game we were eighteenth in the league and our previous fixture had been a home defeat to Notts County, who were bottom of the table and would stay there.

To prepare us for the cup tie, the club flew us out to Fuengirola on the Costa del Sol, where in January they have even better weather than we do in the north-east of England. There was understandable muttering from some of the fans about this after the depressingly bad show against Notts County, but it was deemed to be the best preparation. I didn't object. A golf day was arranged for our first full day there, with some training during the evening. The BBC's *Football Focus* team, fronted by Eddie Butler who was really a rugby journalist, were to come out to do a feature on us while we belted golf balls round a picturesque, southern Spanish course; the sort of tough assignment with which the lads at the Beeb's sports department like to challenge themselves. The feature would go out the day before the game, thereby giving an additional plug to *Match of the Day*.

We checked in at the hotel at around 7 p.m. and held a meeting an hour later. Mick and Trevor Hartley said we were allowed a few drinks, but imposed a midnight curfew. This was the sort of thing my mother used to do with equal effect – and Yvonne was far more frightening than Mick Buxton. We all readily agreed to the curfew, then strolled out into the warm, crepuscular Spanish air without the slightest intention of keeping our word.

We headed for Fuengirola's main square. It was Tuesday, so the square was fairly quiet. At first. The local bars were most welcoming and it was one in the morning before anyone took the trouble to check the time. Not one person in our party had left that bar. Oh well; we were late now anyway so we thought we might as well continue, and moved to another pub. It seemed a good idea at the time, your honour.

At approximately 2 a.m., Micky Gray, Martin Smith and Craig Russell lurched through the doors of whichever watering hole the rest of us were in. Micky was crying and approaching me for protection.

'Big man! Big man!' he wailed. 'Someone out there's just kicked me in the face.'

My natural sense of injustice at this meant that I was ready to extract retribution. Why not? I was young, fit, physically imposing, loyal to my friends and – most importantly of all – had about a gallon-and-a-half of San Miguel inside me. I walked out into the street behind Micky, shadow boxing, followed by some equally stupid teammates.

'Who was it Micky? Who? Who? Who? Tell me?' I was ready for action, wondering who they would get to play me when this was made into a film.

We looked round and saw on the other side of the pub car park that about thirty local youths had gathered; glowering, shouting, threatening and indisputably outnumbering us. At this point even being young, fit, physically imposing, loyal to my friends and containing about a gallon-and-a-half of San Miguel somehow didn't seem sufficient for the task in hand. I wasn't a complete idiot.

A couple of them came over and began to thrash out a treaty with Phil Gray and Derek Ferguson; probably the two least diplomatic people there. Negotiations broke down at an early stage when a Spaniard began to chase Phil around the car park with a pint glass in his hand. They ran past me and I managed to stop the irate local. I gestured to the assailant that he ought to put down the weapon and that he and I should sort out matters properly. He eventually understood and, while he was still putting the glass on the bonnet of a car, I took a short but swift run-up and nutted him in the mush with quite some precision. He rolled under the car.

Admittedly this was underhand. But when the Marquess of Queensberry sat down to write his rules he did so alone, undistracted by irate Spaniards wanting to stick a pint glass up his arse.

Whatever. My lack of wisdom instigated a mass brawl. Not everyone in the squad joined in with the activities, although I couldn't be sure who had opted out, as I was otherwise occupied. I suspect it was the cleverer ones.

I had one gentleman with his back to a wall and was rat-a-tat-tat punching him. As he fell, he grabbed the new shirt my wife had recently bought me and pop went the buttons in various directions. Sirens could now be heard and we still had enough wherewithal – just – to abandon the scene with immediate effect. We then made our way back to the hotel, in my case bare-chested, by a less conspicuous back-street route.

Today, virtually everyone in the West has a phone in their pocket with the facility to take pictures, which can then be seen anywhere in the world within a minute. Thinking back to Fuengirola and our Christmas parties, this isn't necessarily a good thing.

Martin Smith later gave us an unexpurgated version of the assault on Micky Gray that had instigated a potentially huge disgrace upon our club. It turned out to be virtually self-inflicted. This is what had happened:

Micky, who could be intoxicated on a standard packet of wine gums, had drunk a few bottles of lager and began to feel the call of nature. Rather than go to all the trouble of using a toilet in a bar (he considered this to be a logistical nightmare), he simply relieved himself against the rear wheel of a Suzuki 125. The owner of the vehicle saw this and began, quite justifiably, to remonstrate. In Málaga it is probably safer to sleep with someone's wife than it is to piss on his bike. However, Micky did not comprehend how he could possibly be in the wrong and took a swing at the bloke, whom he thought was behaving unreasonably.

Micky's already limited skills as a pugilist were further restricted by San Miguel, which meant that his punch connected with nothing but the night air and, like a character in a bad sketch, he went flat on his face. The same face was subsequently administered with a retributive kick from the scooter-owner, who then walked away. Micky's version of events had omitted considerable detail. Had Martin given me this prequel earlier I would have done nothing because really it served Micky right, and a whole squad of First Division footballers would have been preserved from some of Fuengirola's more widely attended fisticuffs.

We shuffled back into the hotel at 3 a.m. and were informed that some of the others were in a bar at the top of the town (Micky Gray had gone to bed). The curfew was by now something of an academic point, so we decanted ourselves into a taxi to join them at this bar, which was called El-Something-Or-Other. The place was inhabited by a number of young ladies dressed for a party and the drinks were vastly overpriced. Had this been a few hours earlier when we had clearer heads, we would have realised within seconds that it was a brothel. As it was, it took some time for this information to register. Perhaps it was called El-Knockio-Shop.

We were shocked to the marrow. Five quid for a can of Heineken in 1995 was nothing short of outrageous.

At around 6 a.m., we were back at the hotel for two entire hours of unbroken sleep. Before that, I noticed that my hand had swollen considerably and I slept with it in a bucket of ice that the staff had given me. We were pumped for information at breakfast by Kevin Ball, who had done the captainly thing by actually adhering to the midnight curfew. Micky Gray eventually joined us to louder cheers and more good-natured abuse than his pumping little head would have liked. He was wearing dark glasses to disguise the biggest shiner that any of us had seen since... well... the one that Bally had worn at Christmas.

The golf day was a success and I had a better round than was generally expected of someone with a swollen hand, two hours' sleep behind him and a hangover. *Football Focus* got what they wanted, too, although Micky was kept well away from the cameras. In fact the whole trip went well in as much as no one was actually hospitalised (with the possible exception of a Spaniard or two). We genuinely bonded on that excursion. As far as I am aware no one was ever fined or even spoken to about the ridiculously unprofessional manner in which we had conducted ourselves. It was never mentioned by anyone in authority, even though everyone knew about it. Micky's gleaming black eye and my Fred Flintstone hand had aroused instant suspicion and a full account was soon made known to pretty much anyone who was interested. The clientele of the Museum Vaults was apprised of the facts, so you can safely bet that Mick Buxton was too.

The remainder of our time in Spain was conducted with considerably more decorum and we certainly avoided the town centre.

• • •

We returned home and, after reflecting upon yet another diplomatic triumph for SAFC on foreign soil, discussed tactics for the cup tie.

Despite my heroics against Bristol City six weeks earlier, scoring possibly the ugliest pair of goals that any Sunderland player would ever manage, I was still nothing like an automatic choice for the first team. By the time we played Spurs, I had made just two starts all season, so any time at all on the pitch before the *Match of the Day* cameras would be a bonus.

A day or two before the game, Mick took me to one side and told me I would be in the starting XI. At centre-back. I had literally never played in that position in the first team anywhere; not at Sunderland, Hemptinne, Bishop Auckland, St Aidan's or Plains Farm Working Men's Club. Nowhere.

Against a side of Spurs' undoubted attacking ability, we were going to play three centre-backs, Gary Bennett, Andy Melville and me, in the hope of absorbing pressure and scoring on the break. I was extremely pleased yet somewhat bemused. I would be pitted against Jürgen Klinsmann, undeniably one of the greatest strikers in the world at that time. He would captain Germany when they won the European Championships at Wembley the following year. He had already won the World Cup in 1990 and would be named third behind George Weah and Paolo Maldini for the 1995 FIFA World Player of the Year award. If I got bored with Klinsmann I could always go and sort out Teddy Sheringham, who was equally crap. Then there was Nick Barmby and other quality attacking players. It would be like marking the Red Arrows.

It should be said that I was not completely inexperienced as a centre-back, having played there a few times for the reserves. Only recently I had come up against Ronnie Tucknutt, a nippy little striker who turned out a few times for Rotherham United's second-string. He never quite made their first team, but when he left football he opened a thriving ironmongery in Houghton-le-Spring. He could be a handful on the football pitch too. However, if forced to choose, I would have to say that Klinsmann was the better player.

Fair enough, Ronnie Tucknutt is someone I have just invented. But I still think he illustrates a point.

We knew what we were up against, but we were ready. The game kicked off in weather as fair as could be expected near the banks of the River Wear in January and for a long time our game plan worked. We frustrated them and created a couple of decent chances ourselves. Personally, I put in a few good tackles against opponents who were infinitely more famous than me, and my passing wasn't bad either; all live on BBC Television, too. I sincerely hoped that Mr McAuliffe had tuned in.

I was coping reasonably well with Klinsmann, who attempted his trademark dive once or twice. I may have politely mentioned this to him in passing. His English was excellent, but didn't need to be for him to understand the words I was using to describe his routinely dishonest attempts to win free kicks.

Teddy Sheringham played with his chest out and was supercilious, acting as though the whole occasion was beneath him. In fact he was every bit as arrogant as Geoff Thomas had been. The crucial difference was that Sheringham had the talent to back up *his* arrogance. What a player. Not that any of this did him any good in the first half, which ended goalless. So far, so good.

But the shock that the BBC were hoping for would not come to pass. The match was turned in the fiftieth minute. Sheringham hit our post; the ball rebounded to David Howells who passed to Gheorghe Popescu who placed the ball to his right of the goal, bringing out a quite magnificent left-handed stop from Gary Bennett.

The only thing to sully Gary's superb reflex save was the fact that Alec Chamberlain was our designated goalkeeper. The referee, Mike Reed, could have made a name for himself by ignoring the most blatant handball anyone had ever clapped eyes on, but he didn't. He behaved with shameless competence. Gary was given a distinctly uncontroversial red card, before Klinsmann gave Alec no chance with the penalty, deliberately placing it with total precision into the bottom right corner; the sort of dirty German trick we had come to expect. Thirteen minutes later, Sheringham and an own-goal had made it 3–0. Phil Gray retrieved one before Klinsmann scored his second.

It could have been worse with ten men and under the circumstances we had performed respectably, although that didn't mean it wasn't a bad day. Either way, it was an interesting first game for me as a centre-half and a tough, yet invaluable experience.

• • •

The Sunderland–Tottenham Hotspur FA Cup fourth round tie of 1995 would ordinarily be long forgotten by everyone, except perhaps those with a vested interest. But it was restored to public consciousness nineteen years later for the most regrettable of reasons.

Playing at right-back for Spurs that day was twenty-year-old Sol Campbell, better remembered as a centre-back during a highly successful, medal-strewn career that saw him capped seventy-three times by England, playing in three World Cups. He was given a tough time by Martin Smith and was at fault for Phil Gray's goal. But that is not Mr Campbell's abiding memory of the game. In 2014 he gave an interview to Evan Davis on Radio 4's *Today* programme, describing his experience of Roker Park almost two decades earlier – as he remembered it.

He claimed:

Every time I touched the ball it was monkey chants.

As a footballer you start saying to yourself 'what is this all about?' I'm an England player and you've got the whole stadium ringing of monkey chants every time I've touched the ball. It was a scary, kind of confusing moment for me.

Let us pass lightly over the fact that he wouldn't be an England player for another sixteen months, because that isn't exactly at the heart of the issue. He gave another interview later the same day to Victoria Derbyshire on BBC Radio 5 Live.

He told her:

One of my earliest encounters with it [racism] was at Sunderland. Yes it was a long time ago. It was at Roker Park. I was playing for Tottenham in the FA Cup. Basically, every time I touched the ball I was subjected to monkey chants; *every* single, *every* single time I touched the ball.

It was a very confusing time for me. I was nineteen, twenty. I'd never really experienced that level of racism before. It wasn't really recorded.

Not recorded? He's correct about that. The game was broadcast live on national television, with highlights shown later, and no racism was recorded. There might be a reason for that. It must have been 'confusing' because, if it did happen, it was most certainly not on the scale that Sol Campbell supposes. That is not to say he wasn't subjected to any pea-brained racism that day, which is disgraceful and something I wholeheartedly condemn. All footballers will receive a dog's abuse at some time from spectators, for whatever reason. This does not justify racism and hopefully the days we recall from the 1980s in this country, of bananas being thrown at black players, are far behind us. Matters had improved by 1995, but even today there is much to do. Sadly there is still racism among the support of every club; some of it sinister, some of it simply mindless.

But '*every* single, *every* single time I [Sol Campbell] touched the ball' at Roker Park?

I know he is wrong about this because I was on the pitch with him and many, many people I know were in the crowd. Between us we would have noticed if the Nuremberg-style frenzy as described by Sol had actually happened. I don't remember *any* racial chanting. What I also definitely have no memory of – and nor does anyone I have spoken to on the subject – is 'the *whole stadium* ringing of monkey chants'.

That was a ludicrous claim. Undiluted rubbish. No media referred to any racism, as they surely would have done. Martin Smith spent most of the afternoon within a few feet of Sol and has no recollection of any racist incidents whatsoever. Martin and

Sol knew each other personally too from the England under-21 squad and Martin recalls no conversation with Sol after the game. Admittedly and for obvious reasons, Sol's ears were probably more attuned to racial abuse than Martin's or mine. However, Gary Bennett, a black player who made the fifth most appearances in Sunderland's history, didn't notice anything either.

Even a single instance of racism is embarrassing to the huge majority of football supporters. But what Sol Campbell said about that fateful January day requires clarification, because it was an exaggeration, to say the least; bordering on an insult. This is because '*the whole stadium*' suggests that *each and every* Sunderland supporter present was/is a racist, including my family and friends.

His claims in 2014 went largely unchallenged by the media, except in the *Sunderland Echo*. This is understandable as I don't suppose that Evan Davis or Victoria Derbyshire were prolific attendees of Sunderland home games in the 1990s. Sol repeated the claims in his authorised biography, the zanily entitled *Sol Campbell: The Authorised Biography*. Indeed, his comments about Sunderland's supporters were made on a number of occasions. It wasn't a slip of the tongue.

Perhaps I have strayed into cynicism here, but the comments that took him nineteen years to utter created bad feeling on Wearside. I make no claims for the moral perfection of every single Sunderland fan, but the overwhelming majority of them – and British football fans generally – deserve better. I stop short of saying that Sol Campbell, an otherwise fine ambassador for our sport, should apologise – I don't know how he felt – but I don't recognise the version of events that he related.

CHAPTER 8

THE SEASON COULDN'T
END QUICKLY ENOUGH

Sunderland supporters appreciate the quality of the likes of Klinsmann and Sheringham, or their modern equivalents, even if they are playing for another team. Their appearance at Roker was the last of the rare pieces of excitement during the Mick Buxton era. Indeed, nothing of interest to any neutral had happened to Sunderland since the club reached the 1992 FA Cup final. It remained a thrill for me to play for the team I loved, but it can't be denied that as 1994–95 lumbered on, SAFC was moribund.

The fans were acutely aware of this. The game after our cup elimination to Spurs was a 1–1 draw at home to Port Vale, then a 1–0 defeat at Charlton. I won't be insulted if your eyes are drooping at these riveting recollections because I don't remember a great many games from the rest of that season myself. I looked those two up.

The mediocrity continued on Wednesday 8 March when we travelled to Wolves, where I played the whole game but notably failed to enamour myself to the Molineux faithful. It had only been eighteen months since the Geoff Thomas incident and football supporters have elephantine memories. Lightning was about to strike twice.

Wolves had a decent side and would finish the season in fourth place. They now had Don Goodman in their line-up, as well as Mike Stowell, Steve Bull, Peter Shirtliff, David Kelly, Mark Walters, Paul Birch and the Dutch defender John de Wolf.

His full name was Johannes Hildebrand de Wolf, so you can see why he preferred John. John de Wolf of Wolves. His shaggy hair and beard meant that he actually resembled a wolf and he was known on the terraces as 'de Wolf Man'; about as droll as nicknames get in football. As wolfy as a full moon. Could anything be wolfier? It was widely assumed that there would never be a more lupine arrangement in the whole of the professional game, a notion that was disproved in Germany in 1998 when Wolfgang Wolf became manager of Wolfsburg.

John, a Dutch international, had joined from Feyenoord for £600,000 just three months earlier and become an instant crowd favourite. He could certainly play, but the Wolves fans also loved his aggression, ruthless tackling and goading of opponents. The difference between a cult hero and a dirty sod is defined by whether or not the individual concerned plays for your team.

The game itself was a poor one and goalless at half-time, although Wolves had been the better side. All I remember of the first half is that it was a chilly evening in March and I was being smashed into the middle of April by de Wolf. Knee in the back, elbow on the top of the head, smashed from the sides, numerous pushes. It was thoroughly unpleasant and not even subtle. The referee, Philip Wright, ignored my complaints, seeming to adopt the view that a big centre-forward should expect this sort of thing, and took no action. This was much to the delight of John, who was enjoying his impunity.

During the interval I didn't listen to a word that Mick Buxton said. It was remarkable when anyone ever did, but on this occasion even someone who didn't speak like a man swallowing an ocarina would have struggled for my attention. I was seething at what had occurred in the first forty-five minutes and could think only of retribution. It was the solitary thought occupying my head and the prospect of a red card was no deterrent at all. A thunderously bad mood was heightened two minutes into the second half when Andy Thompson scored a penalty for Wolves. The de Wolf treatment continued relentlessly; elbow, knee, toe, kick, thump. None of my attempted retaliations worked. I kept missing or not connecting properly and the frustration was making me even angrier.

But destiny called in its own good time. With an hour gone, Tony Norman put a goal kick just over the halfway line; de Wolf was standing to my left with the ball about to land closer to him than me, and I clattered into him from the side with my left arm when he was in mid-jump. He hit the ground a relatively long time before I did, so I could have moved my feet further apart to avoid landing on him – but chose not to. I landed with one foot on his knee, which was already in a brace, and the other on his calf. He was carried off and did not play again that season. My anger still didn't subside and several other opponents could testify to this. It was back to the days of Plains Farm Club and the home crowd was incensed. I was slightly late with a challenge on their right-back, Jamie Smith, treading on his toe. Mr Wright, having taken no action when I incapacitated de Wolf, showed me a yellow card for that – and it was a complete accident.

I wasn't in the habit of doing these things to just anyone. But both Geoff Thomas and John de Wolf had invited retribution and duly received it. With John it wasn't just a case of 'he would have done it to me'; he *was* doing it to me.

However, I don't think the Wolves fans saw matters in quite the same regard. A West Midlands football phone-in on a local radio station that evening was apparently dedicated to me, although not in a flattering way like an earlier show dedicated to Slade had been. It was all about how I had done this to Geoff and John, I should never be allowed on a football field again; that sort of thing. Had I known about it I could have called and given my side of the story, but it wouldn't have been a good idea. Not much appeasement would have come about because I would have been honest. I was neither proud nor sorry. Both Thomas and de Wolf had reaped what they had sown.

This was the preamble to the death threats I received from Wolverhampton, although to the best of my recollection I was never actually killed. Razor blades were posted to me, as was a good deal of hate mail. Two letters stated that I would be shot if I ever returned to Molineux. Another particularly unconvincing *billet-doux*, purportedly from a chapter of the Hell's Angels, threatened to carry out other unspeakable acts of a thoroughly bad-mannered type. Further threats were made against my wife and kids, even though I didn't have any children at the time. It was all referred to the police. No one really took it seriously, but there is always that tiny piece of doubt and when we returned to Wolves a year later no one would warm up next to me.

• • •

The most important element of the Wolves game was not any personal tribulation. It was the bald fact of a 1–0 defeat for Sunderland. Yet another bad day. The season was deteriorating along with the standard of football we were producing.

I remember very little of what I did personally on the pitch during the remainder of 1994–95. What I do recall is that matters for the club as a whole came to a head when we played the next game, which was against Stoke City at Roker Park on 11 March. We had only won two league games since beating Bristol City in December and were a single place above the relegation zone. Don Goodman had been sold to Wolves before Christmas with midfielder Steve Agnew the only notable recruit. The dissatisfaction was well founded.

Fifteen minutes into the Stoke game, thousands of fans held up red cards to visibly display their disapproval. The protest was aimed mainly at Bob Murray, the owner (although he wasn't chairman at this time). Late in the game I won a free kick when I was clattered by Stoke's goalie, Ronnie Sinclair. Derek Ferguson delivered the free kick and Andy Melville got just in front of me to head the only goal of the game, which softened the mood in the stadium. Slightly. The protest continued outside the Main Stand after the match had ended. It was all becoming very ugly.

I was still being run into the ground by training as a first team as well as a reserve player at Mick's insistence. I never bothered to complain again and, as always, remained happy just to play when I was given the opportunity. Nevertheless, there was a limit to my natural compliance, and something happened that truly infuriated me. We bought Brett Angell from Everton. He would prove to be one of Sunderland's more ill-fated signings of the 1990s.

Brett had been quite a prolific goal scorer at Stockport County and Southend United before joining Everton in 1994 (strangely, Stockport had already loaned him to Everton twice). He was out of his depth in the Premier League, scoring one goal in over a year on Merseyside. He would later return to Stockport, where he resumed his impressive goal ratio, as he did at several other clubs too. By the end of a fairly successful career he had done well at most of his many clubs, but there were two glaring exceptions: Everton and Sunderland. He was loaned out three times by Sunderland before making a permanent move back to Stockport in November 1996. He would score just once for us too, and that was in the League Cup.

Everton paid £500,000 for his services, which raised more than a few sniggers considering his goal scoring record there. Sunderland then took him off their hands – for £700,000 – so both player and sniggers were transferred from Merseyside to Wearside. This was still a significant investment and made him one of our more expensive signings and 117 times more costly than I had been. He would therefore have to play, which meant that I wouldn't. After signing, he started all eight of the season's remaining games while I didn't even make the bench for any of them. Brett never looked like scoring in any of those matches except his first one. What little confidence he retained after his Everton experience dissipated further.

Only a year remained on my contract and Brett's arrival looked, at the time, to signify the end of me at Sunderland. This was mightily annoying and I demanded to speak to the manager about it. After a brief and failed attempt to fob me off by his secretary, I barged into Mick's office, which was in the Main Stand at Roker Park, overlooking the car park and with an unrivalled view of the Citroën garage. He was sitting in his usual Napoleonic splendour, slurping tea from a Popeye mug.

He looked up and made a guttural noise that sounded something like: 'Gyerr fnn urr, Lee'. He may have been eating a custard cream – perhaps even two (honestly, the debauchery of the man).

I was undeterred by his gilded eloquence and launched into a tirade about how I was working myself into the ground, playing in two positions, training uncomplainingly more than anyone else at the club for first team and reserves (I hadn't forgotten his 'tiredness is all in your head' shite), only for him to go out and buy an expensive striker. He may as well have told me I wasn't wanted and that I should look for another club. I had not been dealt with openly and honestly. Brett's arrival seemed to denote that my life was about to be completely rearranged, because when a footballer changes clubs he doesn't just have a new employer, he usually has to find another home in another town too.

New arrivals and added competition for places are an accepted part of football. Players are bought to improve the squad (even if it doesn't always work out like that). If it's you who is shunted out, then tough. That's life. What sparked my anger was no one having the courtesy to keep me informed that a pricey new signing was apparently about to make my already limited first team chances even more difficult.

I really did lose it. After I had threatened to give Mick an even better view of the Citroën garage by putting him through the office window, he finally managed to speak a few words. Of English.

'Calm down man, Lee. Take a seat.'

'Calm down!? I will; I'll put you through that fu—'

'It wasn't me who signed him.'

This temporarily threw me sideways, but it didn't take long to regather my thoughts and I still retained a keen interest in his literal defenestration.

I screamed: 'What do you mean you didn't sign him? You're the manager. A fucking useless one, but you're still the manager'– and further abuse to go with it.

'I never signed him. The chairman did.'

I didn't know whether he meant the chairman, John Featherstone, or the owner, Bob Murray, but this didn't matter much to me either way. A deal had been struck between the boards of directors at Roker and Goodison and that was that. Mick had no input and so cannot be blamed for the disaster that was Brett Angell's move to Sunderland; and a disaster it was for all concerned – except Everton.

It was all most unfortunate. Brett became an unwittingly comical figure. In training, whoever was deemed to be the worst performer in practice games was made to wear this yellow vest. Brett never seemed to have that vest off his back. This didn't do much for my confidence either because he was playing ahead of me. It was at this point I realised that my future was likely to be as a centre-half.

Brett became a fulcrum of amusement for the fans too. He would be loaned out twice the following season, to Sheffield United and West Bromwich Albion. He appeared as a half-time substitute for Albion against Sunderland in our final home game, a game that secured the championship for us, and was mocked most cruelly by the crowd when he came on. It must have been embarrassing enough that Sunderland had given West Brom permission to play him against us, as he was not considered much of a threat. That was before the Sunderland fans gave a huge mocking cheer when he ran onto the pitch and then just laughed. Not the snarling, derisory laughter they would have given to someone like Alan Shearer or Steve McManaman; it was the type of laughter you might hear when someone falls down a manhole. His humiliation at Sunderland was then complete. Nothing went right for this man.

Poor Brett. He was a lovely fellow. A gentleman. I'm glad to say that he did well after his nightmare couple of years at Sunderland and Everton and scored many goals in what was, overall, a very decent career. He was a good striker when he had a bit of confidence. Indeed, he had scored four times *against* Sunderland before he joined us. What didn't kill him made him stronger.

But it all might have been so different had he made a good start. He very nearly did. His Sunderland debut was against Barnsley at Oakwell on Friday 24 March 1995, a game played in a ridiculously high wind. I wasn't even on the bench (I don't suppose that my recent threat to lob the manager from his own office window had enhanced my claim to more first team opportunities).

With the score at 0–0 we took a throw-in deep in their half, which ended with the ball in Barnsley's net. The ball may or may not have skimmed Brett's head. No one else touched it. If Brett did make contact, it was a goal; if he didn't, it remained goalless as per the laws of the game. The referee said that the ball had been thrown directly into the net, so no goal. The final score was 2–0 to Barnsley. We were in serious trouble and only one place above a relegation spot.

Additional farce was injected into the occasion by the first and last appearance of the defender Dominic Matteo in a Sunderland shirt. He was then a twenty-year-old, highly rated prospect and it was something of a coup to bring him in on loan from Liverpool. But in yet another pantomime scene, it transpired that his registration had not been completed in time and that he should never have played at Barnsley. Perhaps no one at Roker Park knew how to operate the fax machine. Maybe the club pigeon had been shot. Whatever the reason, Bob Murray had to plead our case with the FA. They accepted it as an honest mistake that hadn't benefitted us because we had lost the game anyway. They let us off with a £2,500 fine and ordered Dominic back to Anfield. This was fortunate as they could have deducted points, with potentially ruinous consequences.

Mick Buxton was not responsible for signing Brett Angell, or for the Dominic Matteo fiasco, but he was sacked soon after the debacle at Oakwell. Out the window anyway, so to speak. Even his charisma couldn't save him.

There were no goodbyes; he just disappeared. The first I knew of his departure was when someone mentioned it in the changing rooms at training. Barnsley was our fourth defeat in a row and we were only going one way. We were the biggest club in the league, but had lost to (sorry if this sounds patronising) the likes of Grimsby, Millwall, Swindon, Tranmere, Southend and Luton. The fans were embarrassed and angry and Mick had paid for those results. There is more to management than simply not being Terry Butcher.

Bob Murray finally realised that appointing someone on the basis that they were already conveniently employed by the club was an approach that was considerably more easily implemented than it was productive. He was about to enlist the services of someone who would at last transform the club and leave a lasting legacy; a man who, certainly in terms of league position, would become Sunderland's most successful manager since 1955 – and I would get to play my part.

Before all that, he had to keep us out of the third tier of English football.

CHAPTER 9

PROGRESS AND PETER REID

The situation that Peter Reid inherited was not as desperate as it had been two years earlier, but still indisputably precarious. Not only were Sunderland one place above the relegation zone, we were sinking.

As a player, Peter's credentials were not in dispute. He was a famously tenacious midfielder, but skilful too. His best days were at Everton where he won two league titles, an FA Cup and a European Cup Winners' Cup. European Cup glory may have awaited Everton had not English clubs been booted out of Europe following the Heysel Stadium disaster of 1985. He was also an England international, including appearances in the 1986 World Cup.

His only previous job in management had been at Manchester City between 1990 and 1993. His three top-flight finishes there were fifth, fifth again, then ninth. Four games into the 1993–94 season, he was sacked after three defeats and a draw. This seemed harsh at the time. In retrospect it seems incredibly misguided. By 1998 City had dropped down two divisions and been through another five, less successful managers. They would not return to anywhere near fifth in the Premier League for many years; this was a few hundred million quid later in the late 2000s.

Peter joined Sunderland on an interim basis until the end of the 1994–95 season. I don't think it's a plot spoiler to mention that he would be there until October 2002. He had turned down several job offers before coming to Roker Park. His appointment was made quickly; in fact, he appeared before us unannounced. I don't recall any speculative talk about who the new manager might be; there was no time for that.

His personality was markedly different from that of Mick Buxton in that he had one. Peter was full of energy, chat and infectious Scouse enthusiasm. You always knew when he was anywhere within the vicinity; you could hear him. He gave the place an instant lift that we desperately needed because he only had seven games in which to save us.

I was happy that such a well-known, respected and buoyant figure had arrived. There was just one problem: I didn't even make the bench for any of the seven games. Trevor Hartley was still at the club and had Peter's considerable ear. Trevor saw little merit in big old-fashioned centre-forwards. Everyone is entitled to their opinion but, whether or not it affected his judgement, the fact that Trevor and I had never really got on too well can't have helped my cause. Even if my appearances on the pitch had been sporadic since joining the club in 1993, I had always at least been in and around the first team squad. Now I wasn't.

A couple of days into Reidy's tenure, I knocked on his door and introduced myself. I was relieved to discover that he at least knew who I was. I was seeking some sort of reassurance. I had never been certain to start games and had now been ejected from the first team squad altogether.

He said: 'Look. I only took the job five minutes ago and I don't even know how long I'm going to be here. Let me get my feet under the table and then we'll have a look.'

He delivered on his promise. Although I personally had no part to play for the remainder of 1994–95, I was back on the bench for the first game of the following season. In the meantime I could only be a supporter; hoping like everyone else that the other lads could pull it off. They did.

Peter Reid's first game in charge was at home to Sheffield United on 1 April 1995; my twenty-sixth birthday. United were a decent side and fourteen places above us in a play-off spot. Given the respective positions of the two clubs, the Sunderland fans would probably have been satisfied with a draw. Then Craig Russell came off the bench for Brett Angell. With two minutes remaining and the score at nil–nil, we attacked. Craig, a Jarrow lad and Sunderland fan, scored what was probably the most important goal of his career. His shot was half saved by Alan Kelly. It then seemed to take about a fortnight for the ball to trundle over the line. It was one of those that appeared to have been inhaled into the net by the Fulwell End, but in it went for the only goal of the game.

It was one of those games that look far more important today than they felt at the time. Not winning could have meant relegation and a truncated spell in the job for Peter Reid. The victory was an enormous confidence boost and we won 1–0 again seven days later at Derby County. Kevin Ball got that one. In those seven games we won three, drew three and lost one (to Bolton, who would finish third, then win the play-offs). Martin Smith looked especially impressive during this run and safety was secured with a game to spare.

My lack of involvement did not stem my delight. Obviously I wanted to play, but it was a wonderful turnaround regardless of who took to the field. The players on the pitch were my friends and I was still part of the team (my two wonder goals against Bristol City in December remained important). It was all about the club and I remained a fan. The expression 'we're all in it together' has become something of a joke in this country in recent years. At SAFC in the spring of 1995, it was completely apposite. I celebrated as much as anyone else when the job was done.

• • •

Our latest escape from relegation induced optimism of the most cautious type. But it was optimism nonetheless, something that had until very recently been missing, presumed extinct. It wasn't just the artificial lift that clubs often receive when a new manager replaces a floundering one, as indeed we had seen when Mick Buxton replaced Terry Butcher. This was something more; not just 'here we go again'. Even after seven games, everyone seemed to have stepped up and so, therefore, did the whole club. You could feel it. It was tangible.

Peter Reid had a way of instilling confidence into players of all abilities. Training started to become, would you believe, fun: an alien concept in the Butcher and Buxton eras. There were short-side games and lots of laughter, without a drop in work rate. Whereas training sessions had previously been immediately followed by everyone just buggering off home, we began to stay around the Charlie Hurley Centre more, taking it upon ourselves to play head tennis or do other stuff together. It was a new world, and during this time my thoughts were simply: 'You know what? Life is better.'

It can be hard to imagine now just how disorganised and frankly tin-pot things had become. In 2016, astonishment was professed among the media when José Mourinho ordered his squad to train in a car park prior to Manchester United's League Cup tie at Northampton Town. Mick Buxton may have read the story and wondered what was so bizarre about it.

On several occasions, when we were playing away and arriving in whichever town the night before the game, he instructed our bus driver to keep his eyes open for a grassy piece of land. Any old glass-strewn, dog-shit-ridden plot would do, such as you might use for a kick-about when you are eight years old. When somewhere 'suitable' was found we would check in at our hotel, change clothes then return to the bomb site and carry out a training session. Mick thought this was perfectly acceptable. His only concession to the late twentieth century was to insist that there was some street lighting nearby if it was dark. By contrast, Peter Reid introduced wacky concepts such as 'organising things properly' and 'making sure there are adequate facilities'. What a breakthrough.

Training and life generally under Peter Reid was in every respect different from anything I had known since joining the club two years earlier. However much of a thrill it was and remained for me personally just to be a Sunderland player, the best job in the world, there is no escaping the truth: that it had been a dismal time for the supporters and the second lowest point in the club's history (relegation to the old Third Division in 1987 still claims that unwanted prize).

Not that all had been beer and skittles before I arrived, and feelings were heightened by resurgent arch-rivals. Until 1992, at least Newcastle United had shown something like common decency by being crap as well. This was before Kevin Keegan selfishly abandoned that policy. Sunderland and Newcastle were what journalists are obliged to call 'sleeping giants' and one of them was waking up. The wrong one. Although Sunderland supporters are far more interested in their own club, this didn't help the mood. It cost the club some followers too, particularly in places like South Tyneside and Durham, where the young children of Sunderland-supporting parents were going over to the dark side.

We were told 'You can't blame the kids for supporting a winning team.' Rubbish. Not only can you blame them, you can thrash them around the ears with a rolled-up newspaper until they recant. The spineless, glory-hunting little bastards! Damn bad parenting too.

Luckily I'm not one to rant about this.

In the traditional and endless bickering about football that people have in the workplace, Sunderland fans didn't have much with which to deflect the taunting of their black-and-white colleagues. It had been a horrible time in that regard.

• • •

Peter's appointment became permanent and over the summer he was pretty unsentimental about showing people the door. Among those to play their last games for Sunderland in 1994–95 was Gary Bennett, who had played well over 400 games for the club, but was now thirty-three. Tony Norman had played more than 200, but was thirty-seven. Younger players went too, including Stephen Brodie, Anthony Smith, Derek Ferguson and Shaun Cunnington. Our third game of the following season was also Brett Angell's last.

Gordon Armstrong, another to surpass 400 appearances but still only twenty-eight, was eased out by comparison. He came on as substitute on the opening day of 1995–96, which proved to be his last league game for Sunderland. He was loaned to Bristol City, then Northampton Town. He didn't move permanently until July 1996 when he was transferred to Bury, but his time was effectively up long before then.

Gordon was an excellent servant to Sunderland AFC. He was the mainstay of the midfield for over a decade, playing in three divisions and an FA Cup final. He helped to extricate the club from its deepest, darkest pit of 1987. He scored fifty-seven goals, the most celebrated of which was that fabulous headed winner against Chelsea in the 1992 cup quarter-final replay that paved the way to Wembley. As a fan, I would like to take this opportunity to thank him again for that goal alone. His picture now hangs in the Stadium of Light for a reason.

The entrance door swung less often than the exit that summer. We had only signed two new players when the season kicked off. Still, all those departures along with the earlier sales of Don Goodman and Gary Owers meant that we had a radically different squad from a year earlier.

The first of the two arrivals was John Mullin, signed for £40,000 from Burnley. The other 'new' player was Paul Bracewell, then aged thirty-three, who came to Roker Park for the third time following his re-acquisition from Newcastle for just £50,000. This time he would be assistant manager too. He was also invaluable. A teammate of Peter Reid's at Everton during their 1980s pomp, he had done pretty much everything in the game including playing for England. He had won the league at Everton and played in four FA Cup finals (sadly he lost them all). His legs did not now carry him as they once had, but he compensated for this by being totally at ease on the ball, rarely squandering possession and transferring his own confidence to the younger players.

There is a myth, sadly propagated by Steve Bruce in recent years, that anyone with a Newcastle connection coming to Sunderland – and vice versa – will be made to suffer for it; tarred and feathered, then run out of town. Not true. When Bracewell left Sunderland for Newcastle in 1992 it angered many fans on Wearside. Yet he was welcomed back with open arms three years later, despite having been pivotal in the Mags' revival. His Wearside background was never an issue for Newcastle fans either. Sunderland fans later loved Lee Clark when he was on the pitch in red and white (off the pitch he later proved to be troublesome) and there was no one more black-and-white than Lee. In 2014, Newcastle fans were thrilled when Jack Colback arrived at St James' from Sunderland on a Bosman. Dare I say it: they retain a soft spot for the native Mackem, Steven Howey.

The animosity between supporters of Sunderland and Newcastle is famous. But if you do it right, the fans of both clubs will hold you in their affections for ever, regardless of background or previous clubs. There is a very long list of players who turned out for both sides. How fondly they are remembered by the respective sets of fans depends on how well they played – and nothing else. The same principle applies to other staff. Bob Stokoe made almost

300 appearances for Newcastle United and was a Geordie. His statue now stands outside the Stadium of Light. So it was with Paul Bracewell. He was good at what he did, so nothing else mattered.

Another key appointment was that of Bobby Saxton as coach. I successfully disguised any disappointment when he replaced Trevor Hartley. Sacko was a hugely experienced figure who would be a major presence at Sunderland for the next few years. Television audiences may remember him for the Wildean philosophies he shared on the documentary *Premier Passions*, such as: 'Don't let him turn. Get up his fuckin' arse!' 'That's fuckin' mingin' that' and other aphorisms. A very quotable man.

• • •

I still had a year left on my contract and Reidy had not seen me play. But he had said he would give me a chance, so I was retained. Being an option as both striker and centre-back was an asset. My relatively low salary may have been a factor too. I was still on £500 per week with a £600 win bonus. This doesn't sound at all bad for what was called the First Division in 1995, but I must caveat this by pointing out that I was a fringe player and, as any supporter could have told you, wins had not hitherto been a predominant feature of my time at Sunderland. There was also a condition that we had to be above a certain position in the league, I think top six, which we didn't manage too often either. There was nothing for a draw and these rules applied to everyone in the squad.

There was no honeymoon this time to hinder my fitness and I made sure I was especially conscientious in pre-season training. More thought went into the regime than in times past of simply instructing everyone to run umpteen miles, perform millions of press-ups, sit-ups and squat-thrusts – then do some serious exercise. We still ran but we also trained with a ball, which was more of a novelty than you might think. Fitness was still considered to be of the utmost importance, but so was footballing skill. Training was rotated between fitness, skills and actual games.

Professionals and youths were all involved and there was no segregation. There were some pretty decent youths vying to be part of the first team, including David Preece, Sam Aiston, Paul Heckingbottom and David Mawson. But one kid is particularly vivid in my memory, a skinny little article who was still only sixteen. To make it more exciting I shall withhold his identity for now.

This lad, along with Phil Gray, Martin Smith and Craig Russell, were our striking options, soon to be joined by internationals Paul Stewart and David Kelly. I began to feel more than ever that my best chance in the longer term was in defence. With Gary Bennett gone and Kevin Ball now a midfielder, Richard Ord and Andy Melville were the only other available centre-backs. Considering what we were about to achieve, it was a pretty thin squad.

Perhaps the man who developed most under Peter Reid was Richard Ord, who was transformed from someone who was in and out of the side as a left-back, to an imposing centre-half who was a good passer and very comfortable with the ball at his feet: a defender who was also a footballer. In fact, he became quite brilliant. He also came to be the life and soul of the squad, his shyness dissipating and his humour becoming renowned.

Key to this, in my opinion, was that Reidy just made everyone happier. In other industries, a happy workforce is a productive workforce. It's the same in football. We loved the short-side games, and Peter joined in with them. He was not yet forty and his retirement as a player had come only two years beforehand. He still had it. These games were fun, but still high intensity with plenty of kicking and other fouls. Kevin Ball was in his element at this dispensation to wipe out anyone on the opposing side, and one or two in his own – if you can imagine such a thing.

We were treated like blokes, which was the opposite of how we had been treated on the bus home from Swindon in January. We didn't spend every spare moment propping up a bar, but most of us still liked a drink, as did Reidy. His mantra was: 'Go out. Enjoy yourself. Do what you want. Be men. But be respectful. If the police come knocking on my door, you're fucking gone.'

Sorry to break it to you like this, but Peter Reid did occasionally swear. It is one of football's best kept secrets, until now.

We took this golden rule on board and had the most wonderful social lives, while simultaneously understanding that work was work. Training was enjoyable, but still hard. A perfect balance was struck. When we were out 'on the hoy', as they say in Sunderland, it was not a clandestine activity that the management were unaware of. We did as we pleased, but no quarter was given in training because it was the morning after a party; we were worked into the ground to sweat out the booze. Not that we minded, because we were told what would happen and knew what we were getting into. Peter himself would run round the training pitch dressed in bin liners in order to perspire away the previous evening's Budweiser (Christian Dior bin liners, cutting edge).

• • •

The pre-season tour of late July was in Ireland. This time, mercifully, it was in the south. Fixtures were arranged with St Patrick's Athletic, Drogheda United and Athlone Town. We didn't see much of Peter Reid on the tour apart from at the games. He would just appear like the Magic Shopkeeper in *Mr Benn*. Bobby Saxton always took training.

I have always been a Guinness drinker, purely for its health benefits, you understand (it has a high iron content), so when after a 2–0 win over St Pat's in Dublin we were told to please ourselves, it was straight into the club bar upstairs in Richmond Park. Any Guinness drinker will tell you that the delicious stuff they sell in Ireland knocks spots off what we settle for in Britain, so I persuaded some of the other lads to try it. They liked it too. Andy Melville added blackcurrant to his, thereby revealing his bohemian side, although this was rather too exotic for some of the others. Still, I enhanced their collective palate. The Guinness went down singing hymns.

Following the Athlone game, the usual core of us went in search of an open bar. This was tricky as it was Tuesday and Athlone is a small town. But it was also Ireland, so we found one. It was deserted at 9 p.m. but gradually filled up, not just with people, but also with fiddles, banjos, bodhráns and tin whistles. It was an impromptu céilidh. Most of the clichés about Irish pubs are true. Our collective tone deafness notwithstanding, glorious Guinness lent us the confidence to join a sing-along and God knows what time we poured out of there.

My roommate in Ireland was Martin Gray, not to be confused with either Michael Gray or Phil Gray. The club was certainly well replenished with Grays during this period. The night before Athlone, he had kept me awake by shouting in his sleep.

'Ross! Ross! Come here, boy. Leave that alone. Good lad. Come on, Ross. Fetch! Fetch!'

Martin used to miss his dog when he was away. But that was no concern of mine and I just wanted him to shut his yap (Martin, not Ross) so I could sleep. When I rolled in at an unfeasibly late hour the next night after the céilidh, Martin, one of the more temperate as well as dog-loving members of the squad, was sleeping soundly. At least, he was until I staggered in and started clashing about, pissing like a racehorse in the loo then creating more noise than is generally thought possible from a man who is merely removing his socks. Martin began to grunt disapprovingly at the irruption.

'Fuckin' hell, big man! Keep it down.'

'You what?' I slurred. 'Keep it *dooooowwwn*? After the hour we spent at Crufts last night?'

Just for the fun of it, I then stood on his bed, my head scraping against the ceiling, and placed a size nine desert boot on his chest. I began to remove my leather belt and informed him that I was about to administer a damn good thrashing. At this point he must have thought I was even more drunk than I actually was and began to panic.

'No, big man! Don't do it.'

I retired to my own bed, giggling at what I thought had been an extremely humorous piece of horseplay, and soon nodded off, while Martin attempted to do the same thing with one eye open. We're friends to this day, although I doubt if he would ever care to recreate that evening.

We were bonding as a squad in a way that I had never known at Sunderland, and not just in pubs. Steve Agnew was a wonderful addition to the team and to morale. An experienced pro with more than a few stories to tell, he and Martin Scott used to delight in insulting each other. More than ever we genuinely began to look forward to training. We would turn up early at the Charlie Hurley Centre and thoroughly enjoy each other's company. This extended to the ground staff, Adrian and Glenn. We would sit in the pavilion around the tea urn, our conversations about football interspersed with the most wonderful rubbish. It's what blokes do. Almost overnight, Sunderland AFC became a joyous place of work.

The only exception to this was Dariusz Kubicki. This had nothing to do with his ability as a player. He joined from Aston Villa permanently after his initial loan and had quite some pedigree. He had played forty-six times for Poland, including an appearance in the 1986 World Cup alongside the great Zbigniew Boniek. Although Dariusz wasn't always the most courageous player, he was very dependable and had started every single game since his Sunderland debut in March 1994.

The fans liked him, but I can't say that the players shared in this warmth. Richard Ord was probably the least enamoured of him. Dariusz was an odd fish, very insular, sombre and not a mixer, although he had been signed by Mick Buxton who probably considered him the last word in roguish tomfoolery. He was the one who would head straight home after training and keep away from activities outside of football. This was nothing to do with language or culture, it was just the way he was. It wasn't an issue for me. In any group there is usually one who walks alone and in this case it just happened to be Dariusz. Each to their own and it should be remembered that we were there to win football matches and not for the off-field razzmatazz that was a feature of the Peter Reid era.

This managerial appointment would be a lucky one for Bob Murray, the club, the players, the supporters, the press (who considered Reidy to be 'great copy') and for Peter himself. It would not be a perfect seven-and-a-half years, but Peter Reid was to leave Sunderland AFC in an unquestionably better condition than he'd found it.

• • •

A highly significant season had a mediocre start. We lost 2–1 at home to Leicester City, who had just been relegated. Leicester were among the favourites for promotion. They would go up through the play-offs after replacing their manager Mark McGhee with Martin O'Neill in December. It was a tight game and defeat was hard to bear. I was an unused substitute. Obviously I would have preferred some time on the pitch, but at least I was back in the fold, as per Peter's promise.

We then had the League Cup first round, first leg at Preston

North End of Division Three. This was tricky. Preston would go on to win their league and the 1–1 draw was a decent enough result, more so because we'd been far from brilliant. That was the night when Brett Angell scored his one and only goal for us. For the Sunderland fans who made the effort to travel to Deepdale, it was a real 'I was there' moment, like being on Dealey Plaza, or when Dylan went electric. It was also Gordon Armstrong's final appearance for Sunderland.

I was confined to the bench that night too. Brett's final game for Sunderland came four days later at Carrow Road in a goalless draw with Norwich, who had also just been relegated. I replaced Brett with twenty minutes left and had a decent game. I would have scored the winner had some idiot not put a post in the way of my header.

This brought us to the second leg in the League Cup at home to Preston. It was a strange game and in its way quite an important one. The fans had so far been given nothing by way of excitement this season; a defeat and a goalless draw in the league and a draw in the first leg against a side two divisions below us. In other words, more of the same.

I had done enough at Norwich to merit a start up front and was very happy to make it. But at half-time the patience of our supporters was being tested to its limits. Not only were we losing 2–0, but we deserved to be. It was about as bad a forty-five minutes of football from a Sunderland side that anyone could remember. Frustration bubbled over, with Kevin Ball and Alec Chamberlain almost coming to blows on the pitch. It had been a shambles and right then Roker Park was not a pleasant place to be.

The team-talk at the interval consisted entirely of our manager going berserk – and not without due cause. He simply erupted and tore lumps off the whole XI, including me. I felt that individually I had performed quite respectably, winning headers and holding up the ball well. I didn't feel that I deserved to be keelhauled along with everyone else. However, a cursory glance at the vibrating veins on Reidy's left temple suggested that this was possibly not the moment to say as much. His language may have been obscene, but it was also unambiguous.

Within four minutes of the second half, the mood was transformed – largely by me. Immodest, I know, but being the star turn was an occasion to be savoured, so please allow me to cling on to it.

First I controlled a poor clearance on the edge of the Preston box with my left, then bent the ball into the bottom far corner with my right. It was a good finish. Two–one and back in the game. Very soon after that we were level. I flicked a free kick from the right with my head and struck Ryan Kidd for an own-goal. Two–two. It then became a question of whether Preston could hold out. With five minutes remaining, Craig Russell surged into the box and the keeper parried his shot. After a scramble, the ball broke kindly to me and I just smashed it in with my left. The final score was 3–2: 4–3 on aggregate. I had scored two and gamely tried to claim the own-goal as part of a hat-trick (our superbly biased stadium announcer boomed out my name over the PA system for all three goals, but it was not to be).

Still, I was officially man-of-the-match and was awarded a prize for my efforts. The League Cup was sponsored by Coca-Cola in those days and they provided this bounty. In the next round, Paul Bracewell was given a man-of-the-match award for which he received a rather snazzy mountain bike. I'm a cyclist and would have appreciated that. Instead I received a black polyester bomber jacket with a huge Coca-Cola logo on the back. It was hideous, and forty-six seconds after it had been presented to me, it was presented in turn to a swing bin. Martin Gray wouldn't even give it to his dog to sleep in. Ross would have been insulted.

The bomber jacket was not the main consideration of the

evening. It was important to get through the tie. This was similar to beating Carlisle United in the FA Cup early in 1994. It was not a momentous achievement for Sunderland to beat Preston, nor was anyone seriously contemplating a trip to Wembley on the back of it. But the effect on morale had we been beaten, as we very nearly were, could have proved a decisive setback.

Paul Bracewell said at the end of the season:

I think the turning point was the home game with Preston. We had already lost at home to Leicester City on the first day of the season and we were losing 2–0 at half-time in the cup-tie. Then all of a sudden we pulled the game out of the fire and it just gave the lads belief to go on from there.

He still wouldn't give me the bike.

We got away with it. It was also our first win of the season and we carried some confidence into the next game, three days later against my good friends from Wolverhampton Wanderers. This was the day of Geoff Thomas's 'vengeance'. We won that game too, 2–0, and I set one up for Andy Melville. The visiting fans gave me no little gyp throughout the afternoon, but it's easier to ignore at home. Then there was a useful draw at Port Vale. This was progress. Slow, but still progress.

A big bonus of the Preston victory was a League Cup tie against Liverpool, the holders, in the second round. This was another two-legged affair and we lost 2–0 at Anfield, where Micky Gray missed his second most famous penalty (we missed an awful lot of penalties that season). We lost the home leg 1–0 after Martin Smith and Rob Jones, their right-back, were sent off for fighting. But we had performed well and there was much encouragement from the two games. If we could do that against Fowler, Rush, McManaman, Redknapp, Barnes and the rest of a team that would finish third in the Premier League that season, then what could we do against teams in our own division?

(I have to say that Liverpool's superstars of the era were a good set – down-to-earth and friendly. They seemed like an even better set after we had played Manchester United in the FA Cup three months later.)

Not that we were getting carried away. There was a pleasant return to Portman Road where I caught up with many old friends. It would have been even more pleasant had it not been 3–0 to Ipswich; an Alex Mathie hat-trick. Again, though, despite the scoreline, we actually played very well. I remember Bobby Saxton showering me personally with praise afterwards. It was 'one of those days'. The main problem was scoring goals.

Ipswich also saw the first start for Paul Stewart, on loan to us from Liverpool. He was an experienced striker with England caps and had scored for Tottenham in the 1991 FA Cup final. He injured his knee at Portman Road; end of loan. However, he returned permanently in March on a free transfer and proved an important player that season. Like Ball and Bracewell, his experience was a big asset and he was great to have around.

● ● ●

The mention of Paul Stewart and the dark events that were revealed in 2016 compel me into an unpleasant digression. It was then that he went public to reveal that he had been sexually abused as a child by a coach for four years. This came as a shock to me. I had no knowledge of this, or any of the other appalling crimes that were committed against other players of a similar age to myself. Nothing of that nature ever happened to me, and if things happened at any club, then they were never mentioned to me.

But I can see how the environment for undetected abuse was

created. The brutality that took place – at every club – was accepted. 'This is a man's game…' and all that. You had to take it. As apprentices, we would be routinely told that we were useless, we were going to be sacked, we would never be footballers, etcetera. Such approbation was publicly bawled at us too, as was the pointing out of mistakes. Everyone went through it and this was partly why so many trainees failed to make it.

As a sixteen-year-old at Ipswich, I was once told by Brian Owen to go and train with the first team. I was the only youth to be afforded this honour and was excited and nervous in equal measure. Terry Butcher, Eric Gates, Paul Cooper, Frank Yallop, Mark Brennan and other established names of the time would be there. It was daunting.

During the warm-up, Bobby Ferguson singled me out for ridicule because of the way I was running. I felt humiliated and it was the closest I ever came to tears. I have to say that none of the senior players made me feel even worse by laughing. They were embarrassed themselves, presumably because it brought back unpleasant memories.

Several weeks later, I trained with the first team again. I played the ball to a teammate, but was told by a disapproving Bobby that I had made the wrong pass. He then tersely informed me as to what I should have done. Lecture over, we resumed play and when I next received the ball I made exactly the pass he had recommended. This annoyed him.

'Have you fucking not got a mind of your own?'

Bobby and the other coaches did not do things like this because they enjoyed mistreating people. It had a purpose. Indeed, it was well-intentioned. Nietzsche reckoned 'That which does not kill us, makes us stronger', so he might have fitted in well as part of the backroom staff at Ipswich. The point was that the verbals we were receiving in training did not compare with what we could expect from the terraces if we were to ever play in the first team; and the more equipped we were to shrug this off, the better.

Complaining about this was not an option. To do so would make you less of a man and wouldn't do much for your chances professionally. You therefore accepted your fate. Youngsters, hundreds of miles from home and with no recourse, were eager to please and, as we discovered many years later, this environment coupled with the usual threats was ideal for people who were most certainly not acting in anyone's long-term interest. At least I was an adolescent and therefore less vulnerable than the victims, the crimes against whom would only emerge in their middle-age. They were children.

Paul Stewart was in his thirties when he arrived at Sunderland and I was aware that he had an issue with drink. I didn't know there had been a drugs issue too. His problems were something a non-victim can never fully understand and I wish him nothing but the best for the rest of his days.

• • •

On 28 October, almost a third of the way into the season, we faced Barnsley at home. By then we had played thirteen, won five, drawn six and lost two. We were fifth in the table and, although the pundits were not sitting bolt upright at our improvement, this was obviously the best we had been in years. We had scored a modest average of a fraction more than a single goal per game. But we were very difficult to score against. Confidence had gradually built. We weren't wonderful and had won only two home games, but had become better than merely steady. No one was making any bold predictions but, for the first time since I had joined, promotion to the Premier League was not out of the question.

I personally had one of my best days against Barnsley and not just because of events on the pitch, although they helped too.

We were leading by a Craig Russell goal at half-time, but he went off injured on thirty-nine minutes and was replaced by me. Seventeen minutes into the second half I won a header, knocking the ball down to Phil Gray, who played it to Steve Agnew on the right; I then galloped into their box. Aggers duly presented a beautiful cross that I reached before the defender, scoring with, if I may say so myself, a quite spiffing low, diving header.

We were in complete control of the match and had been since it started. It almost goes without saying then that we allowed Andy Liddell to pull one back for Barnsley to instil the wrong kind of excitement in the latter stages of the game. But the final score was 2–1, which meant that I had bagged the winner (yes, it's a team game, but we all want to score the winner). I played well too. We had even met the criteria for a bonus.

Afterwards, I was being ushered around the building to speak with various media as I had scored the winner (I may have mentioned that already). During my wandering I heard an oddly familiar Scottish voice calling my name. I turned around.

'Lee! Lee! Well done today. You had a good game.'

It was John Duncan, my old manager at Ipswich, who had clearly not given a shit when I was told as a teenager that I would never be able to play football again. That was in 1988. It was now 1995 and it's possible that he didn't remember the incident. I did.

By this stage he was manager of Chesterfield again, so I have no idea what he was doing at Roker Park. My initial reaction was one of shock; shock that he had appeared, shock that he had spoken to me, but shock most of all at the simple fact that it was him. I was temporarily nonplussed. That was in the second or two required for the terrible, painful, seven-year-old memories to come flooding back.

Back in 1988, when I was in Suffolk and most of my right knee was in Cambridgeshire, the people at Ipswich were very good to me; a distraught youngster. I had not forgotten this. But I hadn't forgotten Duncan either, who had been the exception to the well-wishing. His callous indifference – 'D'yer know any other trades?' – had appalled me then and it appalled me now as it flashed back. Now that I had made it in football at a high level with no thanks to him (quite the reverse), and on a too-rare day when I was the man-of-the-hour, he appeared to be schmoozing and treating me like a long-lost friend. It took a split second for my mind to register that he wasn't my boss any more. Then my spleen was opened.

I don't recall verbatim what I said to him, but I do know that 'Go fuck yourself!' was at the heart of my short, succinct and un-equivocal speech. He possibly knew the reason for my philippic. If he didn't, then that was even worse. Either way, he was taken aback and left in no doubt as to my opinion of him as a human being.

It took perhaps a couple of hours for my anger to subside, by which time I was at home. I had never expected to see Duncan again and much had happened since our previous meeting. When I had ceased fomenting I began to feel rather pleased with myself and even glad that we had met again.

There is a French term, *l'esprit d'escalier*, which literally means 'staircase wit'. It refers to those moments when you walk away from an argument and get halfway up the stairs, then think of some witheringly witty putdown that you wish you had said earlier, but by then it's too late.

Well I had no feeling of *l'esprit d'escalier* after being reacquainted with John Duncan. 'Go fuck yourself!' is unlikely to make its way into a book of quotations to be whipped out at dinner parties, but it served its purpose. Duncan was jarred, embarrassed and left like a salted snail when I marched away from him. Nothing cleverer, wittier or more incisive would have done the job any better. There is many a more literate response than 'Go fuck yourself!' but none delivers the same satisfaction. It felt good.

It was an unintended consequence, but John Duncan had made my day better still. I have never seen him since and don't suppose he's been searching for me either. Looking more broadly at life, it reconfirmed that I had done myself a wonderful favour by ignoring his 'advice' all those years earlier.

•   •   •

My chances of starting games as a striker had been hampered further by the arrival of David Kelly from Wolves.

Ned, as he was known, was from the Midlands. Like so many others he was able to represent the Republic of Ireland in spite of being about as Irish as Boney M. He won twenty-six caps. Ned had done pretty well at Molineux but had really made his name at Newcastle when they stormed the First Division in 1992–93, with Ned averaging a goal every other game. Upon Newcastle's promotion he was sold to Wolves for £750,000. Although not quite as successful in the Black Country, as well as being a few weeks short of his thirtieth birthday, he eventually cost Sunderland £1 million. This was still a big fee in 1995; especially for a club outside the Premier League (the British record at the time was only £8.5 million, paid to Nottingham Forest by Liverpool for Stan Collymore).

Yet another expensive signing had shoved me down the pecking order. I looked even less likely to feature when he announced his arrival with two goals in his first three games, including the winner at Crystal Palace (when we also missed two penalties). However, Ned's time at Sunderland would not be the highlight of his career. Hindered by an ankle injury that excluded him from the second half of 1995–96, loss of form and sometimes being played out of position, those were the only two goals he would ever score for us. He was never expected to notch as prolifically as he had done at Newcastle, yet it was surprising how badly things went for him.

Far less was expected from Kevin Phillips when he joined two years later; the moral of the tale is that you just never know.

Ned was a good player, an easy-going bloke and I liked him. I was also more relaxed about his arrival than I had been about that of Brett Angell. I was becoming used to the disappointment of new strikers arriving and being selected ahead of me. Apart from that, I was coming to be considered as much a centre-back as a striker. Peter Reid and Bobby Saxton had told me as much. This was a great asset for me as it gave me double the chance of selection that the other fringe players had.

Another reason for liking Ned was that he was completely useless at three-card brag. All you needed to beat him was caution because he never folded; a trait he shared with Mike Hooper, our reserve goalkeeper on loan from Newcastle. Sometimes I would make more than my salary from the card school on the team bus.

Ned also confirmed to me, not that confirmation was required, that I was detested in Wolverhampton. We spoke about Geoff Thomas and John de Wolf. I was completely honest with him about both incidents, which he seemed taken aback by.

• • •

Wednesday 22 November saw us lose 1–0 at Stoke to an early Ray Wallace goal, pushing us down to seventh. We hadn't played badly, but Ned had a real stinker. Whatever he tried didn't work, so a dischuffed Peter Reid replaced him with me. I played well and hit the post. This did nothing to salvage a point, but along with a calf strain for Ned, it did see me selected to start the next game at West Bromwich Albion.

The Hawthorns and Stoke's old Victoria Ground being a matter of forty miles apart, we stayed in the Midlands between games. In fact, we stayed at The Belfry (things really were looking up since Reidy arrived). Ten minutes into the West Brom game, Aggers delivered a right-foot in-swinging corner that I headed in at the Smethwick End for the only goal of the game. We worked hard, but it was not a classic and Peter Reid wasn't overly complimentary about our performance. It was a long afternoon for our supporters. We had played better against Ipswich and Stoke, but lost to both. So heigh-ho. Points over performance any day and we were up to sixth.

Having scored that goal I was keen to celebrate it with our fulsome away following. However, in all the excitement, I momentarily forgot where our fans were, as you do, and ran to the right of the goal instead of the left. This meant that instead of absorbing the joy on the faces of a couple of thousand Mackems, I was confronted by row upon row of Albion supporters who were discernibly failing to appreciate my achievement. Each one of them was glowering and grinding their teeth, the more kindly among them wishing that I would be merely hanged. I hadn't intended to antagonise them in this manner, but there wasn't really the opportunity to explain what had happened.

Two years earlier, I had scored the winner against Birmingham City. Wolves, I think, we have already covered. Now there was the hostility I had inadvertently aroused at West Bromwich, as well as scoring against them. It's fair to say I did not cut the most popular figure in most of the West Midlands in the mid-1990s, although I was becoming a decent outside bet for Aston Villa's player of the year.

After another 1–0 win in a televised Sunday home game against Crystal Palace, we were up to second; an automatic promotion spot behind only Mick McCarthy's Millwall. But I was substituted in that game and back on the bench for the next one – against Millwall at Roker Park. I was disappointed to be sub again, but in no position to quibble, as the manager would be vindicated – with bells on. Phil Gray and Craig Russell were preferred to me. David

Kelly was injured. Phil scored one, Craig scored four (and also missed a prize sitter) and Peter Reid didn't make any substitutions. We won 6–0 and went top of the league. I would have looked a bit of a berk banging on the manager's door and demanding to hear his reasons for not picking me.

Millwall, incidentally, parted company with Mick McCarthy two months later when he went to manage the Republic of Ireland. They only won four more matches and were eventually relegated.

• • •

In between the Palace and Millwall games, great excitement was instigated on Wearside when we were drawn away to Manchester United in the third round of the FA Cup.

That, the thumping of Millwall and our league position created a stampede for half-season tickets. This was the best the atmosphere in and around the club had been in years; certainly since I had joined. In the same month that we were to play Grimsby Town and Tranmere Rovers, we would also be travelling to Old Trafford to take on one of the best sides on earth. I am obliged to say that I mean no disrespect to either Grimsby or Tranmere, but there was only one fixture that the fans were talking about.

The big day was what is referred to in the north-west of England as 'bitterly cold' and in Sunderland as 'nippy'. It was foggy too, especially travelling home on the M62. The away following was simply magnificent, the 8,000 allocation gone in a snap. It was a sell-out, although the capacity then was only 42,000 as Old Trafford was in the middle of redevelopment.

United most certainly did not take us lightly. With two exceptions, they played their strongest starting XI; Peter Schmeichel and Paul Scholes were injured. Kevin Pilkington replaced Schmeichel and lined up alongside Gary Neville, Irwin, Pallister, Bruce,

Beckham, Keane, Butt, Cole, Cantona and Giggs, with Phil Neville, Sharpe and McClair on the bench. To my lack of astonishment, I was a substitute too, which I was still pleased about as the possibility remained for me to feature in this huge fixture.

What to do when faced with such opposition? Let's face it: United's worst player was probably better than our best. With the possible exception of Pilkington, everyone on their team sheet was (is) a household name. I couldn't help but think of cup ties I had been involved in only three years previously, such as Plains Farm WMC versus Redhouse in the Pronto-Plumbers Trophy.

All was going as generally expected at half-time when it was 1–0 to United, although we hadn't played at all badly. Micky Gray was having a stormer, but Nicky Butt had lobbed the oncoming Alec Chamberlain from eight yards in the thirteenth minute. Kevin Ball had gone off injured too.

However, Bally's replacement, Steve Agnew, equalised after an hour. We were attacking the Stretford End when he received the ball from Micky in the diametric centre of their half, knocked it a few yards forward then bent it from thirty yards into the bottom right-hand corner of the net. No pressure whatsoever was placed upon Aggers, and Alex Ferguson was doing his nut. In fact his face went red and would never change colour again.

Eight thousand Sunderland fans in the East Stand went hysterical, as did our additional Sunderland fan behind Pilkington's goal. He could be seen distinctly on television in a beige jacket, leaping around in the fourth row and demonstrably not giving a shit about being outnumbered by 12,000 to one. Whoever that bloke was, he was obviously unable to buy a ticket for the visitors' section and had somehow hornswoggled his way into the Stretford End.

Things got even better. The space given to Steve Agnew was as nothing compared to the room that Craig Russell was afforded when a high pass from the busy Aggers landed beside him in almost the same position. There wasn't a United player within 100 feet of Craig, who took the ball calmly into the penalty area to score with a left-foot shot that went across Pilkington and into the same part of the goal that Aggers had struck three minutes earlier. The delirium was repeated and Fergie went even redder, although the bloke in the beige jacket managed to be a little more restrained this time. Sunderland were on the verge of what would be perhaps our greatest victory since the 1973 final.

But for us to beat a side like Manchester United, it would take 100 per cent physical effort and concentration – as well as some luck. We had used up all of our luck for the afternoon with the scarcely believable amount of space that their usually marvellous defenders had given us for both of our goals. In the eightieth minute, Lee Sharpe crossed the ball to the head of Eric Cantona, not long back from his famous ban for karate-kicking an arsehole. Cantona's header went straight at Alec, who really ought to have saved it, but seemed to shove it into the roof of the net. That was really the beginning of the end for Alec Chamberlain at Sunderland.

The final score was 2–2, and we were far more deflated by such a scoreline than we ever imagined. I did make it onto the pitch when I replaced Phil Gray with a few minutes remaining and also managed to make an impression of sorts. One of the final acts of the game was when a 50/50 ball occurred between Nicky Butt and me. Having sat through most of the game, I had a lot of pent-up energy and was not about to lose out in such an instance. I attacked the ball with everything I had and Nicky, a terrific footballer who was aware of me from reserve games, knew what was coming and began to pull out. He was a peaky-looking specimen at the best of times, but any colour he had was visibly draining from his face, as you might see in a Warner Brothers cartoon. His ensuing somersault when we made contact was quite cartoonish too.

The televised replay at a packed Roker Park came ten days later on a Tuesday (and just forty-eight hours after our league game against Norwich, because Sky wanted to show a one-day cricket match on the Wednesday). The unfortunate Kevin Pilkington was out on his ear (in another three weeks he would be on loan at Rochdale). But Phil Gray still scored past Peter Schmeichel midway through the first half. Scholes equalised on seventy minutes. With extra time in mind, I replaced Paul Bracewell in the eighty-ninth, but the added half-an-hour never happened. A minute after I was introduced, Andy Cole, who had missed several much easier opportunities, planted a superb header past Alec at the Fulwell End. It finished 2–1 to United, who went on to win the FA Cup as well as the Premier League.

After both games there was absolutely no interaction between the United players and ourselves. We were all in the players' lounge at Old Trafford, but not one of them approached any of us. They didn't appear at all after the replay at Roker. This aloofness was unusual from another club and can only have been premeditated. His Ferginess liked to concoct a siege mentality – them-and-us – so this was presumably part of that thinking. I don't know what benefit it gave them, but it certainly didn't do them any harm. It just seemed unnecessarily anti-social, especially when the tie was over and as there was no animosity between players, staff or fans of both clubs that I know of. It also made me feel a little sorry for Cantona and Beckham, as it denied them the opportunity of asking for my autograph.

• • •

So we were disappointed twice in the third round of the FA Cup. However, there was the same consoling thought that we'd had after playing Liverpool in the League Cup: 'If we can play like that against teams in our own league…'

It would take us a while to make this philosophy work. After the cup draw and the annihilation of Millwall, we travelled to Reading where Martin Smith's goal was equalised quite beautifully and late on by their player-manager Jimmy Quinn, who then hit the bar (Quinn must have been about seventy-two by then, but would still play for another nine clubs). Two days before Christmas, we were still top of the league when we endured another bad day at the Baseball Ground in a crucial fixture with Derby County, who would replace us at the top if they beat us. They did. Micky Gray gave us the lead. Marco Gabbiadini took it away a minute later. Derby went on to win 3–1 and knock us down to second. I didn't feature at all that day.

There was then a three-week hiatus in our league season due to the cup tie and the postponement of an away game at Oldham Athletic on New Year's Day. We trained the day before with a view to travelling the next morning. I had been invited to a New Year's Eve party with a few mates, which I would have to forgo. In theory.

Judging from the weather forecast, it sounded extremely unlikely that conditions would allow the match to be played. It was going to be minus-whatever overnight, the roads would be treacherous. Boundary Park is also well above sea level and notoriously windy. But without knowing for certain that the game wouldn't go ahead, I was facing a frustrating night in for nothing. So I rang Oldham Athletic, posing as a loyal punter who was concerned about making a long, arduous and ultimately pointless journey with his young family for a game that was likely to be called off. It stretched my acting abilities to their outer limits.

'Ah, gud arfternoon. My name is Mr Jones and I need to know the likelihood that tomorrow's association football match will take place as scheduled. Awful lot of inconvenience to travel there for no reason, don't you know.'

'Could you hold the line please? I'll have a quick word with the groundsman.'

I listened to *Greensleeves* for a couple of minutes before this very polite and helpful woman returned.

'Hello, Mr Jones. Sorry to keep you waiting. I'm afraid it's bad news. There won't be an official announcement until tomorrow's pitch inspection, but the groundsman says there is absolutely no chance of the game going ahead.'

'Out on the lash for me then.'

'I'm sorry?'

'I mean botheration. I shall have to break the bad tidings to the little ones: what, what. Thank you for your assistance. Gudbye.'

It was a great party, and in the morning I was called with official confirmation that the match had indeed been called off. You don't say. I didn't go mad on New Year's Eve, as a contingency training session had been arranged for 1 p.m. the next day in the event of a postponement, so I was in bed by 3 a.m. I later admitted to Kevin Ball what I'd done. He gave me a look of absolute disgust, failing to give me any credit for using my initiative. No pleasing some captains.

The bad news was that Derby County beat Norwich City on 1 January and were now eight points ahead of us. In between the Manchester United matches, we lost at home to Norwich in a Sunday televised game, a game that also saw David Kelly hobble off in the second minute. He didn't play again that season. We were now down to eighth. We followed this with a dreary 0–0 draw with Leicester at Filbert Street, another televised treat for ITV to broadcast (although there were some very interesting aspects to that game that I shall return to). It did begin to look as though the FA Cup had been an unwelcome distraction. There was some respite with an important 1–0 home win against Grimsby. This was another dull encounter, but we prevailed thanks to a rare goal from Richard Ord, who went completely la-la with joy and ran more than half the length of the pitch to celebrate – something he had never actually achieved when the ball was in play.

The thrills and spills continued with, yes, another goalless draw at home to Tranmere Rovers. We should have won that game too, but at least there was some fun for me when I had the pleasure of nutmegging John Aldridge at the corner of the Main Stand and Roker End. I replaced the injured Andy Melville at centre-back for that fixture, the first time I had played there since the Tottenham game a year earlier. I kept my place for the next game too, which enabled me to further bask in the warm glow of popularity that I felt every time we played against Wolverhampton Wanderers.

I mentioned earlier that Wolves fans had made threats against my life through the post. Mainly second class, so you have to wonder if they were as angry as they claimed. Recorded delivery was only slightly more expensive, while the Royal Mail's Express Death Threat service was only about a quid a pop.

The threats were the subject of some verbal levity, and my teammates all reassured me that they were not to be taken seriously. However, as I also mentioned earlier, I couldn't help but notice that none of the bastards would warm up within forty yards of me before the game at Molineux. It was to be a grim afternoon for us, even if the trained assassin was not about to ply his trade as promised.

Mark Rankine was still there and spent much of his time informing me, with that narky whine, of his idea that I was 'not a footballer' and 'just a bouncer'. Don Goodman was up front for Wolves and was also keen to give me lip for as long as we were on the pitch, although this was slightly different, as Don did this to everyone. That was fine. And of course, the near sell-out home crowd were relentless in giving me their considered opinion, which consisted of a good, round booing every time I received the ball. I must say, I rather enjoyed that part.

What I didn't enjoy was the result. After fifteen minutes, Wolves were awarded a contentious penalty by the referee Uriah Rennie when I was adjudged to have fouled Don in the area. I say 'contentious' as it is the accepted euphemism for 'never a penalty as long as I have a hole in my arse'. I had done little more than head the ball and the contact between us would not have been sufficient to knock down a reasonably sturdy toddler, but Don went down like a shot ostrich. He knew perfectly well what he'd done, but just smirked and made faux-pious comments about if-the-referee-says-it's-a-penalty-then-it's-a-penalty and the like. Andy Thompson scored from the spot. Incidentally, it was the only penalty I ever conceded. Four minutes later, Don scored their second himself. Mark Atkins added another in the second half and the game finished 3–0. This was more than a little harsh on us, but we had missed some good chances and paid for it.

The handshakes at full-time were rather reluctant: arms out, head turned. That is to say nothing of the handshakes that didn't take place at all. The abuse continued until I was back in the changing room. Even today I doubt if I shall be signing copies of this book in the Wolverhampton branch of Waterstone's. The records show that John de Wolf was an unused substitute that day. He didn't attempt to speak to me. In fact, I don't even remember seeing him, although I assume he was as wolfy as ever.

The following week saw yet another goalless draw. This time at home to Port Vale, who were struggling. 'The Entertainers', as we were at this stage being called by no one on God's earth, had now only scored once in six games (but I was playing in defence, so don't blame me). Our promotion push was visibly wilting and would not appear any more dynamic at the final whistle of our next game, which was away to Portsmouth.

But appearances can be deceptive. The fixture at Fratton Park on 17 February 1996 was to prove pivotal for Sunderland AFC and I can truthfully say that I did more than my bit, not least when I scored the most important goal of my life.

It was to be an odd afternoon and, again, we really ought to have won the match. We dominated, and Steve Agnew gave us an early lead. But Andy Melville then completely missed an attempted interception, which allowed Paul Hall to equalise against the run of play. One–one at half-time when it should have been about 5–1 to us. Craig Russell missed yet another penalty. Oh, the chances. We had Pompey by the throat until the eighty-sixth minute, when Carl Griffiths, almost inexplicably, gave them the lead. This was really, really, really against the run of play and was such a convolutedly bad goal defensively that I can barely describe it. I'll have a go anyway.

The ball had pinballed, bounced and bobbled off a number of players around our penalty area before Jimmy Carter accidentally kicked it against Kevin Ball. It then ricocheted off Mel three feet away and somehow landed inside the corner of the box at the feet of Carter (with Paul Bracewell optimistically raising his hands to appeal for something or other). Carter then toe-poked a hopeful shot which I almost blocked, and that would have been comfortably wide of the far post had it not struck Griffiths and rolled, with painful slowness, towards the net.

The ball seemed reluctant to go in, as if it somehow knew it was assisting in a crime. To complete the agony, a casual observer might have thought that Mel, who was having a personal nightmare, had tried successfully to get out of the way of the ball in the nick of time, rather than attempting to clear it. He got his feet confused and stepped over it instead of jabbing it away somewhere. It was an extraordinary goal; cruel and sickening. However, it proved to be the prelude for the turning point in our season, which came extremely late in the game.

The Pompey fans were whistling, the sky was pitch dark and if someone had put the kettle on it wouldn't have boiled before we were back in the dressing room. Nightclub barmaids were leaving home for work. It was that late.

Gareth Hall played a long ball which Phil Gray chased with Robbie Pethick down the left and forced a corner at the Fratton End. Had Pethick got his foot further around the ball, it might have only been a throw-in and altered history. The butterfly effect. Steve Agnew sprinted to take the corner. Aggers would usually raise one or both arms in the way that corner takers often do. In my experience this signifies sod all. The opposition may see arms raised and think that they are about to deal with some cunning, elaborate, scientifically formulated goal scoring idea, when in reality there is no plan other than to ping the ball in and miss the first defender. The arm raising is all cobblers and anyway, on this occasion Aggers didn't even have the time to lift his arms. He could barely lift his legs either.

Everyone except our goalkeeper was in the penalty area (these days he would be there too). It is rare in these circumstances to see any sort of space to run into, but this was an exception. I told myself that if the ball should arc into the right-hand side of the six-yard line, then I would have it. Steve's corner was beautiful and destined for exactly where I wanted it. I ran from the edge of the area, rose above everyone and from eight yards out headed it firmly into the far corner of the net. Alan Knight was in goal for Pompey and had no chance. There was no defender on either post. That was their problem. Gettin.

Peter Reid later said: 'That was a crucial goal. Without a doubt.'

Steve Agnew: 'For me the turning point was the away game at Portsmouth. I scored first and I honestly thought we were going to win. But they scored twice and it looked as though we were going to lose when Lee Howey popped up with an injury-time equaliser.'

Geoff Storey, of the *Sunderland Echo*: 'Howey came to the rescue with an injury-time equaliser. The draw was to have a startling effect on the rest of the season.'

Various others expressed the same opinion. So what was so

damned important about that goal, when at the time it had no perceived value other than to rescue a point when it looked as though Portsmouth would burgle all three? We had only won one game in the eleven league and cup fixtures since the Millwall match. On the evening of 17 February 1996, a draw at Portsmouth did not seem to have done much to arrest this slump. History would disprove this. But why?

Well, to begin with, anyone involved with football – players, managers and fans – will tell you that a draw is considerably better than a defeat, especially when you have equalised and even more so when it comes late in the game. This isn't just because one point is obviously preferable to none. The difference it makes to morale is huge. We took the confidence from the dying-seconds draw at Portsmouth and became virtually invincible for the remainder of the season.

We won the next nine games on the bounce and went unbeaten in eighteen. When we finally did lose it was in the last game of the season and we had already been given our Division One championship medals. Portsmouth triggered it all.

Cynics will be keen to undermine all this by alluding to our immediate relegation from the Premier League the following season. Sunderland became the definitive 'yo-yo club' between 1996 and 2007, when there would be four promotions and three relegations. But at least they had become a yo-yo club, something that hadn't looked at all likely before Peter Reid's arrival. The club had not been automatically promoted to the top flight since 1980. There had been a very fortunate promotion in 1990 when a highly convoluted set of circumstances saw Sunderland finish sixth, lose the play-off final, yet still be promoted. But that good fortune came to nothing – not even yo-yo years. The up-and-down seasons after 1996 ended with promotion under Roy Keane in 2007 and an unbroken decade in the top flight (although relegation was finally inflicted again in 2017 and the yo-yoing recommenced).

In the twenty-one seasons to elapse between 1996 and this book going to print, the club would spend sixteen of them in the Premier League, a statistic I sincerely hope will improve further. This plays a vital role in raising the profile of an economically struggling city. The shipyards and mines are long dead, so the city of Sunderland has but two banners to wave to the rest of the world – Nissan and football. Warts and all, the last couple of decades have unquestionably been an improvement on the two before and this quiet revolution can be traced back to that goal at Fratton Park on a cold February afternoon many years ago. It's all down to me and no one else deserves any credit. None of the above would have occurred without my header. The same goes for the Good Friday Agreement, the rise of the internet and the Arab Spring. I'm dead important, I am. They should have given me a medal. Come to think of it, they did give me a medal.

Perhaps I have overstated things a little. Let's just say it's a good job it went in.

CHAPTER 10

WE DIDN'T WANT THE SEASON TO END

I have omitted to mention two significant new faces in Sunderland's first team squad. I have done so deliberately, to polish them under the table, as it were. It would be wrong to say that their emergence coincided with our long, unbeaten run. Their performances were fundamental to that run – not coincidental.

The first of the two was goalkeeper Shay Given. Outside Wearside, it has been largely forgotten that Shay even played for Sunderland, but Peter Reid more or less invented him. Just two months after his debut for us, he won the first of his 134 Republic of Ireland caps (second only to Robbie Keane). That is not to say that Shay owes the club anything, because in return for his big break of seventeen games for us, he was quite sensational. An overused adjective in football, but in this case perfectly appropriate.

He was still only nineteen when he arrived on loan from Blackburn Rovers in January 1996. Blackburn were Premier League champions and one of the richest clubs in the country. Shay couldn't get near their starting XI, where England's Tim Flowers was automatic choice and Bobby Mimms, a fixture on their subs' bench, was vastly experienced. By contrast, Shay's first team experience consisted of four games at Swindon Town the previous August, where he conceded just one goal. This was impressive, but still not a massive recommendation to a club in our position. However, Peter Reid was undeterred and, somewhat brutally for Alec

Chamberlain, put Shay straight into the first team for a televised game away to Martin O'Neill's Leicester City. This was five days after our defeat to Manchester United. We had been pushed down to eighth position and were clearly wobbling. Leicester were fifth.

I was a substitute at Leicester and as such, one of my duties was to warm up the goalkeeper before kick-off. This consisted of delivering some crosses for Shay to practise on, but mainly pelting as many shots at him as time would allow. There was no point in taking it easy on the youngster, so I smashed the ball at him from all angles and distances and every shot, about fifty of them, was accurate. They were in all four corners of the goal, benders, spinners, follow-ups when he was already on the ground. I really was walloping them too and under no pressure. He saved virtually every one of them. It was only a warm-up, but it was a stunning display nevertheless – and I was the only person to take a shred of notice.

I returned to the changing room, sweating and slightly in shock. I told the lads quite bluntly: 'He's fucking brilliant. He's the best goalkeeper I've ever seen.' I was not joking or even exaggerating. Shay went on to pull off a succession of excellent saves that day and keep a clean sheet, the first of a dozen in his seventeen appearances. He was a huge part of our success, not just because of his own ability, but also because knowing that a keeper of such calibre is behind them instils a great deal of confidence in defenders. Alec Chamberlain was good. Shay Given was world class.

He was a fine lad too with good Irish banter, gregarious, keen to fit in and glad of the opportunity to play. The only fault that anyone ever found with him was his distribution of the ball. Other than that – what a find! From his perspective, in only four months he would come from nowhere to trousering a First Division championship medal and playing international football. In 2011 he was given an FA Cup winners medal when he sat on Manchester City's bench at Wembley while they beat Stoke. Unless you count this (bearing in mind he didn't play at all in City's cup run), his time at Sunderland provided the only winner's medal he would ever receive. This seems quite remarkable, perhaps even a little unfair, given his immense natural gifts.

Sunderland tried to sign him permanently during the close season, but Blackburn, at that time dripping with Jack Walker's multi-millions, were simply uninterested in selling their best young players. They did elbow Bobby Mimms away to Crystal Palace and make Shay a substitute in his place. However, he would only make two appearances for Rovers before signing for some other club where he proceeded to waste twelve years of his life. Shame.

●   ●   ●

As I mentioned earlier, Leicester was another goalless draw and largely unmemorable – apart from Shay. However, there are one or two other recollections I have. First there was the pounding excitement of the home fans when eighteen-year-old Emile Heskey replaced Julian Joachim ('Bruno-ooh! Bruno-ooh!'). Gareth Hall was harshly sent off after a second yellow for a foul on Heskey (centre-back Colin Hill could clearly be seen on camera complaining about the dismissal – and he was playing for Leicester).

But on a personal level, there was some infuriating unpleasantness when I came on for Craig Russell for the final half-hour. For legal reasons I am restricted in what I can say here. I had dished it out as a player at all levels of the game. I was therefore in no position to complain when 'it' was returned with interest. Football is a physical, competitive environment, a macho culture, and personal dislikes are a natural consequence of this. However, some things are just too despicable to ever be acceptable and one of these things happened after I had been accused of diving – something I never did (maybe I should have).

Consensus among footballers is that they would prefer to be kicked than spat at. It is beneath contempt.

I wanted to remove the teeth and vital organs of the person who did this to me, the only player who ever would (although Millwall supporters had spat at me in the past for no particular reason, other than to confirm that evolution isn't over yet). Steve Agnew, who had signed for us from Leicester and knew the spitter, managed with some help from Richard Ord to prevent any bloodshed.

The Filbert Street gobber denies it to this day. I can't name him because I can't prove it, although I can tell the reader, categorically, unequivocally, one hundred per cent, on my children's lives, emphatically and with complete certainty, that I was spat at in the face. And it was appalling; a truly revolting thing to do to an opposition player – or any other human being for that matter. The legal issue is that *proving* someone has done something is not the same as knowing *for a fact* that he did it. The burden of proof in a libel case is with the defendant. The person suing does *not* have to prove that the incident did *not* happen.

Would our spitter be mean and petty enough to take me to court if I named him in the allegation, even though he knows it to be true? We will never know. But as we are dealing here with someone with no compunction about hockling in the face of an opponent, it's safest to assume that meanness and pettiness are two of his confirmed traits. So while he is alive I can't name him with guaranteed impunity. Shame.

• • •

The second young debutant to make a significant contribution in the latter half of 1995–96 had first come to my attention in pre-season training; the skinny kid I mentioned in the previous chapter.

He was a physically unpromising-looking specimen and

appeared to have been constructed from pipe cleaners. On the third or fourth day of training, this bony little chap, still a few weeks short of his seventeenth birthday, received a pass during a practice match. He allowed the ball to run through his spindly legs, casually knocked it past one defender, lobbed it over another before blamming an arrow-straight shot right into Alec Chamberlain's top corner. It was a barely believable goal.

With this sublime display of raw talent, Michael Bridges had announced himself to the rest of an open-mouthed squad. What a player he was. It's frustrating now to think what he might have done but for some bad injuries a few years down the line. I am convinced that at the very least he would have played for England. He was still developing physically when he initially broke into Sunderland's first team; I don't think he had even reached his full height and was about nine stone dripping wet. It would be several years before he was allowed out in a high wind. He made his debut as a substitute in the home fixture against Port Vale. It may have finished goalless, but Michael prevented the game from being entirely boring by making an instant impression with the fans, who recognised natural talent when they saw it. He was wonderfully skilful, with his touch, movement off the ball and ability to effortlessly beat an opponent. He had it all. Peter Reid and Bobby Saxton loved him and so did the crowd.

There was a story after I left Sunderland about Michael starting to earn big money and buying himself a flash car when he was still very young. It seems that Paul Bracewell instructed him to sell it and replace it with something more modest. The coaching staff were keen to keep Michael's feet on the ground. There are two sides to this. I understand what Paul was trying to do, but don't think this was necessary, especially in the case of a young man who was a dedicated professional and is a nice bloke to this day. His parents saw to that.

• • •

The first of our nine consecutive wins following the draw at Portsmouth came at home to Ipswich Town on a freezing February evening. The pitch was like a billiard table, by which I mean that it was green but as hard as slate. It was barely playable. Some old mates were in their squad: Mick Stockwell, Simon Milton and Neil Gregory. They also had Tony Mowbray, Richard Wright in goal, Claus Thomsen, Mauricio Tarrico, Stuart Slater and Steve Sedgley. John Wark was back at Ipswich then for his third stint, but didn't feature that day as he had been given permission to go and celebrate his 150th birthday.

The absence of *Escape To Victory* stars notwithstanding, this was a technically very good side. Had they been more physical they would have finished higher than their eventual seventh. They were by far the better side that night and we could barely get the ball off them. They ought to have bagged the three points, making chance upon chance. But they became the latest side to discover how good Shay Given was. The main source of injustice came in the thirty-eighth minute when Bracewell wellied up a hopeful one; I outjumped Sedgley to head the ball on to Craig Russell who was thereby through on goal and jabbed the ball past Wright.

That, somewhat implausibly, was the only goal of the game. A game that Ipswich should have won about 6–2. There was justifiable disbelief among the visiting players after the match, incredulous that they had lost. We were incredulous that we had won. My heart went out to my old club – in between guffaws. They had done something similar to us at Portman Road. Luck? We took our one chance while they fluffed all of theirs, which was a bad idea on their part if you ask me.

All wins boost the confidence of a side, but this one boosted us more in a slightly unorthodox way. If we could play so atrociously and still win, then we could do anything. I personally didn't have too bad a game, but it wasn't a good team display.

Four days later we were little better at home to Lennie Lawrence's Luton Town, upon a blustery afternoon on a dusty Roker Park pitch. I don't think we mustered a shot at goal that day. We didn't need to. Coincidentally, it was in the thirty-eighth minute again when I nudged the ball left to Craig, who then placed it wide to Micky Gray. Micky aimed his cross towards me at the back post, but it was cut out by Luton's makeshift centre-back, Julian James – and buried into his own goal before a joyous Fulwell End. Sorry if you're reading this, Julian, but it really was a beauty. The own goal was greeted with a cruel but amusing chorus of 'Sign him on! Sign him on!'

Again we hadn't played well as a team and this time neither had I personally. Again it was 1–0 at the final whistle. Again, therefore, we didn't care and neither did the fans. Again we all just thought: 'Roll on the next game.'

Roll on it did. Our next victory was even more farcical and came three days later against Southend United at Roots Hall. We flew to Essex in a little chartered plane; the first time I had ever flown to a match. It was rather misty when we arrived at the ground, but the rule was that there only needed to be visibility across the width of the pitch, as well as from each goal to the halfway line. So the referee, Graham Barber, said the match should go ahead. From our own penalty area we couldn't see the opposition's goal, but overall visibility was still just within regulations. At least it was when we kicked off. Whether it was fog or sea fret was of little interest outside the meteorological community. What concerned us was that in airborne waves it was encasing us in increasing thickness.

Martin Scott scored a penalty a few minutes into the second half and the Southend players began to harangue Mr Barber about the conditions. They wanted an abandonment. Obviously we were of the opposite opinion, partly because we had flown all the way down there, but mainly because we were winning.

'Come on, ref. This is ridiculous. You can't see your hand in front of your face. You've got to abandon this.'

'Don't listen to them, ref. You can see easy. Crystal clear.'

Footage of the game confirms that the match should indeed have been abandoned. This was despite our patently nonsensical claims to the contrary, and the fog only got worse as the minutes passed. If a Southend defender had stabbed me in the jugular with a cutlass, there would have been no other eye-witnesses.

I had worked hard and was tiring, so I was replaced by Michael Bridges with about ten minutes to go. I didn't mind being substituted. In fact, a complaint would have been more than futile because twenty-five seconds later Michael had scored. It was his first goal for the club and he was overjoyed. From the dugout we knew that the ball had gone into the net, but had very little other detail. It was followed by silence as the information filtered through the ground. The Sunderland supporters were at the other end of the stadium and only received news of our second goal by word of mouth. The final score was 2–0, which was a goal glut by our standards.

We didn't care. Two poor performances and a farce had yielded three wins. When you're winning you can get away with anything: bad performances and bad behaviour. Although in fairness to ourselves, we passed the ball well at Roots Hall, controlled the game and were the better side. We deserved the victory, even if not everyone in the ground saw it happening.

The fog had not abated when we returned to the plane, but the pilot said something like: 'Ha'way then. We'll take a chance.' This was not what the more nervous fliers wanted to hear. Yet, after a near-vertical take-off, with passengers clinging to cans of Budweiser (an obvious essential of aviation safety), we were above the clouds and all was well.

The next game was considerably more convincing. We travelled to Blundell Park for a televised Sunday fixture at Grimsby Town, who were struggling. We flattened them. Bally gave us a half-time lead and when Craig Russell got the second it was a matter of how many we would win by. Four–nil, as it turned out. Phil Gray scored from a mile out before Bridges got another one from the bench. I was an unused substitute but still happy. We were becoming a team that no one wanted to play. Our run was grounded in a solid defence. Our nine consecutive victories were to feature seven clean sheets and we would only concede thirty-three goals all season. I'm not entirely sure how we did this, but it was essential as we would only score fifty-nine – a very modest total for champions. Bearing in mind that twenty-two of our goals came in just six of the forty-six games, it was all the more remarkable (for those of you who can't be arsed to do the maths, it means that the other forty fixtures produced less than a goal a game – and we won the league!).

Six days later came the biggest match of the run, before a sell-out crowd at home to Derby County, who were now the only side above us in the division and hadn't lost in twenty matches. They had comprehensively beaten us at the Baseball Ground at Christmas.

We were about to be even comprehensiver. We won 3–0, a score-line that flattered Derby. We were in peak form and so were the Sunderland fans. Craig scored an early one, Aggers added another. The only quibble was that we ought to have been unassailable by half-time instead of a measly 2–0 ahead. No matter: Craig got another. Derby – with Gabbiadini, Chris Powell, Dean Sturridge, Russell Hoult and all – never got started. Three–nil.

A bonus was the return of Paul Stewart. He only played for an hour, but what an hour. The fans can't have been expecting much from him. During his two appearances early in the season he had looked far from match fit. Now here he was returning from six months out with a knee injury. But he barely made an error that day. He held the ball up, won headers and made intelligent runs. The first half was essentially The Paul Stewart Show. It was like watching a different player. All that was missing from him was a goal.

The belief of the fans was now turning into expectation. We were still second, but had just dismantled the team in first. Not only had we won five in a row, we hadn't conceded a goal. Teams were intimidated by us and we began to feel invulnerable. Opposition supporters would happily settle for a draw before matches had even kicked off. It's a wonderful feeling, although Peter Reid would not allow us to get ahead of ourselves. There was still much to do and plenty that could go wrong. But it didn't. We had a will to win and were running like a Swiss watch. Everyone knew their job – and everyone else's – by instinct and by rote.

Three days later we were at Boundary Park to face Oldham Athletic in the fixture that had been postponed on New Year's Day (fingers crossed that Mr Jones and his travelling offspring were in attendance this time). I was back in defence in place of the injured Andy Melville. Oldham had Chris Makin and Paul Gerrard in their side; two very good players. It didn't help them. We dominated, and Micky Gray gave us an early lead. Lee Richardson had the temerity to equalise a minute before the interval, but Kevin Ball scored with a few minutes remaining to win a game that now has a misleading look on paper. Our 2–1 victory with a late winner gives the impression of a hard-fought victory. It wasn't. We dominated again and did a professional job. The winning goal just happened to come later rather than sooner. In and out of the side though I was and always had been, this was the stuff of dreams: being part of a genuinely impressive Sunderland squad. It was even better than dispatching envelopes around an office block for BT.

I hadn't done anything wrong against Oldham, but Melville was available for the game at Birmingham City; another televised fixture the following Sunday. I wasn't even on the bench at St Andrew's, so I was naturally disappointed. But I expected it and didn't mind too much. Mel and Richard Ord were the first choice centre-backs and the manager's selection was vindicated further when Mel scored the second in a problem-free 2–0 win, putting us back to the top of the table after Derby's draw with Watford the previous day. I was still mightily pleased with the team and with life generally. Becoming as much of an option at centre-back as centre-forward was, overall, paying great dividends.

I was happy to make the team when we had been crap. Now that we actually had a good side, I could barely stop smiling.

• • •

The social side of all this was another joy, and something that wouldn't happen today.

Fixtures permitting, most of the squad would be out on a Saturday night, out again for a few on Sunday, train Monday, then train very hard on Tuesday, which meant that we felt entitled to a few in the evening. Wednesday was our day off and could often be an all-day session before we were back in training on Thursday. This was a cycle that continued for many weeks, and all the while we were winning games so no one could complain. We would drink in Sunderland, Newcastle, the Dun Cow in Burnmoor, the Bowes Incline Hotel in Gateshead, or pretty much anywhere with a bar. We would generally end the evening in a Sunderland nightclub – Fino's or Annabel's (both now long gone).

We played cards on the bus on the way to games, but only for fun, so that no one would be depressed when we kicked off because they had been cleaned out. It would be a proper card school on the return journey. The bus's cargo, nestled between the trolleys full of kit, would be tray, upon tray, upon tray of Budweiser, as well as a good many bottles of wine for the more refined among us. Steve Smelt, the physio, would sometimes hand out Mars Bars, just to give our bodies something to work with other than booze, and in fairness they did help us work, rest and play three-card brag. As we had usually swallowed a few cans before the driver had even put his key in the ignition, it was sometimes a physical achievement to alight the bus and land upright on the pavement. Pavements can be deceptively flat.

The team bus was the venue for some of our best nights out. Virtually every away trip involved a diversion into Wetherby on the return journey, so we could fill our faces with fish and chips, or chicken and chips for the more health conscious. The order was phoned in ahead and the chip shop would be kept open until all hours for our benefit (and their own). There were various drop-off points depending on where people lived, with Roker Park the final destination. But for a Saturday game, hardly anyone got off the bus before Annabel's, where we would clump in wearing our tracksuits and stagger upstairs. Dress restrictions were waived for footballers, as were rules about being clearly and utterly crapulous.

That then, is what the average coach journey back from an away game entailed in the Peter Reid era. Work hard, play hard. The level of jolliness was largely dependent on the result of the match, but the drink played no small role too. I couldn't but help compare and contrast all of this gay abandon with the mobile monastery that Mick Buxton had insisted upon after that aborted trip to Swindon on the second day of 1995.

On nights out with my old friends from outside football, there was never an issue in Sunderland city centre with the other revellers. On a bad day the odd comment might be made about how crap the team, or I personally, had been, but it never went beyond banter. Sometimes people might pat me on the back, or pump me for information about what was going on at the club. There were no problems.

Today this sort of socialising from footballers is virtually extinct. You rarely see a player out and about in the town he represents on the field. This is partly to do with the money involved: the potential cost of something silly and unfortunate happening to a footballer on a night out is enormous. Then there is the immediate snitching from social media if the modern player is spotted after 8 p.m. with a Taboo and lemonade.

There is also the issue of the sheer quantity of booze we used to sink. Players are fitter these days and it isn't such a bad thing that the drinking culture, quite spectacular at Sunderland while I was there, has been eroded from the game. But the lack of sociability, the detachment of footballers from the 'ordinary people', particularly at the top end of the game, is all but complete. And that is a shame.

I couldn't have been aloof even if I'd wanted to be. I was still the same bloke from Thorney Close. I just happened to play for Sunderland and was no better or worse than the next fella. Most players of the day had the same attitude. The 1995–96 season was the best time I ever had as a professional footballer; on and off the pitch. Both ends of the candle were burned and life was lived to the full. Britpop footballers. Oh, happy days.

This attitude was prevalent across the game. We were perhaps more than averagely out on the tiles, but were by no means unique. At Arsenal, for example, with Tony Adams, Paul Merson and others, it had clearly gone too far. We were invited each year to the PFA awards in London, but didn't always make the ceremony, preferring instead to embark on a pub crawl. It was the same at virtually every club.

•   •   •

The parties continued to be interspersed with the occasional game of football. Next came a home fixture against Oldham, only eleven days after playing them at Boundary Park. This time we won 1–0. Huddersfield Town came to Roker on 30 March, with Tony Norman in goal. This was a tough one; Huddersfield twice took the lead before Michael Bridges came off the bench with fifteen minutes remaining. He scored two and we won 3–2 (incidentally the only two goals Shay Given would ever concede at Roker Park). Everything was going right for us and for Bridges in particular. However, Huddersfield proved to be the last of the nine consecutive wins.

Watford were bottom of the league when we played them at Vicarage Road on 2 April. But Graham Taylor had returned as manager and although he didn't ultimately avert relegation, they were better organised and forced a 3–3 draw after trailing 2–0 and 3–1. It was a very good, end-to-end game.

The run of consecutive wins was over, but the unbeaten run now extended to a dozen games and, as it was Sunderland's best winning streak of the twentieth century and we remained top of the league by four points, we weren't exactly grief-stricken.

You get greedy. After a tenth win we would have wanted an eleventh and so on. However, it should be noted that the nine-victory run was the club's best sequence in 104 years. Thirteen straight wins were racked up in the 1891–92 season. We couldn't match those lads. On the other hand, they were all dead. Swings and roundabouts.

The hardest-fought victory of the season came at Barnsley. It would have been even harder if what almost happened to me actually did. I was very nearly called upon to go in goal.

Midway through the first half we took the lead through Craig Russell at the Pontefract Road End of Oakwell and looked good for the win. But just before the break, Paul Stewart was sent off for violent conduct. The one-man disadvantage meant that the second half seemed to last for about six months, with ball after ball being played into our penalty area.

With fifteen minutes remaining, another high one came in, with Shay Given bashing his ribs in the mêlée that followed it. Substitute again, I was told to warm up to replace Michael Bridges. But in truth it was to replace Shay rather than Michael, who had only been on the pitch for twenty minutes himself as a substitute for Craig. There were only three subs on the bench in the First Division in those days – and none of the three would ever be a goalkeeper. I was deemed to be the nearest thing due to my height and because I would occasionally go in goal during training. I was unofficially, therefore, the emergency goalie. Fine by me – although when you plan for an emergency there is an assumption that it will never happen. I wasn't a bad keeper or, to put it more accurately, the best of a bad bunch under the circumstances.

I affected, or attempted to affect, a James Bond-like coolness, as though this was an everyday occurrence. In reality, my stomach was revolving like a tumble-dryer. Had the winning margin been two or three, then it might have been a bit of fun. A single goal advantage and the ongoing siege in the Sunderland penalty area meant that it would be anything but.

Mercifully for all concerned, except Barnsley, it didn't happen. Shay was able to continue. I came on anyway for Michael and played as a third centre-back. We held on. It finished 1–0 and all player and supporter bowels were restored to their rightful positions (at least 8,000 Sunderland fans were at Oakwell). It was a tremendous victory and, although we couldn't allow ourselves any sort of complacency, the pundits were now discussing how we would fare in the Premier League – not *if* we would make it there.

Sadly, Shay Given would never play for Sunderland again. He was X-rayed and although no break was found, his injuries were deemed sufficient for him to be withdrawn. So a very cheesed-off young goalkeeper was sent back to Blackburn Rovers. But what a three months he'd had.

Alec Chamberlain came back into the side for the final six games and I was delighted to see him keep five clean sheets. The first two were goalless draws at home to Charlton and away to Sheffield United (then managed by Howard Kendall). He made a particularly superb fingertip save at Bramall Lane.

Three days later, Birmingham City came to Roker. We had won easily at St Andrew's a month earlier and their erratic gorblimey manager, Barry Fry (who famously used forty-four players that season), had made noises about coming to Sunderland to avenge this. 'I want to go up there and give them the fright of their lives.'

His ambition was soon downgraded. The game was over in twenty minutes. Micky Gray scored a thirty-yard corker at the Fulwell End on eighteen minutes; probably our goal of the season. Shortly afterwards, Paul Stewart finally headed the Sunderland goal he thoroughly deserved. It was his last game of the campaign, as he was suspended for the final three fixtures. Craig Russell rubbed salt into Birmingham's wounds in the second half and it ended 3–0.

For as long as I played for Sunderland at Roker Park, there was a table near the door in the home dressing room. The table top was two feet square and sat bearing a number of football essentials: tie-ups, strappings, tape, chewing gum and, for some reason, a large bottle of Bell's whisky which was never opened – until we played Birmingham that night.

All fourteen players on pitch or bench were 'up for it', shaking hands, wishing each other good luck and man-hugging in the minutes before kick-off. At the door stood Bobby Saxton, whisky bottle in hand with its top finally unscrewed, offering every player a generous swig. There were one or two takers, me being one of them for reasons that remain unclear even to myself. As I looked along the line I could see a few of the lads coughing as the alcohol burned home. What would sports scientists and dieticians think of this now?

It would probably drive them to drink.

•   •   •

Perhaps oddly, that was the only one of our last six games that we won; four of those matches finished 0–0. But however uneventful the games themselves were, the excitement on Wearside could be felt in every street, pub and schoolyard. We were six points clear with three games remaining. Superior goal difference meant that a Sunday victory against Stoke City at Roker Park in the next game would guarantee us Premier League football. As it transpired, we were promoted before we had even gone to bed on Saturday.

It is an historical quirk that the goal which ensured our promotion was actually scored by someone who wouldn't play for Sunderland for another seven years. On Saturday 20 April 1996, Paul Simpson gave Derby County a fifty-sixth minute lead over Birmingham at the Baseball Ground. Eighteen minutes later, future SAFC centre-back Gary Breen headed one home from ten inches to equalise. There were no more goals. Derby's failure to win meant that they couldn't catch us and Sunderland were a top-flight club again. That led to a massive night of celebration on Wearside, which, I hasten to add, the players had no part of.

Stoke had a good side and would finish fourth under Lou Macari. In the absence of the suspended Stewart, I was back up front for that game. I was shit too. Lárus Sigurðsson and Lee Sandford played at the back for Stoke and barely gave me a kick, other than up the arse. I was surprised to last the whole ninety minutes. But Stoke didn't get the win they needed more than we did. Poor though I was that day, it was Michael Bridges who missed a sitter that would have won the league there and then; so if anyone asks – he was crap and I was brilliant. Not only that, he was still too young to have a drink afterwards. Loser.

The game was broadcast live to six ITV regions, the telly people hoping to show the win that would take us up. They must have been narked, because not only had our promotion already been decided elsewhere, ours was an almost eventless fixture. It couldn't even provide more than one yellow card.

Unlike ITV, no one connected with Sunderland AFC was remotely concerned with the paucity of entertainment during the Stoke game. We began the celebrations by drenching Peter Reid with champagne in the changing rooms. I don't remember exactly what the celebrations entailed after that – which suggests that they were very good.

The main objective, by some distance, was to be promoted. That had been achieved, but there was still the Endsleigh Division One championship to play for. Medals. All we needed was a single point at home to West Bromwich Albion, who had nothing to play for. I kept my place up front and was much better than against Stoke. I headed against the post and had a volley that clipped the crossbar. It was another game that we ought to have won, but this time it really didn't matter. We were the champions. We had done it. We had done it on a very paltry budget too. The only signing that Peter Reid had made for any significant fee was that of David Kelly, who hardly played.

Cue more celebrations. There was a warm-up area adjacent to the changing rooms, but no one was warmed up in there that day, occupied as it was by a four-feet high stack of booze: slabs of the ubiquitous Budweiser and bottles of dodgy champagne.

After a brief pitch invasion had cleared, we were introduced back to the crowd in twos. I was paired with Craig Russell. The last pair out were Peter Reid and the captain Kevin Ball, who had not played due to a suspension, if you can imagine such a thing. Kevin then had the privilege of lifting that beautiful old trophy. It was presented by Gordon McKeag, who was president of the Football League at the time. Mr McKeag managed to elicit the only boos of the afternoon by virtue of being a former chairman of Newcastle United. He laughed it off. It was all part of the fun.

Before the trophy was raised it was knocked to the ground when a swirling wind swept an advertising hoarding into the table on which it had been placed. Bally lifted the silverware, minus the pirouetting lady who is supposed to adorn its top. He denied that she was the victim of a late tackle. The stricken lady actually spent the rest of the celebrations in the top pocket of my Uncle John's jacket. He was more than a little nervy at the responsibility.

We took the opportunity to do all those arsing about things that footballers do when they win a trophy: wearing scarves, silly hats, curly red and white wigs, waving flags and prancing around with the trophy while the mandatory 'We Are the Champions' by Queen was blaring out. This was what we had all imagined when we were kids. It was a special moment; so much so that Steve Agnew even put his teeth in for the occasion.

For locals like myself, Ordy, Craig, Martin Smith, Micky Gray and adopted Mackem Kevin Ball, it was even more special, because if we hadn't been on the pitch disporting ourselves with the trophy, then we would have been in the crowd cheering those who were.

Receiving a medal was great, but it was of distant secondary importance when compared to the prospect of playing in the Premier League. Only four years into its existence, it was already a global brand and where everyone desperately wanted to be, even people like Paul Bracewell and Paul Stewart, who had done it all. It was an unbelievable feeling and I was now quite easily the happiest I had been in my life. If the Premier League wasn't/isn't the best league in the world, then it was certainly the highest profile (Sky had seen to that) and the most exciting.

That evening, Saturday 27 April 1996, was a rambunctious night out even by our standards. We were suited and booted while we warmed up in the Roker Park lounge for a couple of hours, although I gave my jacket and tie to my heavily pregnant wife, who drove home after dropping me off in a buoyant city centre.

I really only remember one thing about that night. I spent about an hour and a half standing on a table outside a pub called Chaplin's, leading a merry sing-song of about a hundred fans. The playlist consisted of every Sunderland song that we could remember between us. Every third tune was *the song*, partly because people were coming and going and didn't realise that it had already been given umpteen renditions. People may have worried about upsetting me with a ditty that was so terribly abusive towards my little brother, but I managed to assuage their fears by joining in. I conducted the crowd like a pissed-up Simon Rattle. I was never a wallflower at parties, but standing on a table and rousing the natives into song was rather more extroverted than normal for me. I didn't care. My life had been leading up to this moment – nothing else had come close.

To this day, I am reminded by people of that night: 'I remember when you were outside Chaplin's…' It would be nice if they could reminisce about some breathtaking piece of skill on the field of play rather than some piss-artistry on a pub table. But Chaplin's is still a memory to cherish.

The West Brom game was a joy, even if it didn't produce any goals. I had started the match, played well and gone damn close to scoring. The rest of the day was wonderful too.

•　　•　　•

I had unquestionably contributed to the success of the campaign as a whole. If it had (somehow) happened the season before, I wouldn't have felt the same sense of achievement as for various reasons I barely featured in 1994–95. Of the fifty-two league and cup games of 1995–96, I was, as a minimum, a substitute in all but six of them. I hadn't been injury-free, but had taken tablets which enabled me to ignore my ailments. Play now, pay later. Much later.

The day after the West Brom fixture, Sunday, was the civic parade; open-top bus and all that. It began at Roker Park and nudged gradually towards Seaburn Beach with tens of thousands lining the streets. Everyone was worse for wear, even Kevin Ball who was not usually much of a drinker. There was champagne and beer in the lounge while we waited for the bus, which was also well stocked with booze. This was clearly the last thing we needed, as opposed to the last thing we wanted. Still, a proven method for avoiding a hangover is to remain drunk. Sound medical advice for professional sportsmen.

It was bitterly cold and I only had a shirt. But it was an incredible afternoon, with the players accompanying the crowd for a variety of off-colour chants, including several more airings of *the song*. Someone foolishly handed Micky Gray the microphone when we finally made it to the balcony of the Seaburn Centre, and he belted out a song or two that are not normally associated with the Sabbath. That cost him a week or two's wages. He didn't seem to care.

When the event was over, we went out and had a jolly good drink.

Charlie Hurley gave a speech that was considerably more family-friendly than Micky's singing. Charlie was as chuffed as anyone with what we had done (on the pitch, not on the bus) and pointed out that despite all his great days and well-deserved reputation, he had never actually won a medal. On the occasion of the club's centenary in 1979 he was named as Sunderland's Player of the Century. But now I had a medal and he didn't, which can only mean that he was a rubbish player compared to me. Or something.

My happiness had still not quite peaked. On photographs of the bus journey my infant son can, in a manner of speaking, be clearly seen. Elliot would not be born for another seventeen days, 14 May 1996. But my wife was on the bus and her bump was more than a little pronounced.

● ● ●

We still had one game to play, away to Tranmere the following Sunday. The fixture was largely meaningless, but another great day out for the fans who didn't want the carnival to end. They're like that. The team was picked on Saturday with me pencilled in to sit on the bench. Owing to nerves, I would never eat much of a pre-match meal but would have a very substantial breakfast, a full English: toast, marmalade and everything else that the players of today will not even see until they retire.

When I had boarded the bus, Reidy came bounding up to inform me that I would be playing at centre-back instead of Andy Melville. I don't know what the official reason for Mel's absence was, but I'm fairly certain of the real one. Whatever; I was always pleased to make the starting line-up, and with an entire forty-eight hours behind me without a drink I considered myself something of a health fanatic.

For the first time in three months, we lost a game. It was another that we should have won, but Kenny Irons scored against the run of play, before John Aldridge wrung a rather dubious penalty from Martin Scott which he then put away himself. Our supporters, who comprised at least half of the attendance, which was comfortably more than double Tranmere's average, were not particularly concerned. Most of them had drunk even more than we had in the previous week.

I say they weren't particularly concerned. There was one exception to this, and it seemed that one of his abiding passions in life was hating me. The ball rolled out for a throw-in beside the centre line during the first half. I ran to retrieve it and as I did so, an angry, sweating, porcine face appeared above the advertising hoarding. He looked as though he'd been marinated. Our exchange was brief.

'*Howey!*'

Having successfully diverted my attention, he added the epigram: '*You're fucking shit!*'

I thanked him for this eloquent assertion then carried on with the game.

It was bewildering and usually I would shrug aside general abuse. Many years before, Norman, Bobby Ferguson and others had helped me to develop a thick skin. What made this particular verbal pelter stand out was that we had won the league, gone unbeaten in eighteen, given the fans and ourselves a better season than anyone had dared to hope for, restored pride and delivered Premier League football. Personally, I had played in two positions, never complained when I was left on the bench, scored a number of crucial goals, wasn't on big money and had been signed for virtually nothing. Above all, I had never given less than my best for Sunderland, even if I hadn't been the star of the show. At Tranmere, I had only been told at the last minute that I was playing and had actually performed pretty well against the great Aldridge (the division's top scorer that season). What did this bloke expect from me? I was actually enjoying the game and remember Alan Durban, back at the club as chief scout, being very complimentary about me afterwards and I took Alan's compliments seriously.

And yet, because we were losing 1–0 at Prenton Park in an all but meaningless last game of a highly successful season, this bloke evidently felt that nothing less than a show trial in The Hague would do for me.

Of course, everyone is entitled to express an opinion, especially a paying customer. But ask yourself: is hurling abuse at someone who is genuinely doing their best going to inspire them towards betterment, or detract from their confidence and make them perform worse? Don't answer. It's a rhetorical question.

How much this diminishes your performance as a footballer depends on the circumstances. If you have just made an almighty, costly bungle then it is especially difficult to cope with. Players at all levels of the game can be seen to fall apart during games when everything they try is destined to fail; and it takes extraordinary stupidity to think that the acquisition of a huge salary can do anything to override this.

• • •

Further celebrations were squeezed out of the season while opportunity still availed itself. There was a pitch invasion and various demands for our shirts. Micky Gray was left with little more than a tattoo. Then there was another night out, after which the season really was all over. The only issue in the back of my mind was whether or not I would be a part of Peter Reid's plans. My contract was about to run out.

The following Wednesday we were all weighed so that the coaching staff would be able to tell how much we were about to look after ourselves during the close season – or not. The same day, a few of the younger players were released. Brian Atkinson, Alec Chamberlain and Phil Gray were on their way too. Some of the lads would soon be in Puerto Banús for the usual absorption of culture and history. I didn't join them, as my wife was about to pop.

We were finally presented with our medals. We had been given other medals from the Football League sponsors Endsleigh on ribbons around our necks after the West Brom game, but the proper articles were dished out more discreetly. They were about the size of two pence coins, in presentation boxes, with the FA's three lions on one side and 'First Division Winners 1995–96' on the reverse. They were then taken away to be engraved.

Mine was later nicked from a display cabinet in our house in Silksworth. My daughter Claudia was born on 23 May 1999 and christened shortly afterwards (both of our kids were planned so they would first see the world during the close season). We had a party at our home following the christening, with about sixty guests. I was playing for Northampton Town by then and it took me a couple of weeks to realise that my medal had gone. I have no idea who took it, less still why. Maybe Shergar ate it.

It was certainly a strange crime. Wherever that medal is now, it is intrinsically worthless. There is a limited demand for small pieces of metal with 'L Howey' emblazoned on one side. There may be, as you read, master criminals in South American hide-aways, wearing cravats and smoking jackets, smugly perusing their ill-gotten Van Goghs and Caravaggios. A similarly thriving black market is unlikely to exist for my old footy medals.

• • •

Peter Reid wanted to keep me and I was more than happy with this. From 1 August my new contract would be worth £1,100 per week, plus bonuses and a £20,000 signing-on fee. This was taxable, so the signing-on fee was reduced to about £13,000 and considered the breadline in the Premier League.

However, it was money that most people could only dream of and, eight years after being told that I would never play again, five years after being chucked onto a bus from Belgium to Thorney Close, three years after playing for Plains Farm Club in exchange for beer money and two months after being told at Tranmere that I was 'fucking shit!' – *this* was living the dream.

CHAPTER II

PREMIER LEAGUE

Peter Reid's pre-seasons were excellent. Facilities at the Charlie Hurley Centre were further improved in the summer of 1996 and the groundsmen there did a tremendous job.

We would train in different 'stations' for forty-five minutes at a time for agility, stretching, strength and ball skills. One of the strength exercises was for two players to sit on the ground back-to-back with arms hooked. A sort of wrestling match would then take place whereby if you forced your opponent down you were the winner. Kevin Ball took this extremely seriously, if you can imagine such a thing. This was despite him being paired with an enormous Romanian goalkeeper, Bogdan Stelea; an oak tree of a man and about a foot taller than Bally, who was undeterred by this. I don't recall who won, but I do remember wondering if Kevin's eyes were about to leave their cavities during the struggle, so it may well have been stopped.

Bogdan was one of a number of goalkeepers who came and went unnoticed that summer (Keith Welch was another). He went on to win ninety-one caps for his country and two years later was part of the Romania team that beat England in the World Cup. As was often the case, it is unclear why Sunderland never signed him. Perhaps it was money. Maybe he didn't fancy playing in England. Who knows?

The first game of pre-season was at Roker Park on 24 July. This was against Steaua Bucharest for Richard Ord's testimonial. Then it was off to Ireland again for four games there and it was great to be back on tour. I adored my new son, but Elliot wasn't the easiest baby and suddenly the gentle hum of a hotel mini-bar acquired an appeal I had never known before. Besides, I had no say in the matter – it was my job.

On tour there was the usual mixture of hard work and buffoonery, which was recalled twenty years later by our reserve goalkeeper, David Preece, in a column for the *Sunderland Echo*. It was in a piece with the somewhat sensationalist headline: 'On tour with SAFC as Lee Howey tried to kill Martin Smith.'

Mr Preece wrote: 'It was somewhat of a baptism of fire for me.

The matches were followed by "recreation time" which involved more than a couple of drinks that, at times, got a little out of hand.'

He described a question-and-answer drinking game as follows:

As I remember, Martin Smith had given three or four wrong answers in a row and was now in a position where a forfeit was his only choice. His forfeit? Three minutes' Queensberry rules with Lee Howey out on the 18th green (we were staying at a golf resort), with all of us gathered at the window to watch.

Now, I was under the assumption that this was just a laugh. But as it turned out, Lee took his bar games quite seriously and was just short of putting a gum-shield in and wearing a robe with his name across the back. It was at this point I feared for Martin. As Lee swung an arm towards Martin, I remember Andy Melville turning to me and saying 'He's only slapped him there, hasn't he?' I was rather hoping he had. He hadn't, and we all ran out to stop Howey going to prison for murder of the 'Son of Pele'.

I read the piece with barely suppressed rage. How dare David Preece write something this accurate?

I beg to differ on a couple of details. Martin's choice of forfeit was either to drink another pint or, at the instigation of Melville, who was adept at loading other people's guns, to take a single punch from me. It was by now approaching 4 a.m. and Martin could simply take no more grog, to the point where he would literally have preferred to be punched.

'Are you sure?' I asked him. He was. I don't recall going outside, but Martin assures me that we did. The deed was done, after which he may or may not have been upside down. At this stage we drew upon our critically low supplies of common sense, checked his pulse, chucked a bit of water on him then went to bed. I had smacked him on the chin, but had done so without malice – more in a spirit of comradeship. I was always an eager contributor to team bonding.

• • •

Upon promotion in April, Bob Murray made himself chairman again. As he had always been the majority shareholder anyway, this made little difference. He made a few quid available for Peter Reid to spend, but was characteristically cautious.

Tony Coton, a great and experienced goalkeeper then aged thirty-five, arrived for £600,000 from Manchester United (where he had been since January as a replacement for Kevin Pilkington, but had never played). He had played for Reidy at Manchester City and was well known and respected. He was immediately installed as our first choice keeper. TC had also been part of the renowned team of hard-nuts at Birmingham City in the 1980s. He was a fine pro with a good line in dry humour and some great stories. I liked him, but we weren't close. His seniority meant that he was something in between the coaching staff and the players. He was already friends with Paul Stewart and they would regularly converse about various businesses they owned and how the markets were developing. I would earwig these conversations and concluded that they truly inhabited a different planet to me; chuffed to instalments with my £500 per week over the past three years.

My social clique with other players was mainly comprised of the other lads who had won promotion. But Alex Rae was signed early from Millwall and immediately became part of our merry band, which was not necessarily a good thing.

He was a tremendous, tough midfielder and cost Sunderland £1,001,000. The odd thousand quid in that figure was because he played in a friendly at Whitley Bay when a suspension carried over from Millwall had been overlooked. He was also an accomplished spitter. Being next to him in the dugout was like sitting beside a small Glaswegian fountain. Spit, spit, spit. It was his tic. These days, the Opta Stats could furnish us with details of volume, consistency and accuracy.

We have established that my cohorts and I enjoyed a drink. Alex took it to another level and I suppose he is representative of the darker side of football's booze culture of the time. He kept it quite quiet for a while, but a couple of years later he was in rehab. However, Alex is a remarkable bloke. He came off alcohol and has stayed clear of it for many years now. In 2007 he formed the Second Chance project in Glasgow, which does tremendous work in taking people off drink and drugs.

Our new second choice goalkeeper, Lionel Pérez, was a Frenchman. Despite this, he was another top lad. He signed from Bordeaux for £200,000 as cover for Tony. Soon after his arrival we persuaded him to join us in a quaint old English custom in Aidy Marshall's pub in Seaham, The Phoenix.

This custom, which you may have heard of, is known as 'Going for Sunday dinner then spending the rest of the day getting completely blootered'. Lionel soon entered into the spirit of things. By about 9 p.m. he was hugging everyone and declaring: 'I *love* English customs.'

There was one thing that put people off Lionel and oddly it wasn't his extreme Frenchness. It was his smoking. Today it is more likely that a footballer will use cocaine than tobacco, but it was a rarity in the mid-1990s too. No one wanted to room with him because of this, so we decided that he should share with the ever-popular Dariusz Kubicki when we were away from home, and everyone was happy with the arrangement: except for Dariusz, who would be on the verge of tears. Richard Ord derived momentous pleasure from this.

But there was no doubt about the most significant recruit of that summer. It came just two days before the start of the season.

Niall Quinn cost Sunderland £1.3 million from Manchester City, a then-club record buy. Aside from being a magnificent centre-forward, Niall was one of the greatest and most important signings in the history of the club. I had watched him play against Sunderland and always been impressed. On the final day of the 1990–91 season, he scored twice in a 3–2 win for City at Maine Road that sent Sunderland down. I said impressed, not pleased.

For all his glories, Niall Quinn was not to have a successful first season at Sunderland, to the point where at the end of it he felt he owed something to Peter Reid and the fans. He owes nothing now. What he went on to achieve for Sunderland AFC, as a player and then chairman, is unparalleled.

Niall remains a friend of mine. If anyone has an assumption of him as this genial, approachable and highly likeable bloke, then they are completely correct. There is no way to avoid the adjective – he's very nice. He always sees the positive side to a situation, makes time for people and is intelligent, articulate, humorous, garrulous and a gifted raconteur. He is typically Irish in that he has more stories than the Old Testament. Pick a subject and Niall has a tale to tell.

His generosity is famous. This was seen in 2007 when he paid for taxis for Sunderland fans from Cardiff to Wearside after a vindictive air stewardess had them ejected from a plane home for no particular reason. In 2002, he effectively ended the practice of already wealthy footballers bagging testimonial money that they didn't need when he donated all the cash from his own testimonial to two children's hospitals. The Niall Quinn Children's Centre stands within the grounds of the Sunderland Royal Hospital on Kayll Road in the city.

It makes you sick.

However, he isn't a complete saint. The man is an extraordinary drinker. He doesn't just have hollow legs – he also appears to be leaking at the toes. At Sunderland in 1996, this was considered an asset and he fitted in immediately.

Our spending, perhaps hampered by the ten-year mortgage that the club had taken out to build the Stadium of Light where construction had just begun, was modest. Newcastle had recently broken the world record with the £15 million they spent on Alan Shearer. But we weren't going into the top division with no other ambition than to stay in it. We believed we could do something. If we could subsequently start a second season in the Premier League in what would be the best ground in England, the club could really stride forward. The likes of Niall Quinn, Tony Coton and Alex Rae could be the foundation for this. I was delighted, even if the arrival of Niall in particular meant I had no chance of starting another game up front.

• • •

It was during the close season that we were told about plans for *Premier Passions*, the five-part documentary that chronicled our 1996–97 season. It was narrated by the actress Gina McKee, a Sunderland fan. But it's probably best remembered for the pyrotechnic swearing of Peter Reid when he wasn't happy. I can confirm that nothing was contrived, scripted or carried out for the benefit of the camera on that programme. What the viewer saw was exactly how it was, with or without a film crew.

I wasn't wholly comfortable with the idea of a camera being thrust at me when I least expected it, but we became friendly with the crew and after a while we forgot they were filming. Not for nothing are they called fly-on-the-wall documentaries. Occasionally we might have a quiet word about things we would prefer them *not* to broadcast – elbows on the table, split infinitives, cheating at chess, returning library books late; that sort of thing – and they were most obliging. The only time I was miked up and asked questions for a considered response was before we played Newcastle, and they wanted to ask me about Steven.

The man behind *Premier Passions*, Stephen Lambert, went on to create *Gogglebox*, *Faking It*, *Wife Swap*, *The Secret Millionaire* and *Undercover Boss*. These programmes are made internationally and the man must be loaded now. Surely he owes me a drink for starting him off.

•　•　•

We were given our squad numbers for the Premier League. Mine was fourteen (one-four, the first of the fourth, my birthday). I would not even sit on the bench for the opening few fixtures, the first of which was at home to Leicester City on Saturday 17 August 1996. In truth, having this as the first match was probably disappointing to both clubs, who would have preferred to play Manchester United or Liverpool. Leicester were nothing new, as they had been promoted alongside us after Steve Claridge's wonder goal beat Crystal Palace in the play-off final. Derby County had taken the other automatic place.

The Filbert Street spitter was around that day and still refusing to admit what he'd done; or 'talking shit' as other authorities would have it. I was more concerned with the fact that I wouldn't be on the pitch. It was another 0–0 draw. Kasey Keller made a great save from Aggers. Niall Quinn made his debut from the bench and had one disallowed for a push. Still, it was a point on the board. Later there was the added novelty of featuring on *Match of the Day*. We were shown before Manchester United's win at Wimbledon, with the celebrated Beckham goal from his own half.

In Sunderland's first ever game in the Premier League (at that time called the Carling Premiership) Kevin Ball was booked in the second half, if you can imagine such a thing. However, the honour of our first ever yellow card in that hallowed division was awarded to Steve Agnew. I would wager that Bally remains irritated by this.

I travelled with the squad to the game four days later against Nottingham Forest at the City Ground. Since promotion we had improved the squad and it was clearly going to be even harder for me to make the team, or even the bench. In a way it was even more disappointing not to even be named as a substitute, because there were five subs in the top flight compared to three in Division One. Bobby Saxton spoke to me before the game to explain that I was still a valued player and could consider myself unfortunate. As consolation I was told that, even without playing, I would qualify for a win bonus of £600. I think it was £400 for a draw – draws being far more valuable in this league in every respect. I appreciated this fiscal pat on the back. It wasn't about money, but I reminded myself that I was being well remunerated to watch the team I'd always supported. Life remained tip-top.

Anyway I soon forgot my little personal frustration as we had effectively won the game by half-time. At the risk of annoying those who, very reasonably, point out that football existed long before 1992, Sunderland's first ever Premier League goal was scored in the eighth minute by Micky Gray, a Sunderland supporter (he scored four goals that season and all were high profile), belted in past Mark Crossley from about twenty-five yards and a very good strike. Niall, making his first Sunderland start, scored a fluke when the ball bounced against his knee then into the net following Kevin Ball's challenge on Crossley. Alf-Inge Håland retrieved one for Forest before Niall scored more typically with his head. An ecstatic Richard Ord headed another with two minutes of the half remaining to make it 4–1. There were no more goals. What a performance.

The next game was nearly as impressive. It was against Liverpool at Anfield and their imposing forward line of Fowler, Barnes, Collymore and McManaman. Whenever we played Liverpool, Kevin Ball would be tasked with marking Steve McManaman – a phenomenal footballer. Bally was very fit, but by the final whistle that day he was panting like a flabby old Labrador, tongue hanging out and barely able to trot. This was about as well as anyone ever did against McManaman and Bally's efforts paid off. It ended goalless.

Then it was the big one; the one that everyone looked for when the fixture lists were printed in the summer: Newcastle United at home, Sunderland's first derby in three-and-a-half-years.

Whether or not Peter Reid wanted to use me against Newcastle was an academic point. I was injured with some niggle or other. Steven was playing for Newcastle and we had some good-natured words before the game, along the lines of me hoping he got battered in every respect. We avoided the subject of the housing market.

Newcastle began the brighter, but we grew into it and Robbie Elliott fetched down Aggers for a penalty that Martin Scott scored at the Fulwell End. We deservedly led at half-time. But Newcastle had finished runners-up the previous season and would do so again in this one having spent very heavily in recent years. There was no denying their quality. They won 2–1 with goals from Peter Beardsley and Les Ferdinand. The rest of their line-up included Shearer, Lee and Ginola. It's always galling to lose to that lot, but we were clear underdogs and hadn't disgraced ourselves.

I didn't play in the following game either, but at least I was on the bench for the first time that season. We played West Ham at Roker Park in the third goalless draw of our opening five matches. This was broadcast live on Sky, who must have regretted their decision as it was an incredibly dull game. I remember watching West Ham's new striker Florin Răducioiu, recently signed with hopes as high as his salary, and predicting he would be a flop. He was. Still, one of only two goals he scored for the 'Ammers would be against Sunderland at the Boleyn Ground at Christmas, as was inevitable. Harry Redknapp had signed him from Espanyol on the strength of his performances for Romania in Euro '96. This is rarely a good idea, and he soon returned to a giggling Espanyol.

As a point of historical interest, West Ham's bench that day accommodated teenagers Rio Ferdinand and Frank Lampard, alongside Peter Shilton, who turned forty-seven that month.

• • •

On 10 April 1965, Sunderland outside-left George Mulhall set a post-war record of 124 consecutive appearances for the club in a draw at Everton. On 14 September 1996, Sunderland right-back Dariusz Kubicki would have equalled that record at Derby County – had he not been dropped by Peter Reid.

Reidy always maintained that he was unaware of the Mulhall record, a claim that was met with some scepticism by the fans. All I can say is that it was news to me too. But Dariusz, who wasn't even named as a substitute, was well aware of the record and in considerable umbrage when I spoke to him about it. This was the most emotional I ever saw him. I was first aware of the situation when I saw Richard Ord's *schadenfreude* on the bus home.

Ordy needed cheering up after that game. Referee and red card enthusiast David Elleray gave him a second yellow in the twenty-fourth minute for an innocuous push on Marco Gabbiad-ini. We defended stoically until the eighty-fourth minute when, just in front of me, Gareth Hall fouled Aljoša Asanović for a pen-alty. If you look at the footage you'll see that without the foul I would have probably put the ball away for a corner, which made it even worse for Gareth. The spot-kick was converted by Asanović himself and the game ended 1–0.

The fans would never take Gareth to their hearts and this result was a major reason why. It was he who had replaced Dariusz to deny him the appearances record. Dariusz was a favourite on the terraces and the supporters were peeved about it. But they were considerably more put out when his replacement gave away the only goal of the game. Gareth was no one's idea of an all-time great, but the acerbic slurs that came his way, even years later, were beyond disproportionate. Anyone who regards him as 'one of the worst players… blah, blah, blah…' can't have seen much football.

As for Peter Reid's involvement; whether or not he liked Dariusz personally is irrelevant, because he thought Gareth was a more ap-propriate selection for the game. Derby were another promoted side and it was a winnable fixture. It seems unlikely therefore that Peter would have deliberately weakened the team just to annoy someone. You may think that he *did* weaken the team, but it certainly wasn't his intention. Dariusz had quality, but I can say as a central defend-er that the game could be made easier by Gareth for the simple reason that he was more vocal. You need to communicate on the pitch, but this could be difficult with Dariusz, from whom every word on and off the pitch had to be virtually excavated.

The game was another personal milestone for me. When I re-placed Paul Bracewell in the second half it was my first appearance in the Premier League. It was also my first game at the Baseball Ground since the jelly-legged humiliation of three years earlier. I was put in defence to hang on to a point and although I was nervous, it was nothing like as bad. As a centre-back I knew that if I was strong, determined and brave then I would be OK.

So there was another tick on the bucket list. I could go to my grave saying that I was a Premier League footballer. However, as we lost the game it didn't resonate much with me. Perhaps I had a thought or two about it before I went to bed that night, but if I did I don't remember. As somebody, somewhere says every day in the world of football: you move on. You have to. Derby was a bad day, especially for Richard, Dariusz and Gareth. But the next game is never far away.

It proved significant. We beat Coventry 1–0 at home thanks to a beautiful half-volley from Steve Agnew. Sadly that wasn't what made it significant.

Niall Quinn would miss most of the season with the injury he picked up in the first half. He went to ground in agony after an inconsequential-looking challenge from behind by Liam Daish close to the Clock Stand, which was a section of Roker Park and not a section of Niall. It didn't look like much, but he had mangled his cruciate. This was on 21 September. He wouldn't be back until April. Bollocks. He had already made a huge difference and this was a serious setback for the club as a whole. A couple of months later he did his other cruciate in training.

Perhaps I don't much remember my first Premier League appearance because it was against another promoted club in a ground I had played at previously. Badly. But my next game was something very special to me for two reasons. I would play the whole ninety minutes and it was against Arsenal at Highbury.

This was one of the great grounds, even if it was only ten years from demolition. Richard Ord was serving his one-match suspension and I travelled to London knowing that I was going to play, glowing inwardly at the prospect. I had actually played there previously, in the aforementioned Floodlit Cup match for Ipswich as a teenager; I scored too, in a 3–2 win. Obviously this was a much bigger occasion and I absorbed every moment of it, starting with the famous marble entrance and the bust of Herbert Chapman. Then it was a right turn to the capacious changing rooms, the communal bath, the single baths and everything else you might need. It was a very impressive, imposing place, even before considering its abundant history.

I reacquainted myself with an old friend from Ipswich too, Chris Kiwomya, then an Arsenal striker but not playing that day. We reminisced about punch-ups from our youth. Ah, the joys of boyish violence. I never thought that he would play for Arsenal, or that I would line up against them. We were playing them as peers too. I wasn't there because we had been pulled out of the hat in a cup draw, which can happen to anyone. We had earned it.

I partnered Andy Melville at centre-back, where we were to take care of Ian Wright and John Hartson. What could be easier? John was only twenty-one then, but he remembered me from his days at Luton Town and politely asked me to 'take it easy'. Their other nine starters were David Seaman, Lee Dixon, Nigel Winterburn, Steve Bould, Martin Keown, Tony Adams, David Platt, Patrick Viera and Paul Merson. Ray Parlour was a sub. They were all household names, whereas I don't suppose there was too much Lee Howey-related chatter among the Arsenal fans before the kick-off. So what? If days like this didn't serve to remind me why I had worked so hard, amid so much pain, for so long, then nothing would. I was ready for them.

Ian Wright was, as you know, a simply brilliant striker who rarely ceased his yap during the match. This wasn't in a nasty way; it was just his well-founded self-confidence coming to the fore. I remember thinking: 'I hope he goes on to host a Saturday night game show called *Friends Like These*. That would be great.' A few years later I got my wish.

The match itself, played upon a flawless surface on a beautiful late September afternoon, was a very strange one. Melville and I soon settled and were passing the ball well. I made a few good challenges too. We went on a couple of dangerous attacks and Steve Agnew had a decent chance. There was nothing in the game – until the twenty-first minute.

That was when Martin Scott was shown his second yellow card in four minutes, both for late challenges on Lee Dixon, the second of which was not especially bad. In the thirty-ninth minute Martin was joined by Paul Stewart, who also collected two yellows – both for handball. Again, the second was somewhat harsh. He jumped and was pushed by Bould into the flight of the descending ball and couldn't help but handle it. His second card was later rescinded and a one-match ban averted. But that wasn't hugely helpful on the day of the game, which we now had to complete with nine men.

In between the two dismissals, Peter Reid was sent to the stand for a furious invective against the referee, Paul Danson (who in 1999 was removed from refereeing Sunderland's FA Cup tie at Lincoln City as the fans were still fuming about him). Having started with a 4–5–1 formation, we now reverted to a less orthodox 4–4–bugger-all and did nothing for the remainder of the half except make clearances. It was defence versus attack, like a training exercise. Tony Coton took as much time as he could get away with when taking goal kicks, all of which were walloped crudely into the stands. It was goalless at half-time; an accomplishment in itself. It may sound odd, but Ian Wright berated Mr Danson to his face for 'spoiling the game'. His sporting blood meant that he wanted to win as much as anyone, but against full-strength opposition.

Reidy and Bobby Saxton remained positive and, undeterred by trivialities like a two-man disadvantage, actually had a plan to *win* the game. We were to keep it tight for half an hour, then bring Michael Bridges or Craig Russell off the bench, catch Arsenal unawares, steal the points, then wait for poems and plays to be written about how we had done it. The plan was not so far-fetched.

The longer the game progressed, the more irritated the home fans became and the more belief we gained.

Alas, t'was not to be. Hartson finally headed his team into a lead with seventeen minutes remaining. Bridges almost equalised. Had he done so, our supporters, who were in particularly magnificent form that day, would have laughed as much as celebrated. But Parlour finished us off near the end and it finished 2–0.

We had all played well and there was nothing more we could have done. Personally I had proved, if indeed it needed to be proved, that I was not intimidated by anyone and that I could compete with the best if I was on my game. Whatever misgivings people may have had about me, I like to think that a lack of gumption was not among them. If I had been asked to run through a brick wall, my only query would have been 'Which one?' It was the only way I could play.

Regardless of the result, Highbury is one of the great memories of my professional career, up there with lifting the First Division trophy. I had played a full Premier League game for Sunderland in a great ground against celebrated opposition and had done so adeptly. What's more, I had earned the right to be there and it was a fixture that would be long remembered by Sunderland fans.

But I would still have preferred to win, even if that meant scraping a 1–0 win with a dodgy penalty in a tedious match. As Barry Davies said on *Match of the Day* that evening, 'Arsenal won the match. Sunderland won the day.' Thanks, Barry, but I would have preferred it the other way round.

Arsenal were managed that day by Pat Rice. Arsène Wenger had just been appointed but would not be in the dugout until their next game. It was also the first fixture back at Highbury for Tony Adams, who had been out of the game in order to deal with his much publicised alcoholism. I can't say that the travelling Sunderland contingent was overly sympathetic, unless a rousing chorus of 'Who drank all the beer?' counts as sympathy.

Other compassionate comments from the visitors' section included: 'Fuckin' puff! 'E probably only drinks the same as us.'

• • •

I was back on the bench for the next game because Ord was available again. This was at home to Middlesbrough, live on Sky. The crowd was pleased to see Ordy back – until he was sent off in the fifty-eighth minute when we were losing 2–1. He trod on the chest of Nick Barmby and Graham Poll gave him a straight red. However, Craig Russell equalised to give us a useful point against a very expensive side that included Ravanelli, Juninho, Emerson and Barmby. Comparatively speaking, our remaining ten men had cost about the same as a round of drinks. It was a moral, if not an actual victory and was another performance that said much for the spirit of our very small squad. It was about to become smaller.

We flew to the Dell to play Southampton – and what a peculiar little ground that was. Walking on studs from changing room to the pitch was a fraught business, down steep stairs and narrow corridors. It was an achievement to reach the dugout.

We were stuffed 3–0. It was Tony Coton's 501st league game. It was also his last. Following an accidental collision with Egil Østenstad, he was put on a stretcher with his leg broken in five places. Lionel Pérez would play in every remaining game of 1996–97, with Phil Naisbett then David Preece promoted to the bench. But we had a critical shortage of experienced goalkeeping cover.

Lionel became an instant crowd favourite. He couldn't do much to stop Southampton, but made some fine saves in the next game against Aston Villa at Roker Park and kept a clean sheet. Midway through the first half we were awarded a penalty, which was taken by David Kelly, who had recently returned from injury. Mark Bosnich saved it, but Paul Stewart pounced to score the rebound and the only goal of the afternoon. This was an excellent result. Villa would finish the season in fifth and their team that day included Bosnich, Dwight Yorke, Ugo Ehiogu, Gareth Southgate and Andy Townsend. We were now eleven games into the season and in thirteenth position. Mid-table. It was all going very well.

• • •

Richard Ord's latest suspension now took effect. He had been given a three-match ban for his straight red against Middlesbrough, plus one more because he had already been sent off against Derby. I was therefore looking forward to a minimum four-game run in the side. One man's misfortune is another man's opportunity. Or it should have been.

I started the game against Leeds United at Elland Road on 2 November, but was destined not to finish it. Leeds were another useful side and Melville and I had to mark Brian Deane and an aging Ian Rush. A Mark Ford goal put us 1–0 down at half-time. Aggravatingly, Mark was only 5ft 7in. yet scored with his head (it was also the only goal he ever scored for Leeds). But we were far from out of it. Deane had caused me no problems whatsoever and I had given him several clatterings. All good fun (and let's face it, not exactly a novelty at Elland Road).

Peter Reid and Bobby Saxton did most of the talking during the interval. But another member of the backroom staff at that time was none other than Sam Allardyce, a former Sunderland player and old mucker of Reidy's from Bolton Wanderers (Sam had recently been sacked as Blackpool manager by their chairman Owen Oyston, who issued the dismissal from his prison cell where he was doing a six-year stretch for rape). Sam followed me to the toilet in order to offer me some advice. What he said exactly was not recorded, which was just as well for him. If he had been afforded the same level of discretion when he frequented Wing's Cantonese Restaurant in Manchester twenty years later, he might still be manager of England.

Like his former teammate Joe Bolton, Sam had been what is often referred to as a 'no-nonsense defender' in his day. This was reflected in his counsel to me.

'Fuckin' kick him, Lee! Whack 'im where it 'urts. Nut 'im. Bite 'im if you need to. Just do it! Hammer the bastard. Kick 'im. Stick a knee in his…'

Like me you probably don't need any aspect of his speech to be explained to you. He wasn't being what you might call cryptic.

Anyway, the expurgated version of his advice was that I should be as aggressive as possible with Brian Deane. This seemed odd as I had not exactly shirked on that front during the first half. But, pliable as ever, I took deep breaths then returned to the field to carry out Sam's instructions. He had worked me up and I was like an angry bear, but without a legitimate reason for being angry. Brian soon got the message and knew what to do. He had come up against many a player like me and used an old trick I was familiar with from chapter two. He turned his foot slightly and I smashed my ankle against his studs as I tried to kick him; I was gulping with the pain. Not that I was about to let this show. This was a big opportunity for me and I was determined to use it. But physically I was in too much trouble and had to come off.

As I had been hurt by Brian in the course of attempting to hurt him, I could hardly lay blame at his door. However, I have to say: that's what I got for listening to Sam Allardyce (blame him for everything; it's fashionable). There is controlled and uncontrolled aggression and I had foolishly abandoned the former for the latter. It was my job to be tough and dish it out, even if I had to occasionally take it back. Fans love a good aggressive tackle, but not an assassin. I left Elland Road on crutches. After the Leeds game there was a fortnight off for an international break, which gave me two weeks to work on my recovery. We had a new, young, highly recommended physio called Nigel Carnell.

One of the strange things about Nigel was his reluctance to run onto the pitch during a game to treat a player. You would have thought that this was an accepted prerequisite in his job, but he would send on our other physio, Gordon Ellis, in his stead. This provided a problem for Gordon on one occasion. For fear of being seen on television, when he entered the field of play to treat Bally he did so wearing a hood to cover his face and distinctive bald head. It wasn't that he shared Nigel's nervousness of being seen in public; or rather he wouldn't have done had he not been officially on the sick from his other job.

The first thing Nigel did back at the training ground was tell me that I didn't need crutches. He then put me on a trampoline session on one of those little trampettes so beloved of small children. It was a twenty-minute session followed by a half-hour run round the peri-meter of the training ground. When I returned home I was in agony.

The next day I expressed my concern that my ankle might be broken. The idea was dismissed out of hand. On seeing the running I had done at Leeds in the minutes immediately after sustaining the injury, Nigel reckoned there couldn't have been a break and sent me back to work. After a few more bounces on the trampette, I was in greater pain than ever and spoke to Gordon, who happened to be passing. Gordon knew that I wasn't the malingering or exaggerating type; he drove me straight to hospital, where an X-ray confirmed that the ankle bone had become detached, turned further and was gener-ally in a condition whereby bouncing up and down on a trampoline like a giddy cocker spaniel was the last thing it needed. It ought to have been in a cast and my recovery was set back significantly. I wouldn't return to the first team squad until March, four months away.

Tony Coton, meanwhile, was struggling with even worse wounds. His bone had healed, but had done so bent and misshap-en. So his leg had to be re-broken and a rod inserted. There were other lesser injuries among the squad too. Nigel Carnell MCSP, SRP, parted ways with the club soon afterwards. He was young at the time and I understand he now has a glowing reputation.

In 1998, while still employed by Sunderland AFC as a coach, Tony Coton sued the club alleging a failure to provide suitable disability cover, negligence and breach of contract. There would be wider repercussions.

• • •

Christmas of 1996 fell during my recuperation, with the players' night out duly arranged for some or other midweek in December. The idea was to have a jolly little soirée with a fancy dress theme. It was inconceivable that anything could go wrong. Again. For a start we decided to stay out of Newcastle this year.

I went as Batman. This was proper Batman too with latex body armour and a cool mask. None of your Fathers For Justice rubbish. I changed at home in the bedroom and when I came downstairs the two German shepherds I had at the time pounced at me. I had to whip off the mask and explain to them who I was.

The evening began in Seaham at The Phoenix where Aidy Marshall laid on some food. There was also the obligatory stripper and other entertainments. Kevin Ball was dressed as Little Bo Peep in bright yellow pigtails and a pair of rather fetching kitten heels. To borrow from *Blackadder*, he looked about as feminine as W. G. Grace. Tony Coton was still on crutches and therefore went for the obvious: Long John Silver. Niall Quinn was Friar Tuck, Richard Ord was a Mountie. There were three musketeers. Alex Rae came as Madonna. Several Nazis turned up including Martin Scott, who was tastefully decked out as Adolf himself.

We ended up in Sunderland city centre at a place called Idols. I was chatting at the bar with Bo Peep and a couple of Nazis, when a commotion commenced a few yards away. Soon after I was told we were all to go outside where it was 'all kicking off'. What now?

What happened was that Ordy's wife was in the bar when some bloke became over-friendly with her. Ordy was distinctly unhappy and decided upon immediate retribution. As you know, the Mountie always gets his man. The problem was that Mrs Ord's unwanted friend had ten or fifteen mates with him, so a pitched battle commenced.

It was easy for partisan spectators to see who was on which team. There were quite a few spectators too; the public is seldom able to resist the combined lure of pageantry and extreme violence. Everyone was fisticuffing. Even Tony Coton was belting someone with his crutch. The fact that I was throwing punches in the epicentre of a huge fracas meant heightened significance for my Batman costume. This occurred even to me at the time. An appearance by Robin would have been most useful.

Robin never arrived, but Gill Bridge police station was only about a hundred yards away and the cops soon turned up to disperse everyone. To them it was a run-of-the-mill punch-up and they were content to send everyone packing, rather than give themselves a skip-load of paperwork by filling the cells with a load of eedjits in fancy dress. There were no arrests.

The following morning, nursing one of my more extravagant hangovers, I was to be picked up from home by Gordon Ellis and driven to Hartlepool to meet a consultant about my ankle. Gordon was late. From my bedroom I eventually saw him approaching our cul-de-sac and went to the front door, but there was no sign of him from the garden. He was hidden behind the street's bend where his car had become stuck. Distracted by looking for my house, he had absent-mindedly mounted a neighbour's rockery and was unable to vacate it, wheels turning impotently with no terra firma beneath them. The rockery owner accepted Gordon's apology and fortunately another neighbour had a hydraulic jack with which to return him to the highway.

Gordon had also been with us the previous night and his agitation was increased because he couldn't find his SS officer's cap, which would cost him a £30 deposit on his costume. He was also wearing a Hitler moustache that had been drawn on him as a jape. It wouldn't wash off. I was still honking of drink and it's fair to assume that the consultant wasn't overly impressed with us. She still pencilled in my operation.

From Hartlepool we headed for Roker Park where training had finished and Niall Quinn wanted to speak to me.

'Thank God for your dad, Lee.'

My dad?

Following the mass brawl outside Idols, Niall and Tony Coton, two of the wiser heads in the camp, had made a discreet departure. At least, it was as discreet a departure as could be expected of two famous footballers dressed as Long John Silver and Friar Tuck in a busy city centre. They sought sanctuary in a nearby Indian restaurant, but were given grief by an adjacent table of fellow diners who were shouting 'Waste of money!' and other insults at them, clearly keen to instigate a fight. Another one.

It is often forgotten among the idolatry to follow Niall on Wearside that he was not hugely popular there during his first year or so. The gentlemen in the restaurant were piqued that the club they supported had spent almost £2 million on Niall and Tony. The fact that Tony had then broken his leg in five places and Niall had endured agonising injuries on each knee, was something to be taken as a personal insult. This absurd 'reasoning' was compounded by Carlsberg plc and things were about to become nasty.

Enter Norman, his brother-in-law John McClements and his friend Ronnie Cowie, who were also dining out. The lads who were acting the giddy goat knew my dad, who left them in no doubt as to what would occur if they didn't improve their table manners. That was the end of the show and Niall still mentions the incident when we meet.

Shortly after I had listened to this tale, the police turned up at Roker. There was a sergeant and an officer who happens to be a friend of mine, Mickey Crowe. They wanted to discuss the contents of a video cassette they had with them. This was CCTV footage of the merriment outside Idols the previous evening (I understand the VHS tape still exists). The cops knew exactly who they were watching – and who was doing what.

But the senior officer had that special type of unsmiling sarcasm that only police sergeants possess, and he used it to full effect as we were forced to watch the video. The first miscreant to be singled out was Kevin Ball, who could be distinctly seen rearranging the features of an antagonist.

'We would like to speak with this young lady in the yellow pigtails, if anyone knows of her whereabouts,' said the sergeant. 'She may be dangerous, so please do not approach her.'

Next to be singled out was Richard Ord.

'We intend to contact our colleagues in the Royal Canadian Mounted Police to see which of their officers is currently visiting this area. He is clearly in contravention of his oath of office.'

Then it was my turn.

'And who was this caped crusader? The Northumbria constabulary has no need of vigilantism.'

Then it was Martin Scott and his fellow 'Nazis'.

'We have reason to believe that these individuals have connections to a known far-right group...'

And so on. The sergeant knew everything and was basically giving us a good-natured warning as to our future conduct – as well as having enormous fun personally. The bollocking we got from Peter Reid was way in excess of anything that the police said, but underneath this I suspect he was quite pleased that we had all stuck together, looking after each other in a way that a real team does.

We won the fight too.

• • •

The three other games that I would have played in, as a minimum, were away to Tottenham, home to Sheffield Wednesday and away to Everton; a defeat, draw and a win respectively. The 3–1 victory at Goodison Park was Sunderland's first since 1981 and only the second since 1956. There wouldn't be another on this happy hunting ground until 2013.

Win, lose or draw, it was massively disappointing to have waited so long to enter the top flight then only be able to spectate, particularly games that I would almost certainly have played in had not my ankle been held together by carpentry. In fact, I was angry as well as frustrated. This was exacerbated by the knowledge that I would immediately be back on crutches as soon as the season ended when I would have the screws removed. I can't have been easy to live with during such a prolonged downer. My wife would drop me off at The Cavalier pub in Doxford Park and leave me there, sick as a juggler's rabbit.

On Boxing Day we – and Richard Ord especially – exacted some revenge from Derby County by winning 2–0 with goals from his good self and Craig Russell. Kevin Ball broke his jaw in that fixture, but we were now in eleventh place. Exactly halfway through the season and halfway up the league. As well as could be expected.

We played Arsenal three times in eleven days, drawing at Highbury in the FA Cup before winning 1–0 in the league game at home. The Gunners fielded their usual team of instantly recognisable internationals at Roker, whereas we gave a Premier League debut to Darren Williams, signed from York City the previous October for £50,000. There was also a second start of the season for John

Mullin, who had arrived from Burnley the previous season for even less. The winner came when Arsenal's captain turned Ordy's cross past David Seaman. The goal was announced enthusiastically and at many decibels over the PA system.

'Sunderland's first goal of the afternoon was scored by number six: *Tony Adams!*'

This was naughty and dashed ungentlemanly. In fact it was totally unacceptable – but funny. No more was said about it. Dennis Bergkamp was sent off for a horrible high challenge on Paul Bracewell. This was handy because Dennis was one of the best footballers ever to play in the Premier League. However, in the cup replay he scored an exquisite side-footer into the top corner as Arsenal won 2–0.

Being out of the FA Cup was not a huge consideration. The fact that we wouldn't win any of our next thirteen matches – was.

•   •   •

To alleviate the boredom, one of the less discussed symptoms of injury, I would occasionally limp down to Yarm, about thirty-five miles south of Sunderland. Steve Agnew lived there and was a friend and neighbour of Gordon McQueen, the former Manchester United and Scotland defender and by then a coach with Middlesbrough under Bryan Robson. Steve, Gordon and I were having a few beers one day when we were joined by Martin Scott, Gareth Hall, Andy Melville – and Fabrizio Ravanelli, who also lived nearby.

It had been a sensational story when Boro signed Ravanelli. He was an Italian international and his last game for his previous club had been in the 1996 Champions League final, scoring for Juventus as they beat Ajax. He was a striker of international renown and must have had a number of options. So the assumption, rightly or wrongly, was that this superstar had gone to Middlesbrough purely for money. By the end of the day I began to suspect rightly.

Boro had paid £7 million to Juventus for him. This was then the third highest fee ever stumped up by an English club. He was on a reported salary of £42,000 per week. Even if this figure is not quite accurate, he was still one of the highest-paid footballers in the world. I discovered in the course of the afternoon that he managed to consolidate his immense wealth by being as tight as a duck's arse.

Ravanelli loved playing darts and did so for about three hours. Although this might be because darts was free whereas a game of pool cost 50p. While he was chucking arrows, round after round of drinks was bought by other people, including his red wine. It never occurred to him to part with his own cash. By the time I'd had a few I began to speak with theatrical loudness about how this unfathomably tight-fisted Eyetie wasn't paying his way. Regardless of income – you stand your round. Surely this is accepted procedure across the world, including Italy. If it isn't, then the United Nations ought to take decisive action.

Aggers told me that Ravanelli seldom paid for anything. Apparently he would take in his gas and electric bills for his club to pay. His shopping receipts were also reimbursed. I found this hard to respect and not just because I hadn't come from the most affluent of backgrounds. My parents always paid their way and the same was the least I expected from a multi-millionaire. He felt as though he owed nothing. I felt as though I owed him a whack on the shins if we were ever on the same pitch. I don't remember the name of the pub we were in, but I presume it wasn't a Wetherspoon's house as he didn't stuff his pockets with sachets of sauce.

You get your round in and that's that. It's the law.

CHAPTER 12

FRUSTRATION

We already had a small squad and my injury meant there was little cover at centre-back for Richard Ord and Andy Melville. This forced Peter Reid back into the transfer market, and in January 1997 he bought Jan Eriksson from a Swedish club called Helsingborgs IF for £250,000. I wasn't happy about this, as it was the old familiar tale of me losing precedence over a new signing. Jan was twenty-nine and an experienced international with thirty-five caps. He had scored for his country in their win against England at Euro '92 when the Swedes reached the semi-finals. I might not have played again that season; or so it seemed.

Jan was a decent bloke who spoke excellent English. As a player he was physically strong, although he was slightly smaller than he appeared on television. In February, Reidy took us back to The Belfry to prepare for a visit to Aston Villa, by which time Jan still hadn't played a first-team game. I had returned to training by then and was taken along. Jan had to play because Mel had picked up a knock. In fact, we didn't have much of a squad left. Three of our five subs that day, David Preece, Darren Holloway and Paul Heckingbottom, had never played in the first team.

I watched from the Trinity Road Stand as Villa won 1–0. A shot from Savo Milošević squeezed in after a slight deflection off Jan. He had an OK game, but I felt confident on this evidence that if I was available I would be selected ahead of him. I was right about this. It was the only game he would ever play for Sunderland.

The fans were puzzled by the signing of Jan Eriksson. They may have thought he was going to force Ordy or Mel from the side. When he didn't do that they must have supposed, 'Well, Reidy must think he's a better replacement centre-back than Howey.' Nope. This begs the question of why Jan was brought in at all. There is no conspiracy theory to reveal here. It was simply one of the countless transfers in football that didn't work out. The following January, he moved to Tampa Bay Mutiny. A knee injury forced him to retire in 1999 and Mutiny were dissolved two years later. Cheery stuff. Still, the fact that I was preferred to an established international boosted my confidence significantly.

At Blackburn Rovers on 1 March I was mightily pleased to be back on the bench, even if I didn't get off it and we lost 1–0. This marked the end of a tough time for me professionally and personally. Three days later at home to Tottenham there was a similar but worse story. This was probably our least competent performance of the season. We lost 4–0 and were three down after twenty-six minutes. Horrible.

Strangely this was followed the next Saturday by possibly our best performance of the season. We beat the champions Manchester United 2–1 at Roker with goals from Micky Gray and John Mullin. But the slide continued at Hillsborough in midweek when we lost 2–1 to Sheffield Wednesday. That was when I finally made it back on to the pitch, if only for the final ten minutes. I was given another short run-out at Stamford Bridge, the last time I would play up front for Sunderland. Unfortunately the game was lost by the time I was introduced and we went down 6–2, which was a harsh scoreline.

• • •

Harsh or not, we were no longer comfortable and our form was alarming. To arrest the slide, Peter Reid brought in Allan Johnston, a 23-year-old Scotsman who had been a hot prospect at Hearts before moving to Rennes in France. Sunderland gave him his big chance. He was a good-natured, quiet bloke as well as a wonderfully gifted winger. I liked him a great deal.

Another arrival was 36-year-old Chris Waddle, a former England teammate of Reidy's. If you know anything about football in the 1980s and 1990s, you will also know what an incredible player he was. Sunderland signed him from Bradford City for £75,000. Everyone knew how good he was even at that age, to the point where opponents wouldn't even try to tackle him, they would merely attempt to jockey him into passing the ball to a less gifted colleague. He had never possessed pace, but didn't need it. He was also a Sunderland fan.

Despite his talent and fame (he remains a virtual god in Marseille, for example) Chris was another big name who was just one of the lads; another storyteller who liked a laugh and a drink the same as everyone else. I would occasionally be in the social company of Waddler, Niall, Paul Stewart, Paul Bracewell and the like and find this difficult to reconcile with the fact that I was in the same team as them; men I had watched admiringly on television as a kid and when I was playing for a tiny club in a one-horse town in the middle of Belgium.

We also finally managed to recruit some experienced goalkeeping cover for Lionel. The former England goalie Chris Woods would be on the bench for the rest of the season, although he would never actually play.

• • •

Andy Melville was injured at Chelsea and would not feature again that season. This meant that I would replace him in defence and not miss a minute of the seven vital remaining games. The first of the seven was at home to Nottingham Forest who, on current form, were the worst team in the league. This was a big opportunity. We didn't take it.

Dean Saunders and Pierre van Hooijdonk were up front for Forest. Van Hooijdonk was enormous and had been the subject of some hype following his recent move from Celtic. I therefore took great delight in aggressively winning an early header against him and drawing an enthusiastic cheer from the crowd. I was confident and we were in control. Alex Rae went close, Michael Bridges hit the bar, but we didn't take the lead until an hour had passed, when Kevin Ball volleyed in the debuting Waddle's corner at the Fulwell End. Having offered little, a plodding Forest equalised when their full-back, Des Lyttle, scored late with a hopeful prod that bobbled through a crowd of players.

The draw was a damn bad result and no one had done anything wrong. It didn't help Forest either as they would finish bottom of the league. We then had two weeks to forget about it before the short trip to St James' Park on 5 April.

• • •

This would be the only derby I ever played in for Sunderland and my solitary proper appearance at the Temple of Doom. Never before had I experienced such an adrenalin rush. It was something beyond pride and this time I used my emotions positively. I knew that becoming carried away and getting myself injured or sent off would be disastrous, but I would have died for Sunderland that day. Literally. My life for three points? Fair exchange, no robbery.

A few days before the derby, I went to my parents' house for dinner and Steven was there too. Inevitably we chatted about the game. He was coming back from injury and had an outside chance of playing.

My contribution to the badinage was: 'If I get a fifty-fify with you, I'll break your fucking legs.' He laughed at this until he noticed

272

that my stare hadn't dropped. This earned me swift admonishment from our mother ('We'll have none of that at the table!'). *Plus ça change.* As it turned out, Steven didn't play. Not sure why.

People who compare other derbies in England to Newcastle–Sunderland and imagine that they even come close are talking drivel, quite frankly. Derbies in London, Manchester, Merseyside, the Midlands or anywhere else are tea parties, where antipathy is confused with loathing. There is genuine hatred between Sunderland and Newcastle. This isn't something that should necessarily be a source of pride; it's just the way it is.

Things reached such a pitch that visiting supporters were barred from both derbies in 1996–97. It was a daft idea that was never repeated. The futility of it was something that followers of both clubs could actually agree upon.

This game and everything surrounding it was as dynamic as ever, despite the supposed fan ban. I say supposed because there must have been a couple of hundred fearless Sunderland supporters dotted around the ground that day. Naturally they included the legendary Davey Dowell, who had procured a ticket from Kevin Ball. Davey was ensconced in his seat a few rows back, minding his own business and obviously not wearing any colours as we warmed up twenty minutes before kick-off. That was when Bally spotted him and gave him a cheery wave with a hearty 'Hello there, Davey!' to accompany it. Possibly Sunderland's greatest ever fan had to turn round and pretend to be looking for the person that Bally had been yoo-hooing at. That's what we loved about Bally; he was a complete bastard.

The atmosphere by 2.55 p.m. could have been chopped up and applied with brown sauce. It was heightened even further for the locals on the pitch, which for me included Bally, long since subsumed by Wearside. The others for Sunderland were Richard Ord, Chris Waddle, Michael Gray, Michael Bridges and myself. For

Newcastle there was Robbie Elliott, Steve Watson, Lee Clark and Alan Shearer.

You must be on the pitch to truly appreciate the incredible noise that is created in this fixture. It's even louder down there and the sound is not that of singing – it is tens of thousands of people creating as many decibels as possible by any method. I remember screaming at Ordy in the early stages of the game, and he couldn't hear a word. We were about ten yards apart. This was not like any other game. It was perhaps cranked up further because the home fans expected victory, and a convincing one at that.

Why wouldn't they? It was fourth against fourth bottom. Already that season Tottenham and Manchester United had hammered us, whereas Newcastle had beaten them 7–1 and 5–0 respectively. They had an enormously expensive side while our costliest starter that day (making his debut) was Allan Johnston at £500,000 – one thirtieth of what Shearer had cost. The Sunderland fans, many of whom were watching a beamback of the game on a large screen at Roker Park, were fearful.

I wasn't. I just wanted to get on with it. My dad had spoken to me of the dangers of being too pumped up and doing something silly. The irony of Norman being the one to issue this advice was not lost on me, but that didn't make it any less prescient. A few minutes into the game, a high ball was played up to Shearer, who was standing in front of me. My height advantage meant that he was never going to win the header. He was feeling for me to establish exactly where I was without taking his eye off the ball. When he realised how close I was (I was literally not giving him an inch) he threw a backwards headbutt squarely into my face a split second after I had inevitably won the header, making it look like an innocent clash.

This reduced my ambitions, for the time being at least, to booting him up a height. He knew what he was doing and did such things routinely, although he may also have been told by Steven that I was liable to do something stupid if he were to make me angry enough. I tried my utmost, but couldn't get sufficiently close to him for any sort of retribution. So I decided that someone had to suffer vengeance and took it out on David Batty. This was a poor second prize and I was booked for my trouble.

It would surprise me if Shearer remembers the incident; more so if he admitted to it. A year later he booted Leicester's Neil Lennon in the face in the full glare of television cameras, but was still completely exonerated when the FA claimed to believe some extraordinary banana oil about him innocently attempting to free his trapped foot.

We endured an early onslaught, but otherwise there wasn't much in the first half-hour to denote the gulf in class to a casual observer (in the unlikely event of such a person existing). Then I intercepted a careless ball from Ginola in midfield, which I stroked to Waddle (if in doubt) who was just inside their half. He fed it out to Micky Gray on the left. Micky cut inside and struck a fine low shot past the keeper from eighteen yards.

Oh, my.

We went berserk, particularly Ordy and me. We were still fans as well as players, and as roomies we had spoken of little else for weeks. In theory, this should have silenced the place, but it became apparent at that moment just how many Mackems had sneaked into the ground. Before half-time, Shearer missed a one-on-one with Lionel Pérez. The home supporters became ever more anxious, angry, frustrated and quiet as the game progressed. How on earth could Sunderland be winning? The enormity of an away victory did not need to be impressed upon anyone. This was not supposed to happen.

Sadly it didn't. It took them a while – the seventy-seventh minute to be precise – but Warren Barton headed down a hopeful

Ginola cross, which landed behind me at the feet of Shearer, who had, typically, peeled away to score a tap-in. Even then we almost reclaimed the lead. Bally walloped one from the edge of the area into the face of Shaka Hislop, who made a save without knowing much about it. Thus ended a fine game of football and a draw was still a good result for us – and a bad one for them.

While it was 1–0 in the second half, I struck a powerful header direct from a Chris Waddle corner. I really did meet it well. But it hit Hislop. Six inches higher and it would have been a goal. Two–nil, no way back for the Mags and a gigantic step towards safety. I alluded earlier to my goal at Portsmouth that set us off on a run to promotion, toppled governments and discovered new planets. Well, that would have been considered triviality itself compared to a second at St James'. Ballads would have been written about me, T-shirts printed with my image on the front, and I would never have to pay for a drink in Sunderland ever again.

If, if, if, if, if…

But here's a funny thing. Twenty years after my meaty, oh-what-might-have-been header at Newcastle, someone sent me footage of it – and I had no recollection of it whatsoever.

Unusually for a derby, only one yellow card was shown all afternoon. To me.

• • •

Next Sunday we were at home to Liverpool and it was a somewhat dispiriting experience. When we saw their team sheet, we assumed that Robbie Fowler would be a lone striker. So it was agreed that I would mark Robbie tightly with Ordy covering. This plan was put into the long grass when it transpired that Steve McManaman would also play as a striker, something he rarely did. John Barnes was behind them 'in the hole'. Those three saw a great deal of the ball and were quite magnificent. They caused us carnage, although it was only 1–0 at half-time.

I hadn't got near either striker, not even to foul them. As I sat at the interval, I felt for the first time in my life that I really was out of my depth. Fowler and McManaman had done this to more celebrated players than me and would do so for some years to come. I had nothing to answer their ping-ping, pop-pop, one- and two-touch football. My confidence descended further when I missed a good chance with my head when I really ought to have scored. I was so self-absorbed that I didn't hear a word the manager said.

Not long into the second half, it was 2–0. Fowler and McManaman now had a goal apiece. It then seemed to be an issue of how many Liverpool would put in; an alarming thought. I had endured my worst forty-seven minutes in a match.

Then, inexplicably, my problems went away. Liverpool seemed to think that they had won and almost appeared to lose interest, which is dangerous against any opposition. Paul Stewart scored from a Waddle corner with most of the second half remaining. As all bad commentators say, we now had a game on our hands.

However, there were no more goals and the better side won. We hadn't played badly overall, but this was irrelevant, as we needed points. We were now in a relegation spot for the first time that season and there were only four games to go.

• • •

The following Saturday, we went to play Middlesbrough at their recently opened Cellnet Riverside Stadium. Obviously it was always going to have a humdrum atmosphere compared to our previous away game at Newcastle, but, allowing the head to usurp the heart for a change, this was a more important fixture. Middlesbrough were one place and one point behind us, with two games in hand.

Although I was less stressed playing in defence than in attack, as we warmed up, the anxiety of this game gave me a headache. In fact it was rather more than a headache; it was a stabbing pain to the back of my head that I still occasionally suffer from, and I had to pop a couple of paracetamol before kick-off. But I eased myself into the game by giving Fabrizio Ravanelli a couple of juicy whacks in the opening minutes. Wallop! That's what happens to round-dodgers.

He summed himself up with the instructions he kept repeating to his junior strike partner, Mikkel Beck.

'You run. I stay here.'

Ravanelli wanted to be what we called a 'goal-lagger' at school, while Beck did all the work. Fine centre-forward though he was, this was not what the occasion demanded. Beck did as he was told. Perhaps there was a drink in it for him, although I doubt it. He ran to wherever Ravanelli pointed, to no great effect.

Darren Williams had been brought in by Peter Reid to man-mark Juninho, the decidedly tricky Brazilian. Darren was only nineteen and perhaps our fittest player, so this sounded like an eminently cunning strategy – until we found out that Juninho was on the bench.

We would just have to find something else for Darren to do. So, seconds before the break, Chris Waddle took an in-swinging free kick from our right. I was waiting on the edge of the six-yard box, but the ball never got near me. Darren rose higher than anyone and, unchallenged, put a superb header into the empty net.

Juninho was introduced early in the second half. The man was about as skilful as footballers get and we spent much of our time yelling at one another to clatter the little sod – if indeed any of us could get close enough to do so. He was routinely skipping past everyone and it was as though there was more than one of him.

But it wasn't enough for Middlesbrough. The game finished

1-0 and restored a great deal of our confidence. Surprisingly, it was Sunderland's first victory at Middlesbrough since 1962, when Brian Clough scored the winner.

I worked out that the thirteen players we used that day cost about £2.5 million. With the phenomenal amounts of money Bryan Robson had spent, Boro had been heavy favourites. Just to twist the knife further, Darren Williams was a Middlesbrough native too. It was probably his greatest moment, even if it did cost his parents their front window. The match was accurately summarised later in the supernal 2001 book *Let There Be Light*:

> It was amusing to watch *Match of the Day* and see 7 million-pound striker, Fabrizio Ravanelli, being made anonymous by Lee Howey, who cost about a tenner. That said, the winning goal was scored by Darren Williams whose fee was easily in the hundreds.

It was a devastating blow for Middlesbrough. After that, they would win only one of their remaining five games and finish second bottom in what was a strange, strange season for them. Having spent many millions on Juninho, Ravanelli, Beck, Emerson, Festa, Branco and others – plus their massive salaries – they had obviously expected more. They reached both the FA and League Cup finals in 1997, but lost them both.

Their season was encapsulated when the FA deducted them three points for failing to play a fixture at Blackburn. They claimed, somewhat dubiously, that they could not field a full team due to illness. To retrieve the points, they enlisted the expensive help of George Carman QC. Carman was the most celebrated barrister of his day. In criminal trials, he had successfully defended Jeremy Thorpe, Ken Dodd and one of the Guildford Four. He had won libel cases for various newspapers, as well as Imran Khan, Tom Cruise and Nicole Kidman, Mohamed Al-Fayed, Richard Branson and Elton John. Two of his victories effectively put Jonathan Aitken in jail for perjury and financially ruined Gillian Taylforth.

He didn't get Middlesbrough their three points back.

• • •

The pressure to avoid the drop is always intense for the usual professional and financial reasons. At Sunderland in 1996–97 there was added onus because we would be playing in a new stadium in August.

The Stadium of Light was the finest sports arena in England when it opened and it's still one of the best now. Which division we were in marked the difference between playing Manchester United before a raucous full house or facing Bury in a less animated and less-than-full house. Bob Murray pronounced himself 'petrified' at the prospect. The Stadium cost an initial £19 million. Relegation would cost about £10 million: an enormous amount, even if it does seem quaint today.

Two days after Middlesbrough, Paul Stewart, Chris Woods, Allan Johnston and Steve Agnew were given a tour of the new place while it was still under construction. Sitting in a hard hat on the floor of the unseated terrace of what became the West Stand, Paul mused aloud that the front row would be considerably further from the touchline than we were used to at Roker Park. He then alarmed the tour guide by leaping to his feet and bellowing: '*Stewart!* You're fucking *crap!!!*'

He sat back down and reflected: 'Ah. I'll still hear that.'

• • •

The next fixture, our third last, was a Tuesday night home game against Southampton, who were two points and one place behind us. This was every bit as crucial as the Middlesbrough match. But by contrast, this one was a disaster.

Despite it being at Roker, we booked in for the afternoon at the George Washington Hotel along the road, for the pre-match meal and a rest. I was rooming with Ordy again. We were already aware that Niall Quinn would not be starting the game and were perplexed by this. Twenty-two minutes into the match, Alan Neilson played the ball into the air above our penalty area from the Southampton right. As I was about to head it, it curled away from me and I only got the slightest of touches on it instead of the firm header intended. The ball landed precisely between Gareth Hall and myself, perfectly at the feet of Egil Østenstad, who took his goal well.

Quinny was brought on for Johnston immediately afterwards and Southampton's defenders couldn't cope with him. He had one cleared off the line before hitting the bar from the rebound. Then he went close with a volley. The defenders might not have been coping with him, but they were somehow contriving to keep a clean sheet. The game was really only played in one direction after Southampton took the lead. I hit their crossbar with a header and there was a sequence of other near-misses.

Peter Reid buoyed us at half-time with a speech that was later broadcast on *Premier Passions*.

'I don't give a fuck about losing, but I'll tell you what I give a fuck about. Losing *shite!*'

No one could quite bring themselves to tell him that all he had to do to attain grammatical correctness was employ the adverb 'shitely'. It wasn't a high priority at this stage.

Somehow, there would be no more goals. In other circumstances we might have dismissed it as 'just one of those nights', but the result was all that mattered, because when we kicked off our next game we would be in the bottom three. An international break meant that we now had eleven days to swear, kick things and generally rid ourselves of frustration before facing Everton in the last ever league game at Roker Park. With Neville Southall, Gary Speed, Duncan Ferguson, Nick Barmby (again), Dave Watson and the others coming to town, this was not expected to be easy. The match took place on Saturday 3 May 1997, two days after Tony Blair's landslide general election win. If we were to avoid relegation, he would probably have claimed credit for that too.

Despite the pressure, training was no different from normal and the mood was as light-hearted and positive as it had ever been. There was no point in thinking about Southampton, or anything else that we couldn't change now. It was all about Everton.

History weighed upon me. I was quite emotional about this fixture, but I think it was in a positive way. Roker Park had been around since 1898, so it held immense sentimental value for every Sunderland supporter, myself included. We were all excited about the new stadium, but my heart remained at Roker, even if its demolition was the right thing to do. A mercy killing. Whatever the result might be, it would be a source of considerable pride for me just to have played in the game.

We had more than one reason to be nervous and for the first third of the game, it showed. Adding even more to the tension was that although they were in twelfth place, Everton were not mathematically safe. They needed this too. Then on thirty-five minutes everything changed. Attacking the Roker End, Micky Gray floated a high cross towards the back post which Duncan Ferguson, quite inexplicably, shoved away with his left hand raised far above his head. This led to the most fraught, gut-churning penalty kick imaginable. The importance of it did not need to be mentioned. Whoever was about to take the kick deserved credit for doing so, even if he was about to make a complete arse of it.

He didn't. As he proved again in 2016, Paul Stewart was (is) a man of stout heart. Looking considerably calmer than he must have felt, he appointed the ball to the spot before smashing it un-stoppably to the right of Neville Southall to score the final ever goal at the Roker End. We would have no further problems that afternoon.

Strange as it may seem, Peter Reid's chat included: 'Relax. The worst thing that can happen is you get beat. So fuckin' what?'

The stress was virtually expunged on fifty-seven minutes when Southall handled the ball marginally outside the Everton penalty area in the 'D'. Chris Waddle then took a free kick that could not have been bettered by any other footballer on Earth. It travelled like a surface-to-air missile, past the wall and into the top left-hand corner of the net at the Fulwell End.

The way I celebrated, I may as well have been in the Fulwell End. The record attendance at Roker Park was (officially) 75,118 against Derby County in 1933. By 1997, a full house was only 22,000, but the 22,000 watching us play against Everton made the place as deafening as anyone could remember. We were animated by the fervour. Every time we won the ball a roar went up, the fans put-ting wings on our feet, fire in our hearts and all those other things that poets waffle on about. A magnificent occasion with which to end an era. When that sort of momentum is with you, you win. It was one of the best games to play in of my entire career, although I personally didn't have a great deal to do.

The honour of scoring the last goal at Roker Park went to Allan Johnston. Waddle crossed from the left with his 'wrong' right foot and Allan headed it away at the back post. Cue more noise, more delirium and more belief. Of the seven goals we had now scored since Waddle's arrival, he had created five and scored one. That was about the last thing to happen on the Roker Park pitch during its ninety-nine years.

Well, almost.

Duncan Ferguson had become increasingly agitated as the game progressed. He had conceded the penalty, received no joy from Ordy and myself and had been subjected to repeated and highly effective pestering from Darren Williams, who was having a fine game. When Darren had taken the ball from his toes for what must have been the twentieth time, Ferguson's temper went the same way as the three points and he was about to dispose his ire upon Darren, who was significantly smaller than the 6ft 4in. Scotsman. Most people were.

But Ferguson was only an inch taller than I was* and his failure to pick on someone his own size infuriated me. I stood between the two of them to growl as much at Ferguson, adding that he was, in my estimation, a 'Scotch twat'.

Perhaps this presents me in an heroic, albeit inarticulate light, so I should add that the first thought I had after speaking was: 'What are you thinking of, Lee? It's Duncan Ferguson!'

In 1995, he had become the first British footballer to be jailed as the result of an on-field assault: headbutting an opponent while playing for Rangers a year earlier. After serving his forty-four days, he was praised by a Scottish Prison Service spokesman who used the ill-considered phrase: 'He kept his head down.' It wasn't his first offence either.

I stood my ground and pretended I wasn't fearful. Perhaps he was mindful of his past, as well as the yellow card he had already received for the handball, but nothing else occurred. Besides, his teammates dragged him away. It looked to the crowd like common 'handbags'. It didn't feel like it.

At full-time, it was 3–0 and I headed down the tunnel where I kept

---

* I was 6ft 3in. then. Today I am 6ft 4in. This is due to my knee being corrected, my back being fixed and, because I no longer force them into ill-fitting football boots, the arches of my feet are in their proper shape again. I am also a shoe size bigger. This is about as late as a growing spurt gets.

an eye out for Ferguson, but he had lost interest. We returned to the pitch to perform a lap of honour, then had the inevitable drinkies.

•   •   •

I didn't want to leave Roker Park that day, but had to. A minibus arrived at the ground to collect Richard Ord, Martin Smith, Micky Gray and me. The remaining seats were then filled with Ordy's mates from Murton. We were on our way to the NYMEX, now the Manchester Arena, for a boxing match that night. Sunderland's Billy Hardy was challenging Naseem Hamed, a bit of a berk but a sublime fighter, for the WBO and IBF World Featherweight titles. What a day for our city this would be if Billy could pull it off.

After a roadside pick-up of ten cases of refreshments from Aidy Marshall, we pulled in again a few miles down the A19 where we were joined by an attractive stripper called, I believe, Goldie. She demonstrated her art, although she was followed in the car behind by her husband, lest you should think it was in any way tacky or distasteful. She alighted after about half-an-hour. I have no idea who hired her.

We watched Robin Reid win a tough bout against Henry Wharton before Billy took to the ring. Ordy and I bought two drinks each in anticipation of a long fight. We roared at his entrance as we knew how good it would make him feel. This was his hour.

Except that it was some way short of an hour. The whole fight lasted for one minute and thirty-three seconds – including the count. Hamed jabbed and broke Billy's nose with his first punch. Billy felt as though he'd been hit by a heavyweight, or a charging rhino.

We had arranged to meet Billy at a hotel afterwards, but he was understandably not in the mood and retired to bed. Most people will never know how he felt; years of training for that moment. But I have to say that Billy Hardy was a fine boxer. Not for no reason was he given the chance to fight Hamed in the first place. Billy was also a European and Commonwealth champion, not a mug.

We arrived home at around 7 a.m. I may have dreamed this, but I think we left Micky Gray in a fountain in Manchester. If he drowned, he didn't mention it later.

Saturday 3 May 1997 was undoubtedly one of the big days.

• • •

Our final game of the season was at Wimbledon. There were various permutations for the statisticians to ponder. We could lose but still stay up if there were favourable results elsewhere. However, we kept ourselves to but one simple thought:

If we won, then we were still a Premier League team.

We made no assumptions. Why would we? Wimbledon were guaranteed to finish no lower than eighth, had beaten us comfortably at Roker in December and no one ever relished a trip to Selhurst Park. However, the Everton result had restored some confidence, training was fun and I was offered great encouragement in public from complete strangers. The Wimbledon game seemed to be the sole topic of conversation on Wearside. Indeed, much of Wearside would be at the game. Three weeks earlier, 7,979 were at Selhurst to see Wimbledon beat Leeds. When Sunderland came to town there were 21,338.

When we arrived at the ground, we noticed that Wimbledon were still trying that sad little trick with the loud music and were met with the same collective roll of the eye they had received in 1994. Silly people. My nerves had known easier times, but that was nothing to do with the puerile antics of the opposition; it was entirely attributable to the magnitude of the game. We just had to make sure we were OK when the whistle blew.

We were. When we stepped out of that tiny tunnel to start the match we couldn't have been in a better frame of mind. Almost all of the noise was generated by the hordes of visiting fans. If Concorde had flown three feet above the Arthur Wait Stand you wouldn't have heard it. I was concentrating on breathing deeply and willing the referee, Dermot Gallagher, to start the game. It would all be fine once the game was underway.

Wimbledon kicked off. I was momentarily distracted from the game a few seconds into it when a streaker came bounding onto the pitch. After Goldie the previous week, it seemed that indiscriminate appearances by naked women were becoming an accepted feature of life. She had leapt out of the Whitehorse Lane Stand, run over the centre line, inexpertly kicked the ball and was now trotting rapidly in the direction of myself and the adjacent Dean Holdsworth.

She was wearing black training shoes, white ankle socks, a thong that was pink-sequined at the front and plain white at the back – and nothing else. Her flaxen hair flowed midway down her flawless alabaster back, sumptuous, pert, natural breasts glistening in the early summer sunshine, all complemented by a bewitching smile and transfixing eyes of deepest aquamarine. Apart from that I barely noticed her.

It transpired that there was a coordinated spate of streaking models at various Premier League grounds that day as ambush marketing for something or other. Holdsworth had recently been in the papers after being caught *in flagrante* with a glamour model of some prominence (particularly above the navel) who was not Mrs Holdsworth. As the young lady on the pitch drew ever closer, he turned to me and said: 'Christ. I'm in enough trouble already. I hope she's heading for you.'

'So do I, mate. She's fucking beautiful.'

She went straight for Holdsworth. Once she had been escorted away by stewards, who were attempting to look as though they regarded the matter with extreme seriousness, we recommenced.

The respite from the tension was fleeting. I passed the ball to

Paul Bracewell, who had an uncharacteristic rush of blood and wellied it into the stand. Yes, even Brace, with all his experience, medals and caps, was feeling it too. I was open-jawed at this and any hopes we entertained that this might not be such a difficult encounter after all were dissipated there and then. We weren't in such a great frame of mind as we had told ourselves. It was windy, the pitch was dry and hard as oak, so the ball bobbled much of the time. It was frantic. Holdsworth and Jason Euell were difficult opponents. I was intent on doing whatever it took to stop them; easier said than done. The first half was scrappy and goalless and I was glad when it ended. On the other side of the Thames at this stage, Coventry were winning 2–1 at White Hart Lane. As usual, Tottenham could not be relied upon for anything and as things stood we would be relegated by a single goal.

Not that we players knew this. Nor did we want to. Nothing was to deflect any of our attention from the matter in hand, as opposed to matters not in our hands. We played some decent football in the second half and made a couple of chances. Waddle passed when he should have shot. Stewart should have scored with his head from Craig Russell's cross. But the most awful moment came four minutes from time. Wimbledon booted the ball down their left. Ordinarily I would have let it float out for a throw-in. But time was running out and we were still going for victory, so I kept it in with my head. My target was Ordy, who I hoped would come away with the ball and build an attack.

Howl, howl, howl, howl!

It landed at the feet of a grateful Holdsworth, who skipped past Ordy and Micky Gray then played it inside to Euell. From twelve yards, Euell scored. At the other end I headed one backwards to Michael Bridges, who missed his volley in the six-yard box. Full-time: 1–0. We applauded the fans, which was the least they deserved, but I was desperate to get off the pitch.

Micky Gray remained optimistic that other results would save us. Coventry were still leading 2–1 but had fifteen minutes to play. For Sunderland supporters old enough to remember, this was horribly reminiscent of Jimmy Hill's cheating in 1977, which was instrumental in Sunderland's relegation that year – and Coventry's survival. Although twenty years on, the delayed start was legitimate. I was alone in the dressing room while everyone else gathered optimistically around a radio. A Tottenham equaliser would be our salvation, but Coventry held on and stayed up yet again by a single point. A concerto of misery ensued.

Our forty points would have seen us safe in just about any other season. I had no faith in good fortune and the fact that I was proven correct in this did not make me any less inconsolable. That night I got as drunk as it's possible to be without rendering yourself unconscious. Richard Ord told me later that I had 'trashed the bus toilet' in a drunken temper. I had no recollection of it.

I awoke the next day, still in a pit of despair. In fact, I still haven't got over that relegation. It isn't the Wimbledon result that I think of as much as the draw against Forest and, worse still, the defeat to Southampton. That oh-so-important victory at Middlesbrough didn't in reality amount to much because we went down anyway. We were relegated fair and square after thirty-eight games and our demise could be attributed to any one of the twenty-eight games that we failed to win; so it is somewhat irrational of me to blame everything on the Forest and Southampton results. It's just that I do.

• • •

Of course, there should be a sense of perspective. Relegation is not the worst experience a man will endure in his life, even if seems like it at the time. Besides, the long-term damage to Sunderland AFC was limited.

We had players who would obviously be leading lights in Division One: Rae, Gray, Johnston, Ball, Smith, Scott, Quinn. They would be joined by Jody Craddock, Lee Clark, Chris Makin, Nicky Summerbee and the sensational Kevin Phillips. The only surprise was that it took two seasons to return to the Premier League when a record 105 points was won in 1998–99. There was the added pleasure of playing in England's finest football venue, the new Stadium of Light.

The 1997–98 season ended in glorious failure with the play-off final defeat to Charlton at Wembley, 7–6 in a penalty shoot-out after a 4–4 draw (Clive Mendonca doing much of the damage). Ten games into that season, Peter Reid decided that Richard Ord and Andy Melville were not working out at the back and replaced them. This gave Jody Craddock his big chance, but beside him was Darren Williams, who was not really a centre-back. He was too short, for one thing (although it must be conceded that he had some very good days in that position). Promotion was followed by two successive seventh-place Premier League finishes, Sunderland's highest since 1955. These were exciting times on Wearside.

We will never know what the butterfly effect might have been, if any. But I believe that I would have been selected ahead of Darren and I can't stop myself from pondering the griefs and glories I could have been a part of at the club I loved. So you may wish to know: why was I not involved in this enthralling, tumultuous era? The answer is quite simple.

I got pissed and signed for Burnley.

CHAPTER 13

BURNLEY: OH DEAR

The Everton match was not quite Roker Park's final curtain, although it was the last proper fixture there. A friendly had been arranged against Liverpool to say farewell to the old ground on Tuesday 13 May. The reason for this was that Liverpool had been the first visiting team to play there, on 10 September 1898.

The idea was to have a sort of party, celebrating the old and embracing the new. Former players would be wheeled out, turf would be ceremonially dug up and there would be a fireworks display after the match. However, two days after relegation, no one was in the mood to whoop it up and the whole thing became something of a chore. For the record, John Mullin scored and Sunderland won 1–0; the same result as in 1898.

Despite the general despondency across Wearside there was a full house and, to their credit, Liverpool fielded a strong side that included Robbie Fowler, John Barnes, Mark Wright, Jason McAteer, Rob Jones and Michael Thomas.

I did not play. The day before, the screws had been removed from the ankle injury I sustained at Elland Road. Before kick-off I took my son onto the pitch for a kick-about; or the best a man on crutches could do for a kick-about. This was the day before Elliot's first birthday and he was only just walking, but he was faring better than me in that regard. Before a packed Fulwell End he kicked a ball that just about rolled into the net. The fans behind the goal gave a good-hearted and appreciative roar, upon which he burst into tears. This drew a pantomime 'Aaah' that failed to placate him.

My main duty for the evening was to hang about and socialise with both teams in the bar afterwards. This wasn't too much of an encumbrance.

For the first time in my life I arrived at work with a screwdriver. There was some souvenir hunting going on and I didn't want certain items getting into the wrong hands, i.e. hands other than mine. There was one item in particular that Kevin Ball, who also didn't play, was keen to stick up his jumper. All I can say is that I saved him from himself, although I denied everything.

$$\bullet \quad \bullet \quad \bullet$$

Peter Reid's first signing of the summer of 1997 was Lee Clark for a club record £2.75 million. This caused quite a stir (by contrast, the arrival of Kevin Phillips a few weeks later drew barely a murmur). Lee, or Nash as he was known, was not only a Newcastle United player but he was as much a fan of the Mags as I was of Sunderland. He was shown off to the press at the building site that was almost the Stadium of Light, where he said all the right things. More importantly he did all the right things on the pitch.

Having become a pivotal member of Sunderland's promotion-winning side two years later, he was transferred soon afterwards but had in effect been sacked. His position became untenable when he was photographed in an anti-Sunderland T-shirt. He attended Newcastle's 1999 FA Cup final defeat to Manchester United and enjoyed a few shandies. He only wore the T-shirt for a few seconds to please some Newcastle fans who had egged him on, but pictures were taken that soon made their way onto the internet, thereby making Lee Clark a very early victim of social media. It was a stupid thing for him to do; it was supposed to be a bit of fun but he really hadn't thought it through. He still regrets it, but maintains that he wanted to leave anyway as he couldn't bear to play for Sunderland against Newcastle. Whatever; it meant that he was off to Fulham and a player who quite clearly should have been in the Premier League would spend four seasons out of it.

I sympathised with him when it all went wrong. There was no malice in what he did. It was merely horseplay with some mates. Had I been in the reverse situation, then I would have put on an anti-Newcastle T-shirt without a blink. Lee's was a salutary tale for footballers everywhere that they would now have to be considerably more wary in public.

I liked Lee and bear him no ill-will whatsoever. It is too often forgotten that he was superb for Sunderland during his two years there, as well as being a model professional until that fateful afternoon. I knew Lee slightly before he arrived and roomed with him on yet another pre-season tour of Ireland. I don't think he approved of the social hours the rest of us were keeping.

Other new arrivals on that tour were Phillips, who would become a club all-time great and England international; goalkeeper Edwin Zoetebier, who would collect a UEFA Cup winner's medal with Feyenoord in 2002; and Chris Byrne. The last I heard of him he was wanted by police in connection with some stolen boilers from a Plumb Center in Burnley. Also with us on a trial basis, although he was never signed, was Marinko Galič, an established international defender who would play for Slovenia in the 2002 World Cup – where they lost every game.

The final game of the tour was in Dublin against Shelbourne. After a 2–1 win we were given the customary instructions about pleasing ourselves afterwards, but if we weren't on the bus at 9 a.m. the following morning we would, without exception, be left behind.

Niall Quinn had arranged for us to go to some nightclub that was apparently owned by Bono and The Edge. After a while a couple of the lads were dancing with some very attractive women; well dressed and fine figured. Niall was guffawing at the sight of this. So was I when he explained that the ladies were in fact either gentlemen, or had previously been gentlemen. John Mullin in particular took some convincing and wanted evidence.

The next morning we somehow made breakfast and then the bus. Aboard the bus, Steve Agnew was perusing the Irish *Sun* and couldn't help but notice the two-page spread about one of the transsexuals who had been in the nightclub. Another member of our party, who I haven't the heart to name, had not been seen at breakfast. However, at 8.59 a.m. he rolled up in a taxi and shambled aboard. No one said anything, but Ordy simply placed the newspaper in his lap. I don't know what had happened to our man in the eight hours or so before that; quite possibly nothing. But he kept very quiet that day.

• • •

I didn't play against Shelbourne. My final appearance for Sunderland was in the 2–2 draw against Portadown at Shamrock Park on 19 July 1997.

I didn't vacate the bench during the goalless draw with Ajax; the inaugural game at the Stadium of Light. I felt certain I would not be involved in the first game of the season at Sheffield United either. Jody Craddock's arrival meant even more competition to play centre-back and frustration was setting in again.

Several senior players had left. David Kelly was off to Tranmere, Paul Stewart to Stoke, Paul Bracewell would soon join Fulham and Dariusz Kubicki went to Wolves (who never asked me to join, funny that). But first to leave was Chris Waddle, which disappointed more than a few of the fans. He went to Burnley to replace Adrian Heath as player-manager and took Chris Woods with him.

I just wanted to play so I rang Richard Ord's agent and asked if there was anything doing at other clubs. After training one Thursday afternoon, at about four o'clock while I was having a barbecue, Peter Reid phoned me.

'Lee. We've just accepted an offer from Burnley for you. Let me tell you, we don't want you to go. But I know you've been a bit frustrated lately, so it's entirely up to you.'

I told him that I wouldn't mind listening to what Waddle had to say. Four hours later I had checked into a hotel in Burnley. After dinner, in came Mr Waddle accompanied by Burnley's reserve team manager Gordon 'Sid' Cowans. I had admired Sid for many years, mainly from his glory days at Aston Villa where he was a midfielder of the highest order. He was still playing now at thirty-eight, having been signed from Stockport County a few days earlier, and his presence helped to seduce me. Also in attendance were assistant manager Glenn Roeder and Chris Woods, who was a goalkeeping coach as well as a player. The agent was there too.

Chris Waddle gave me his pitch; what he planned for this grand old club and how I fitted into his plans. As more drinks went down, negotiations reached ever increasing technical levels and became intricately detailed in their content.

'Go on, Lee. Sign. It'll be great.'

'I dunno.'

'Pleeeease.'

'Dunno.'

'Go on. Sign. I'll buy you another drink.'

'I'll think about it.'

'Go on.'

'Er.'

'Go on. Go on.'

'All right then. I'll sign.'

By then it was 3 a.m. Oh dear. Worst decision ever.

• • •

I can't say that I regret going to Burnley. It set me on an indirect path to meeting the woman who is now my wife and mother of my two younger sons. But in purely professional terms, it was about as bad a choice as I could have made. For a start, it meant that I had dropped down two leagues in the space of three months, as well as leaving the club that was dearest to me. Still, I was more likely to be playing first team football and I would be working with some very good people.

There was no outcry from Sunderland fans when the news of my departure broke and my name is unlikely to crop up in their conversations about the club's all-time greats. However, I hope they think fondly of me. I will always consider it a privilege to have played for that fabulous football club, and in return I really did give my all during my four years there. How good my best was is something you can discuss among yourselves, but I assure you I could not have tried any harder. Burnley paid £200,000 for my services, which meant that, even if my wages between 1993 and 1997 are put in the liabilities column, Sunderland made a profit on me. For an initial outlay of £6,000 and a very modest salary, Sunderland AFC squeezed eighty first-team appearances out of me in defence as well as attack. I was lucky enough to score a few goals too, some of which were very important. I contributed to the 1996 promotion, which was a big step forward for Sunderland as ever since they have, until 2018 at least, either been a Premier League side or a top three Championship side. This seemed impossible before 1995–96.

I wasn't Lionel Messi, or even Niall Quinn. But be fair; what more could any reasonable person want from me?

• • •

In the correct order, a desire to play first team football, eloquent persuasion and Guinness had played a part in my decision to move to Burnley, but the money wasn't bad either. Despite dropping two divisions, I was to be paid a basic of £1,400 per week; £300 more than at Sunderland. I signed a three-year contract with a signing-on fee of £20,000 at the start of each year, so £60,000 if I lasted until a third year. An added attraction was that Burnley is a fine club with a rich history. They were founder members of the Football League in 1888 and have been champions of England twice; the same as Tottenham Hotspur.

At around the same time, Chris Waddle signed Mark Ford from Leeds (the same bloke who scored against Sunderland when I broke my ankle), Mike Williams from Sheffield Wednesday, Neil Moore from Norwich and Steve Blatherwick from Nottingham Forest. I have already mentioned Gordon Cowans and Chris Woods. Some decent players were already there, including prolific goal scorers Paul Barnes and Andy Cooke, David Eyres, Glen Little, Chris Brass and goalkeeper Marlon Beresford. Waddle wanted us to play football attractively and on the ground.

Having informed my wife that I was now a Burnley player, the club put me up in a very comfortable hotel and told me to report for training. So far so good, but certain realities struck me at the first session.

When I was a kid, I would be picked up and taken to football by my dad's mate, Ronnie Cowie. Ronnie drove a BMW and simply looking at this machine was enough to make me coo (bear with me if you're not interested in cars). I decided that as soon as I could afford it, I would have one. It wasn't until I was at Sunderland that I bought myself a red BMW 316, later a black 318 and six months before signing for Burnley a 325i convertible that was kitted out like an M3. It cost about £24,000, which wasn't much less than the price of my first house. I appreciated my money. It was still only four years on from my days at BT and I could also remember eating the same cheap meal every day for two years as an apprentice at Ipswich.

When I arrived at Burnley's training ground in this vehicle I immediately felt conspicuous because my new teammates were turning up in Peugeot 106s, Ford Escorts and the like. I rather wished I had gone by bus. Mike Williams had done the same as me, having also been a Premier League player the previous season. It was like popping down to the local in a tuxedo and the last thing I wanted was to set myself apart in any way.

The training ground itself was on the outskirts of the town in Padiham and was, quite frankly, a hovel. I understand it is considerably more swish these days, but in 1997 it could not have been spoiled by arson. The rooms within appeared to have only been deemed suitable for professional footballers when cattle refused to use the buildings. It was a long, long walk from the changing rooms to the pitches, over fields and a bridge. Surprisingly, the playing surface was decent, although susceptible to waterlogging, what with Lancashire being familiar with prolonged periods of rain. Despite my time at Hemptinne and Bishop Auckland, I had since become accustomed to better. Having suddenly descended two leagues, I would just have to get used to worse and the realisation of this was instant.

Of more concern was the atmosphere in the squad. Glen Little and another midfielder called Gerry Harrison patently didn't like Glenn Roeder. For the first time ever in a dressing room, I felt like an outsider. Not part of a team, but someone who had been brought in to do a job. A 'them and us' situation developed rapidly between the new intake of players and staff, and those who had been there for a while.

My debut went quite well. I was up front against Lincoln City at Sincil Bank and I scored the equaliser. It was the League Cup first round, first leg. We drew 1–1 and went on to win the tie.

Then someone stole four pairs of boots from me. At Sunderland I had been sponsored by Nike; not for money, but I never went short of boots and other kit. Brian Marwood, a Seaham lad and former England player, was a marketing manager at Nike. He called me to say that the arrangement was now over as I had dropped out of the Premier League. However, he told me to call into the shop in Doxford Park and take a bag of gear as a sort of severance. This included four pairs of Nike Tiempo, top end footy boots, two pairs for soft ground and the others for firm ground. The day before my home debut against Gillingham, all four pairs were hoisted from the training ground. How very hospitable. There was a shrewd idea around the club as to the identity of the culprit, but nothing provable.

A more immediate problem than this whodunit was that I had no boots. Our games teacher at St Aidan's would have made me play in my brogues, but that wasn't an option here. David Eyres had a deal with Adidas in Stockport and managed to procure me a pair of Predators, which weren't exactly to my liking, but it was either them or socks. I was grateful.

I was back to centre-forward and we were dreadful against Gillingham. Glenn Roeder was berating David Eyres, who snarled increasingly in consequence. An opponent bore David's wrath and he was sent off. This meant that I played centre-back for the second half, where I was more at ease, and was also given the captain's armband. I did quite well and we drew 0–0, but it was a poor show overall and the rancour in the dressing room at full-time was something I was glad to retreat from. I returned home to Sunderland afterwards, where I had time alone to cogitate over just what the hell I had got myself into.

Back on the training ground, Chris was attempting to instil his philosophy: don't just thump the ball, full-backs should push up, centre-backs should be available wide, keep the ball down and beat the opposition with passes. Perhaps it was too sudden a change for some of the squad, who were simply unused to receiving the ball in tight situations in their own third of the field. In those days it was more common to launch the ball down the wings and the play-from-the-back idea was a novelty. This meant that we would too often lose the ball while the crowd was baying for us to 'just get it up the pitch'.

Perhaps the manager, himself one of the most naturally able footballers of his generation, was expecting too much of players in the third tier. His methods worked at times and we played some attractive stuff. But as the season progressed the fragility of our defence, as it learned a more technical approach, became apparent. I was trying to establish an understanding with the other centre-back, Steve Blatherwick, which was proving difficult because of his inexperience. He had barely played first team football at this stage. He was a big, solid defender and could head a ball further than most players could kick it. But he found it hard to adapt to the Waddle model. The problems at the other end were even easier to identify. We didn't score in any of our first six league games and only managed five goals in the first ten. No great expertise was required to identify the problem. Solving it was a different matter.

After three goalless draws and three 1–0 defeats, we took our derring-do to Bootham Crescent, where for the first half we played well against York City. We were one up at the interval thanks to Paul Barnes. But the second half was a disaster. A goal kick to your team is generally considered to be one of the game's less precarious situations. However, at Burnley in September 1997, we could craft danger for ourselves from anything and this one was especially creative.

Two minutes after City had equalised, Marlon Beresford, a fine, fine goalkeeper, ran up to take the kick, whereupon he stubbed his toe on a protruding section of Yorkshire. The ball trickled a metre or so outside the penalty area where City's striker Rodney Rowe capitalised on this thoughtful gift, effortlessly stroking the ball into the net. He didn't even say thank you. This was only part of the inevitable capitulation and York won 3–1. All the clichés about what happens when you're bottom of the league were proving to be annoyingly correct.

My father was at the game with my Uncle John (McClements) and was characteristically honest. Norman said that I had not performed badly. Trust me, if he had thought I was crap he would have said so. He also thought we had the makings of a decent side if we could stop the silly mistakes.

Back at training on Monday there was a 'clear the air' meeting in the weights room. Chris, who had verbally assailed us after the game at York, made the point that he didn't think everyone was giving their utmost, but set apart Chris Brass and myself for exoneration. This was a nice compliment, although it didn't exactly swell our popularity with the rest of the squad. A well-attended but uncontrolled slanging match ensued, so I wouldn't like to quantify just how much air was actually cleared. Paul Barnes stormed out, ranting 'This is fucking shite!'

It certainly didn't raise morale. The next game was a 4–0 defeat at home to Stoke City in the League Cup. Peter Thorne and Graham Kavanagh scored twice each and generally did whatever they fancied. Steve Blatherwick and I had an execrable evening, although we weren't alone in this, and that included Waddle. He dropped himself for the next game.

If I had to pick one game that epitomised my time at Burnley then I would plump for the fixture at Brentford on 27 September 1997. Brentford, who were bottom of the league, took a very early lead but we settled down after that. I played well myself and Mark Ford equalised shortly before an hour had passed. It was a very watchable, even game. My main concern was that Mark was a little too motivated and had been spoken to several times by the referee, Rob Styles, who had already booked him. As captain I firmly told Mark to calm himself down because we could win if we kept eleven men on the pitch. Can you see what's coming next?

Neil Moore was playing centre-back alongside me and in the seventy-fifth minute he lost the ball, leading to a chase between myself and Marcus Bent, who was by some margin the faster runner. I did my utmost to stop him legally, but the upshot was that we were both left on the ground and I was dismissed for a professional foul. Fifteen minutes later, sitting alone in the visitors' dressing room at Griffin Park, I heard the unmistakable roar of a home crowd celebrating a winning goal. This was the only red card I ever received in either the Premier or Football League.

For the record, four other red cards were waved at me in my time. The first was for Ipswich reserves against Crystal Palace (fighting) and two were in Belgium (fighting). The last one was in the death throes of my career for Bedford Town against Hitchin Town for a second bookable offence. That second yellow was the only time in my career I was ever booked for dissent. A Hitchin striker made his way into our penalty area and performed the most blatant dive this side of Tom Daley. It was still enough to fool the linesman, who waved his flag vigorously. He waved it even more vigorously a few seconds later after I had given him every insult possible within such a limited timescale. I was down the tunnel before the referee had produced the red card.

Three weeks after my dismissal at Griffin Park I had my nose smashed at Wrexham. What a jolly season I was having. Twenty minutes or so into the game at the Racecourse Ground, I took a few steps backwards to head a long Wrexham goal kick. As my head connected with the ball, approaching from the right was their forward Karl Connolly, who managed to jump and flick his head back into my face with unintended precision.

We both descended to the turf, him clutching the back of his head and me supine and holding the bridge of my nose together. My teammates gathered round as our physio, Nick Worth, attended. He told me to move my hand so he could see, which resulted in an Itchy & Scratchy type blood squirt. The claret fountained six inches upwards and Mark Ford nearly passed out at the sight of it. Poor him. Karl left the pitch shortly before I did and, as I stood up, Waddler asked if I would be coming back on. I would.

Before that I was taken to the medical room. Karl Connolly was already there and being examined by the doctor. I (pardon the pun) butted in and asked Karl if he was going back out.

He replied: 'Fuck that. I need stitches.'

Taking that as a 'no', I told him to get off the bench as I would be. The doctor explained that he would be unable to give me an anaesthetic before he sewed my nose back on.

'Just do it, please. Use a stapler if you like; it won't be any more painful.'

Ten minutes and eight stitches later I returned to the pitch and made it to half-time. As I sat in the dressing room my head began to pound and I could literally feel my face swelling. The inflammation became so bad that my vision was seriously impaired when I returned to the field. It was like being a kid and putting empty toilet rolls over your eyes, trying to look through them like binoculars. I lasted about ten minutes, subbed after trying to clear the ball and missing it by an estimated twenty-six feet. Still, my agony helped us to yet another scintillating goalless draw that the fans would be talking about for literally minutes to come. Great days.

No they weren't. We then had a midweek game at Plymouth in which I participated with a plaster over my stitches. None of that *Phantom of the Opera* facemask nonsense you see today when a player has endured so much as a burst pimple. We were proper men. Rrrrrr. I now have a scar on the bridge of my nose that actually looks like a letter C; so no one can say that Karl Connolly never made an impression on me. His second initial will adorn my sneck for ever.

Anyway, the game at Brentford was when the atmosphere at Burnley really palled. By the end of November we had won just three of our nineteen league games and were eliminated from the FA Cup. We drew 3–3 at Rotherham (a division below us) in the first round. One of Rotherham's goals came from a clearance by Chris Brass on the edge of our penalty area. It struck an opponent on the knee and hurtled into our net. Some ignorant cynics had the audacity to compare it to my world-class strike for Sunderland against Bristol City in 1994. We lost the home replay 3–0 to the ever-burgeoning discontentment of the Turf Moor faithful. It was shown live on Sky too, just so everyone could share the joy. In fairness, Trevor Berry scored a wonderful chip for the second goal, although that somehow failed to ameliorate our supporters' mood.

I personally was given a disproportionate amount of stick. Being a well-paid and relatively high-profile signing meant that more was expected of me, and my mere best was not enough. Many years later, Chris Waddle said: 'Whoever I bought was going to be well-scrutinised; £30,000 was like £3 million and every penny was well-accounted for.'

Andy Cooke, by contrast, was something of a crowd favourite. Chris put him on the bench for the next game and replaced him with me as centre-forward. This was despite me being ostensibly a defender by now and barely having played up front for some time. The news was not received politely. Our opponents that day, Northampton Town, had only just been promoted but were sixth. They would end the season at Wembley, where they lost the play-off final to Grimsby. They were managed by Ian Atkins and my erstwhile roomy, Ian Sampson, was centre-back. They also had

Kevin Wilson, who I knew from Ipswich. I had warm conversations with all of them before the kick-off.

None of this mutual backslapping meant that I was about to ease off on the field. Short on confidence, although not desire, I decided to regress to the days of Plains Farm and become as horrible as possible to play against. In anyone's estimation, the game was not 'one for the purists'. By half-time my aggression meant that I had inadvertently broken the nose of Ray Warburton, who played on. I had also caused a cut to Ian's head. They both responded in kind. Still, even the purists would have to concede that violence was all that stood in the way of the game becoming entirely drab.

In the second half I dived to head the ball in Northampton's six-yard box and was kicked in the ribs. Accidental, but painful. As I lay there, wondering if I was still intact, I was spat at by some Burnley fans whose mood had been further inflamed by Ali Gibb giving Northampton the lead. Festooned in gob, I rose groggily to my feet, shook my head and jogged away. A few people disapproved of my ingratitude for the saliva shower, as though such incidents were somehow perfectly acceptable because we-pay-our-money. I was then booed every time I received the ball. The peak of my career had passed. It had left me at Selhurst Park six months earlier.

Burnley's support was and remains superb. It is a small town, but virtually everyone who lives there supports their local club, despite the proximity of Manchester and Merseyside. They are undeniably passionate. However, at every club there is a dimwit contingent (remember the Sunderland fan at Prenton Park?) who imagine that verbal and, in this case, physical abuse of players is okey-dokey and even in the interests of their club, despite the overwhelming evidence to the contrary. Most supporters are aware of the reality and, with the exception of this tiny percentage, I still say Burnley fans are among the best.

It was horrendous. Chris Waddle went on the radio after the

game to defend me – my attitude was first-class, I was a model professional, etc. This was gratifying, even if it didn't help much. This was the beginning of the end for me at Turf Moor.

Incidentally, we beat Northampton 2–1.

I returned to centre-back for the next game against Bristol City at Ashton Gate, a ground I like. The abuse was more concerted there, with about forty Burnley 'supporters' (look up the definition of 'support' in a dictionary) yelping obscenities at me during the warm-up. The other lads were very supportive and urged me to ignore them. This isn't easy, but a thick skin is essential in football. I had a decent if unremarkable game, which did nothing to revise the opinions of my unstinting detractors as we lost again, 3–1, despite leading at half-time. In fact, we played quite well as a team, but results are everything. If you play badly and win, you're OK.

I played on for the next few games with a pelvic injury. There was quite some pain just above my pubic bone. So I popped my usual brand of anti-inflammatory tablets and got on with it. Defeat at home to Wigan was followed by defeat away to Fulham, with Paul Bracewell in their side. The latter game was televised from Craven Cottage on the Friday before Christmas.

Again, we played passably well.

Again, we lost – to a late Danny Cullip goal.

Again, playing passably well is a fat lot of use when you can't score a goal. I would have been given man-of-the-match by Andy Gray on Sky, were it not for the policy of giving the award to someone on the winning team. I was complimented, but fine words butter no parsnips and, if ever a man needed his parsnips buttered, it was me at Burnley.

After a goalless draw with Chesterfield, another barnstormer, we travelled to Gillingham on 3 January for our latest defeat. By now my pelvic niggle was becoming more serious and, although I lasted the whole game at Priestfield, my season was virtually over.

More bad news. I underwent X-rays and an exquisitely painful cortisone injection into the bone, which consisted of being stabbed five times with a needle by our club doctor, Norman Bates.

I would manage three run-outs as a substitute in March, but that was all that would be seen of me in the remainder of 1997–98. Matters did not improve greatly in my absence, but enough points were squeezed to mercifully avoid relegation. I was an unused sub on an extremely jittery final match of the season at home to Plymouth Argyle, who were on the same number of points as us before kick-off. We had to win and hope that Brentford would lose at Bristol Rovers. Our wishes were granted and with them came the true highlight of the season: its end.

We needed a holiday and I was one of a few of the lads who had planned one in Puerto Banús. We flew out a day or two later. When we arrived at the airport to depart, Chris Waddle rang me to say that he'd resigned. He had spoken with the chairman, Frank Teasdale, and was on his way. He wished me well and that was that. His experiences had put him off management for life. Chris Woods, Gordon Cowans and Glenn Roeder were to leave too.

The only thing for it was to temporarily forget about everything and enjoy a few days of laughter and hooliganism on the Costa del Sol. So we did.

• • •

After Puerto Banús and some time back in Sunderland, I heard that Burnley had appointed Stan Ternent who, amid some rancour, had been dragged from the management position down the M66 at Bury. We were a division below Bury, but a much bigger club. I was aware of Ternent and knew that he was 'old school', which did not concern me. I was ready to go again whoever was in charge.

Stan's playing career had been confined mainly to Carlisle

United. As a coach and manager he had been round the doors, but was originally from Gateshead and, like me, a Sunderland fan. He actually signed for Sunderland as a player, but a knee injury meant that he only managed two appearances in something called the Texaco Cup, so he became a coach for a while at Roker Park in the 1970s. I held no assumptions that any of this would mean favourable treatment for me. Indeed, I didn't want any.

This was just as well. In my opinion, whatever limitations Ternent may have possessed as a player, coach and manager, his credentials in those fields would easily surpass his merits as a human being.

How to describe Stanley Mephistopheles Ternent? Physically he was short, grey and granite-featured. His personality is more difficult to present on the printed page. All I can do is compare him to someone you are all familiar with. So think of someone like Adolf Hitler, but arrogant and bad-tempered.

Ternent was about as modest as Cassius Clay; the sort of bloke who could peer into the night sky, at the countless stars and the ever expanding universe – then wonder why he still felt so significant. His manners reflected this and he was one of life's finger-clickers. He also considered himself to be the last word in cleverness, without silly things like evidence to back this up. He's still out there now, waffling away to anyone who will listen about how he would have taken Burnley to the Premier League had it not been for that pesky collapse of ITV Digital, which apparently only affected Burnley. In fairness, he had done well at Bury and would be promoted with Burnley (he may have mentioned it), although he was finally given the boot by the club in 2004 after they had regressed to relegation-fighting ways.

He was intimately acquainted with the more progressive management theories: screaming, swearing, bullying, losing your temper every three minutes and telling everyone in sight that they were fucking useless. The Yosemite Sam of football. He tried these complex techniques immediately upon arrival. On his first day at pre-season training he made an entrance that almost put paid to the hinges of the changing room door and, undeterred by barely knowing most of us, launched into an immediate tirade.

'Yer all a useless load of shit.'

Note 'useless' as well as 'a load of shit.' I let it pass. Tautology would turn out to be the least of his shortcomings. He continued.

'Yer were a fucking disgrace last season. Yerra buncha cunts. An absolute shower of shit.'

He felt compelled to use these little pet names, as though anyone was labouring under the misapprehension that 1997–98 had been a season of unbridled glory. Then he delivered his 'plan'.

'I'm gonna run the fuckin' legs off yerz and wer gonna be fitter than anyone.'

That was 50 per cent of his strategy. The other half was even more depressing.

'Can anybody take a long throw-in?'

Someone, it might have been Paul Weller, raised his arm.

'Right. Yer in my fuckin' team.'

Paul was a good player with other aspects to his game, but a long throw was what Ternent seemingly coveted above all of them. Paul turned out to be injured for most of the season (by the way, if you ever meet Paul, make a joke about re-forming The Jam; I guarantee he has never heard it before and he will laugh for an hour).

I kept my head down and did the training. The new manager hadn't exaggerated the amount of running he required, although it wasn't as bad as Terry Butcher's regime. I played at centre-back during the pre-season friendlies alongside Neil Moore. I played left and Neil was right, which didn't help my right knee as kicking with the left means planting the right. But I was in the team and so kept shtum.

• • •

For pre-season we travelled to Devon, where our accommodation was the University of Exeter's halls of residence. We played Tiverton and were told afterwards that we could have a few beers, on condition we were back before midnight.

A jolly time was being had in Exeter city centre when, at about 11 p.m., we had a happy yet unintended meeting with the Sunderland squad. They were in the area to play Plymouth Argyle, Yeovil and Weymouth. It was lovely to catch up, but one o'clock seemed to arrive earlier than it should. I was then invited to visit their hotel by Niall Quinn, the *de facto* ringleader (bridle your surprise if you can), to play cards and have a few more drinks. It was a plush hotel, its salubriousness accentuated by the comparison with our halls of residence. I was back in my own bed by around 4.30 a.m. The perfect crime?

Of course not. At 7 a.m. there was a bang on the door to abruptly inform me that there would be a meeting before training. I made it there, not in absolutely pristine condition, it has to be said, but I was well practised at this sort of thing. We sat on the training pitch in the sun, although I was looking for some shade.

Ternent began a speech. Amid the obscenities, I could make out something about rules and regulations. He had stayed up until 2 a.m. and therefore knew when everyone had returned to the digs. The exceptions to this were those of us who had been out way beyond 2 a.m., thereby giving him no idea as to exactly when we had got back. Neil Moore, Mark Winstanley and I were to be sent home in disgrace. This didn't quite imbue me with the intended terror and I decided to have a couple of hours' kip before packing. My sleep was interrupted by Mark, who was quite nervous about the situation, wondering what was to become of us. I hadn't until this point realised that you were supposed to take any notice of curfews.

As I packed, there was another knock at the door. It was Sam

Ellis, the assistant manager, who had quite reasonably come to ask for an explanation. I told him the truth, with one omission. Sam listened intently and then gave a few seconds of silent thought to the situation before passing sentence.

'You're fined £200 but you're not going home. Just stay here with us.'

An apology was due to Sam and Stan Ternent. I duly delivered it and that was the end of the matter. A two hundred quid fine and a bollocking.

The one omission in my otherwise honest version of events to Sam was that I had won £400 at cards.

• • •

I hadn't moved to a house in the area and would either stay in a hotel or at Glen Little's place, or commute from Sunderland. I was given a reprieve from this when Ronnie Jepson, a new signing and an amiable chap, invited me to a day at York Races. I was glad of the invite and while I was there I met Peter Swan, a former centre-back for Burnley who was then at Bury. Through my brother I knew Peter quite well and was among a few people invited back to his place in Wakefield. Peter told me that our manager was trying to sign him back to Burnley. Apparently Ternent had told him: 'Hang fire. I'll get that big twat out.'

This referred to me and I took exception to the statement. Not all of it: I was big, and my status as a twat had long been confirmed. It was the bit about getting rid of me that was at issue. Peter's candour and straightforwardness made a silhouette of Stan's underhandedness. I needed to be on my guard. Consequences of the incident in Exeter would perhaps be more serious than I had thought, although I think I was a marked man even before that.

Back at training I was walking the light-year or so from the changing rooms to the pitch when Sam Ellis appeared and began to make what appeared to be polite, desultory chit-chat about what I had been doing at the weekend, what my travel arrangements were and so on.

After training I was called to the manager's office. I sat outside the door for forty minutes with no clue as to why I was there. Eventually Stan finished his colouring-in and summoned me inside.

He glowered then barked: 'Ah've 'eard yer commuting.'

'Yes.'

'Right. Yer fined a week's wages.'

'What for?'

'Yer were given £7,000, tax-free relocation money when yer signed. Yer still haven't moved inter the area.'

This was true. I had initially rented a place in Harrogate, forty miles away. But my wife hated it and returned to Sunderland, while I continued to travel. Ternent had a point, but the way he set about making it was obviously designed to instigate an argument. Fore-warned is forearmed. I arranged with Glenn Little to rent his spare room, then explained the situation to my wife. I would return home when I could. At least I was in the team.

Not for long. I played in the first two league games and in both legs of an abysmal League Cup defeat to Bury. In the second leg I received a knee in the back, which prevented me from training and left me smarting more than a bit. This was four days before the next game, at home to York City. On Thursday, Ternent asked me how I was feeling. He was concerned; not for my back, which had throbbed since Tuesday, but because he was desperate. We had a mounting injury list and he needed me. The only alternative was eighteen-year-old Chris Scott, who was simply out of his depth (a grand lad, but his next club was Leigh RMI). I told Stan I was struggling quite badly, which was the truth. I was always desperate to be in the first team at all my clubs. We agreed to see how I felt the next day. That was Friday and he spent much of it hectoring and begging me to play. True to my pliable form, I agreed. I would pop a couple of tablets and play.

The York game was in its infancy when I began to die on my arse. Due to the pain, I could barely run and their forward line was quick to realise this. Ternent had made a mistake in persuading me and I had been wrong to agree. However, late in the half we took a free kick that was cleared, then punted back into their penalty area, presenting me with the opportunity to score with a diving header. My header struck the outside of the post; I probably should have scored, but was instead left writhing on the pitch in increasing agony from my back. The ball was cleared again, but my immediate priority was oxygen.

Somehow I managed to last the half. In its dying minutes (and the adjective is used advisedly) we took a throw-in down the left, deep into York territory. Virtually immovable by now, I was standing a few yards from the dugout where Ternent's cutting edge ideas on motivation were being put into practice.

'Gerrin ter the box, you!'

'I can't. I'll never get there.'

'*Get yer fucking lazy arse up there!*'

That was it. I told him to fuck off as loudly as possible.

The throw was taken before the whistle ended the half a few seconds later and I stormed off the pitch in a combustible frame of mind, furious at what I had been given in recognition of playing in constant physical discomfort for this man. This was the only time in my career I had ever considered playing to be a favour to a manager, rather than what it should have been – a privilege.

To rein in my temper in the immediate aftermath, I sat in the dressing room with my head between my knees. Ternent huffed into the room and began to weave his managerial magic by (what else?) telling everyone in turn how useless they were. My turn came, loudest of all.

'And *you!* You will never, *ever*, talk ter me like that again. And you will *never* play fer this football club again.'

I stood up, took my shirt off and threw it in his face, then headed for the shower. What was he going to do? Stop me from playing for this football club ever again? He'd just said he was going to do that anyway.

He then said much the same thing to Mark Winstanley, Steve Blatherwick and Mike Williams. It was true too. The four of us had played our final game for Burnley.

Posturing to the fans, Ternent then gave his version of events to a press conference broadcast on BBC Radio Lancashire, among other outlets. Effectively he managed to sack us with maximum publicity and drama; a touch of class and the sort of professionalism we had come to expect of him. That said, blaming players who were signed by another manager is quite a shrewd move if self-interest is your motivation.

The result of the York game itself was a relative triumph. We only lost 1–0.

It did my back no favours, but I drove back to Sunderland, where I told myself that if I really was out of Turf Moor then it was probably for the best. A few drinks with the lads will always make life seem better, even if it really isn't. At about 7 p.m., I was called by Sam Ellis, instructing me to be back at the ground by 9.30 a.m. the next day.

This I did. Mark Winstanley and Steve Blatherwick were there too and we were kept waiting for forty minutes while Ternent had his cuticles treated or whatever. I was to be mulcted again; another week's wages for going home. It seemed that not only was I expected to live in Burnley, I was to remain within its boundaries unless granted permission, like a 1990s feudal system. Things like wishing to see my wife and toddling son were of no interest or consequence.

I was then ordered to go outside where 'Mick's going t' run yer inter the fuckin' ground'. This referred to Mick Docherty, another former Sunderland and Burnley player and the son of the redoubt-able Tommy Docherty. He was a lovely fellow and apologetic about having to do the dirty work. After an hour of the usual running and leaping about we were told we could leave. I went back to Sunder-land and returned to the training ground the next day, whereupon I received yet another summons to see Davros. As always when he spoke, t'was like poetry.

'Yer went back ter fuckin' Sun'land again, didn't yer?'

'Yes.'

'Fined another week's wages.'

'You can't do that.'

'Ah can. Ah've told yer, yer need permission off me. Yer've been given this money...' blah, blah, blah. I was also informed that I would not be training with the first team. I would have to wait until after the sessions had finished and then be worked by Mick on my own – and that this would be my life until I left the club. That night I didn't drive back to Sunderland, I stayed with Glenn Little.

I contacted the PFA to explain the situation, but they couldn't do much for me. Ternent found out and told me not to do that again, adding: 'The PFA won't beat *me*.' What a line. He must have been a big fan of bad films.

I complied, not wishing to incur yet another fine from this megalomaniac. However, I ensured that I turned up for training each morning stinking of drink. I would have a skinful the night before to ensure that I was hungover and incapable of training as hard as Ternent wanted (Glenn was doing the driving). Simply to annoy him, I was drinking whether I wanted to or not. It was a rare example of someone getting pissed on principle. Everything I did was at quarter pace; going through the motions, then repeating the charade the following day.

After perhaps three weeks of this, I travelled back to Sunder-land. How Ternent found this out I have no idea, but he did. Sam

Ellis rang again to say I was to report at Turf Moor once more at 9.30 a.m. the next morning, because Brian Little wanted to sign me for Stoke City. I had decided I would go there without hearing any more about it.

I arrived at the appointed hour and was made to wait the now customary forty minutes while Ternent counted his felt tips. Eventually I entered his office, where he was sitting with his feet on the desk (his little legs had done well to get them there). You could have warmed your hands on his arrogance. What was one of God's more serious errors about to say this time? He began with his catchphrase.

'Fined a week's wages. Yer went 'ome again, didn't yer.'

'Yes. I wanted to see my wife and son.'

No ice was cut by this. Nor was the fact that my wife was now pregnant again. There is no point in arguing with someone who eschews reason to such a spectacular degree. So I asked him about Stoke.

'Ah've told them ter fuck off.'

He probably had too. He was never one to defer an opportunity of telling someone to fuck off, just because a simple 'no thank you' would suffice. He liked to call a spade a cunt.

I was then back outside for more solitary training. I contacted the PFA again, but still they couldn't do anything. I was acutely aware that he was trying to make life intolerable, but miserable though I was, I was also stubborn and simply plodded on with the relentless training, irritating him with my mere presence. I desperately wanted to leave but wasn't going anywhere unless it suited me.

A week later I was called by Ian Atkins, who was managing Northampton Town. Would I go on loan to Sixfields? I told him 'yes' and that I would walk the 170 miles there in my socks over broken glass and dog shit if necessary (I didn't want to let him know how keen I was). This time Ternent agreed.

•　•　•

My debut for Northampton Town was at Colchester United on Tuesday 10 November 1998. We lost 1–0. I have no recollection of the game whatsoever and had to look it up. But my home debut eleven days later I remember vividly. We played Reading and lost 1–0 again. I played as striker in both matches. As you can imagine, I was distinctly off the pace, having trained neither properly nor entirely soberly for some weeks. I hadn't played first team football for three months.

I was substituted at half-time. This was dejecting and it was difficult not to dwell on my Premier League experiences, which had only been in the previous calendar year. Mental strength was required. I was buoyed by Ian Atkins, our player-coach Kevin Wilson, who I knew from Ipswich, and Kevan Broadhurst (yet another of the renowned team of hard-nuts at Birmingham City in the 1980s); three good men. It was wonderful to be dealing with human beings again. They treated the players like adults and not eight-year-old miscreants. I explained to Ian that I was far more comfortable at centre-back. He agreed and it worked out very well. We picked up a useful point at York in the next fixture and I had a great game. This was followed by a 1–0 victory over Chesterfield at home with the goal scored by my good self. Life had instantly changed for the better. The crowd was singing my name – without adding anything about my brother.

We had an excellent dressing room spirit and my social life was revived too. Duncan Spedding asked me to come on a night out, although he was a three-pints-of-lager-and-then-home man whereas I – let's say – wasn't. He never asked me again. I soon found out whose social habits were similar to mine and it became like Sunderland days. I didn't go out at all during my time at Burnley, partly because I was never the most popular man in that town.

The loan went swimmingly and once it had ended, Burnley accepted Northampton's £50,000 bid to make the loan permanent. Because I had not asked for a transfer, I was entitled to another £20,000 from Burnley as per the contract I had signed. Naturally,

Ternent didn't want to pay and phoned me to say so. Deluded that I would do anything to facilitate the move, he told me: 'Yerl have ter waive the twenty grand.'

'Er … no.'

'What?'

'No.'

'Wodderyermean "No"?'

'I want what I'm owed.'

Incapable of any other approach, he began bellowing again. *'Well yer not fuckin' signin' fer them then!'*

'OK. See you at training on Monday.'

I contemplated a submission and forgetting about the money. But pride and, let's be honest, the prospect of hoovering £20,000 conspired to make me refuse. I would not let him win.

An hour later Ternent's secretary, a lovely woman who deserved better (I wish I could remember her name), called me. She was sobbing because her chivalrous boss had taken his anger out on her. She said that he had gone as maniacal as expected and was now discussing the matter with the chairman. An hour later, this gift to mankind called me again himself. I was to be given, I think, about £13,000 severance pay, which worked out roughly the same for me as it was tax-free. I agreed.

It felt like a small victory. It didn't compensate for the months of nastiness, but I was free to enjoy football again. I joined North-ampton and was contracted to the summer of 2001 for £1,200 per week plus another £20,000 signing-on fee at the start of each year. I've had worse weeks.

• • •

In 2003, Stan Ternent's book, *Stan the Man: A Hard Life in Football*, was published. In it he tries perhaps a little too hard to be seen as 'one of the game's characters'. Its tone is predictably strident and the book is full of incident.

Some people liked it; although less kindly critics alluded to its flammability as its chief recommendation. He does give a mention to little me and my exit from Turf Moor after the York game. The years had not eroded his dudgeon. Here is an extract – giving his version of the effective sackings of Blatherwick, Winstanley, Williams and myself – which, no doubt due to his single-minded pursuit of literary excellence, contains one or two minor factual inaccuracies. So anything in brackets has been helpfully inserted by me.

It was nothing personal (*hmm*). The club needed major surgery. Not just an incision, an amputation. My main responsibility was to the Board and fans. I didn't give a toss how the players reacted…

Howey had an unbelievable clause in his contract (*not true*) which allowed him to commute to Burnley on a 70-mile round trip from Harrogate every day, even though he was constantly moaning about his bad back (*I had never mentioned my bad back until three days before the York game, although I eventually had a good moan in 2014 when three vertebrae in the same back were finally fused together by a surgeon*). There was no way I could ever override this clause (*???*), even when he sold his house in Yorkshire (*I never owned a house in Yorkshire*) and started to drive to work each morning from Sunderland (*my bank statements suggested that he had little difficulty in overriding the imaginary 'clause' with fines*).

I wasn't unnecessarily harsh (*space precludes*).

The consequences varied for the four of us who were sacked. I would be OK. Mark Winstanley went to a few clubs including Shrewsbury and Carlisle. Steve Blatherwick played about 250 games for Chesterfield. Mike Williams just disappeared.

Ternent said publicly at the time that it was just 'business'. It wasn't good business. It didn't occur to him that he had immediately lowered the amount he could have received for us by informing the world that we would never play for the club again. I was sold for a quarter of the fee that Burnley had paid for me. Add to this the salary I received for doing nothing, plus the £13,000 they had to pay me (but minus the fines), and it becomes clear it was not the greatest move by them.

Ternent thought I was 'not good enough'. He was entitled to his opinion and it's true that, for a number of reasons – him being one of them – I did not do well at Burnley.

But *I* am entitled to differ from his opinion. I had performed better at a higher level for four years at Sunderland and the hope was that if I could play to the same standard in the third tier of English football, then all would be well. He was not to blame for everything that went wrong for me in Lancashire, but playing for a better manager might have helped.

My lowest point under Ternent came during my wife's second pregnancy. In my lone training period I contacted Gary Rowell, who lived in the Burnley area. He ended his career at the club and I am not embarrassed to say that he remains a hero of mine for what he did at Sunderland when I was a kid. Although we only knew each other slightly, we arranged to meet for a drink in the knowledge that we would still have plenty to talk about. I was quite excited.

I had to stand him up. My wife called me in obvious distress. She was heavily bleeding and terrified for the baby. I won't milk the tension; Claudia would be a wonderful, healthy, loud baby. But I wasn't to know that and immediately drove home where, mercifully, matters turned out to be nowhere near as serious as feared.

The least important element of the incident was that it made me late for training the following day. I was fined for that, and for going home. I don't suppose the manager would have been interested in wishy-washy excuses like potential miscarriages.

Stan Ternent. What a … character.

CHAPTER 14

NORTHAMPTON, DOWNWARDS AND THE END

Northampton Town had some very useful players. There was Paul Wilkinson, Dave Savage, Kevin Wilson, goalkeeper Andy Woodman, Ian Sampson, Richard Hope, Chris Freestone, Carlo Corazzin, John Frain, Colin Hill, Duncan Spedding and Dougie Hodgson.

Dougie was an Australian who might have gone on to greater things had he not broken his neck in training.

Ian Hendon and Steve Howard would arrive later in the season. Steve was a big striker from Durham and a nightmare to mark. He would score over 200 goals in his career, but would also receive nine red cards, which is a lot for a centre-forward. He wasn't nasty, but he was aggressive and sometimes in his earlier days would tackle like a centre-forward. But the years improved him. He learned how to challenge without annoying referees and was an indisputably good player.

But let's not shy away from the fact that we didn't have *enough* good players. We were relegated that season. Defensively we were pretty solid, conceding fewer goals than any other side in the bottom ten (sixteen fewer than Burnley and with a better goal difference). The problem was at the other end. We only hit the net forty-three times in our forty-six games and I, a defender, finished as second top scorer with six. Carlo Corazzin scored sixteen, but the other strikers seemed to be either too young or too old (Kevin Wilson was thirty-eight when the season ended). This was in the days when goals scored took precedence over goal difference. Going down is always horrible, but I found the season overall to be most enjoyable. I liked and respected Ian Atkins. I always had. I held Kevin Wilson and Kevan Broadhurst in equal regard. The players in turn were treated like adults.

On Boxing Day 1998 we were away to Notts County, featuring Gary Owers. We were allowed home for Christmas Day and told to make our own way to a place near Nottingham where we would board the team bus. I had consumed too much festive fare. Not booze: pudding. Still, there were others who had looked after themselves far less well. I scored a tremendous header, similar to the one against Portsmouth in 1996. Much good it did us; we were already three down.

Ian Atkins wasn't pleased and told us that everyone who would be involved with the home fixture against Fulham two days ahead, was going straight back to Northampton on the bus. My car was to be driven by Richard Hope, as he would miss the Fulham game through injury. This made me extremely jittery as it was a very powerful BMW, the rain was torrential and Hopey was still only twenty – as well as being daft. I was mightily relieved to see Hopey and, more importantly, my car back at Sixfields before us and intact. This owed more to good luck than good driving.

'Cor! That was brilliant, Lee,' trilled Hopey. 'You can do 120 and your foot's hardly touching the pedal.'

• • •

Fulham were then being bankrolled by Mohamed Al-Fayed and would win the league at a trot with a squad that included Chris

Coleman, Steve Finnan, Kit Symons, Paul Bracewell, Paul Pe-schisolido, Peter Beardsley, Geoff Horsfield, John Salako and Barry Hayles (when we played them the following season in the League Cup it also had Andy Melville, Stan Collymore, Stephen Hughes and Lee Clark). They were never going to be stopped, so it was creditable for us to secure a 1–1 draw.

Their manager was Kevin Keegan and he still wasn't speaking to me after I had been escorted from St James' Park six years earlier when he was in charge of Newcastle. He did manage a perfunctory, half-hearted handshake such as Arsène Wenger specialises in.

This huff of his had been born on 16 October 1993. Sunderland were not playing until the next day, so Steven secured tickets for our dad and me to see Newcastle's game with Queen's Park Rangers. Usually under such circumstances I would want Steven to play well, but the Mags to get hammered. This time though it was different. Steven was injured.

The visitors won 2–1 and my attempts at controlling my emotions were not a success. After ten minutes, Les Ferdinand received a through-ball from Ray Wilkins to give QPR the lead. My anonymity was betrayed by the little celebratory dance I performed, as well as my lungful scream of 'Gettin, ya bastard!'

I had to be restrained by Norman, who was more used to the situation. It was not the wisest thing I could have done because the natives already knew who I was. I had scored the winner for Sunderland against Birmingham a week earlier. Shortly afterwards, I was politely but firmly told by a steward that I would have to leave and that I would be escorted down to the players' lounge. A few blokes behind us were showing a keen interest in dismembering me. Honestly; some people have no sense of humour.

Keegan found out and told Steven I was not to be allowed in there again. Back at Northampton in late 1998, he showed that he was more than adept at bearing a grudge.

• • •

There was to be one personal highlight for me that season on its final day, which Fate decreed would be at home to Burnley, who had howitzered up to fifteenth under Ternent. We drew 2–2 and I scored our second goal.

Upon arrival at Sixfields, I shared heartfelt handshakes with some good people and said hello to Sam Ellis. Sam had given me a tip for York Races which came in at 16/1, so I was prepared to overlook much. I also presented Stan Ternent with the acknowledgement I felt he deserved. None.

The game kicked off on a pitch that was surprisingly wet and muddy for 8 May. I was more than usually keyed up and put in a few good early tackles. We had a mathematical chance of avoiding relegation, but not a particularly realistic one (it turned out that we would have gone down anyway, even with a win).

In the course of challenging for an aerial ball from a Northampton corner, I flattened their goalkeeper, Paul Crichton. I was on the ground myself in the aftermath and Gordon Armstrong, by then a Burnley player, smacked me on the crown in a not-playful manner. It was an unusual show of hostility from Gordon and he made a dismissive comment as he did so. My eyes widened as I rose to my feet, growling and fulminating at him.

'*Gordon!*' He spun round.

'What?'

'You fucking *know!*'

What he knew was what I would do to him given anything resembling an opportunity. He apologised and the matter was forgotten about until many years later when I typed the previous few paragraphs.

My moment came in the eightieth minute. A free kick was lofted into Burnley's penalty area, which I headed goalwards. It was a decent rather than unstoppable header, but the conditions were against Crichton and the ball slid through his hands and over the line. He was a good goalie, but they all do it eventually. Our fans celebrated this scrappy strike, but we could still hear the grinding teeth of the visiting supporters. The Burnley fans were having a moment that every football follower has experienced. It-would-be-that-bastard-who-scored-wouldn't-it.

I had a distinct feeling of vindication, but was not in any way tempted to antagonise the Burnley supporters. They had paid my wages, when I wasn't being fined. Even though I was receiving a very audible booing every time I received the ball (something that is far easier to take from opposition supporters), the thought never occurred. However, I was tempted to get closer to Ternent. Not to gloat, but just to see if it was actually possible to fry eggs on his face at that moment. I had a drink after the game with some of my old teammates, who told me that Ternent had brutally excoriated the less than admirable Crichton in front of everyone, as though the keeper was unaware of his mistake, or could somehow then rectify it.

Anyway, an eventful, interesting, but ultimately unsuccessful 1998–99 had ended.

• • •

Initially I resided at the Westone Hotel in Northampton, then the Marriott, until I found a place to rent at the start of 1999–2000. My wife and now two kids remained in Sunderland, which meant that I was in the pub a great deal. There wasn't much else to do and we were still very much in football's drinking era. The truth is that my marriage had begun to crumble and by the end of the following season it would be over.

We strode into the next season with a collective determination to win immediate promotion – and lost the first two games. But the next five matches saw four wins and a draw. Steve Howard and Ian Hendon stood out. Corazzin began to score again after a slow start. As for myself, I was now thirty and understood the requirements of a centre-back better than ever. I felt as though I could play a bit too, but what I really thrived on was the physicality of it all; and the further down the football ladder you go, the more physical it is. Few people are in a better position to attest to this than me.

I was a senior pro and, in an unforeseen move, became the eyes and ears of the staff, making sure that the younger players were doing what they ought to. I was quite vociferous about it too. That didn't mean that I abandoned the social side, which was pretty much as it had been during my most enjoyable times at Sunderland. I could still drink gargantuan amounts and train properly the next day, which drew some admiration of the wrong sort from the youngsters. I'm not sure how I feel about that now. I suppose I was the Tony Adams of Northampton Town, if you'll allow the self-flattery, with much to teach from what I had done wrong as well as right. Something else we did that would cause outrage today was make regular trips to Pizza Hut for an all-you-can-eat-without-needing-an-emetic. It was all fun. We trained at Moulton College, and whoever between Hopey, big Steve and myself drove, would also pick the music for the journey, but had to buy chocolate bars for the other two. Nice life.

We looked after each other on the pitch too. Before I arrived at the club the previous season, Northampton played a goalless draw against Lincoln City. The game was only remembered because our right-back, Ian Clarkson, suffered a bad leg break which would in effect put paid to his time as a Northampton player. This was due to what was, by all accounts, an extraordinarily nasty challenge by the Lincoln striker Lee Thorpe, for which he was merely booked. Lincoln were subsequently relegated alongside us and when we played them at home the following season, Ian politely asked me if I wouldn't mind awfully smashing the bastard if the opportunity arose.

Anything for a friend, and Ian was a thoroughly splendid bloke. In the second half, the ball was played down the Lincoln left, over the head of our right-back Ian Hendon, with Thorpe running on to it. I went over to cover and caught the ball. I also caught just about every part of Lee Thorpe with all fifteen stone of me. With a certain balletic quality, he travelled headlong into the advertising hoardings six feet away and then struck them as though he had been shot from a cannon. The physio treated him for quite some time, but the game could continue while he was down as he was off the pitch. Result. I glanced surreptitiously at our bench and saw Mr Clarkson sitting contentedly, grinning like a lottery winner.

Thorpe was eventually reassembled and returned groggily to the pitch, for some reason showing displeasure. He attempted a swagger, which is a tall order for someone who can't be entirely sure where all of his limbs are. He cocked a finger gun but, realising that people tend not to be overly intimidated by mime, he switched from charades to explicitly telling me that he knew people who would shoot me up… etcetera.

This at least got a laugh. The more ruthless associates of the criminal underworld were rarely to be found admiring the stained glass windows in Lincoln Cathedral. But this fact failed to stem the ranted yet very entertaining horseshit of an inane young braggart. He wouldn't shut his yap, so I clattered him again and still I wasn't booked – although he was. Eventually they substituted him, possibly to spare him from a variety of punishments. We went on to win the match 1–0. I suspect he'd had better afternoons.

I must add that Mafioso knocks on my door remain infrequent at best. I encountered some authentically scary people on football pitches. Lee Thorpe wasn't one of them.

• • •

Ian Atkins left the club in October and was replaced by Kevin Wilson. We drew at Southend on Boxing Day and were fifth in the table. I was really enjoying football again, but had injured my toe. Our physio, Dennis Casey, told me to rest it and that I should be OK to play against Darlington two days later. I was keen to be involved, as Martin Gray, Brian Atkinson, Marco Gabbiadini and Paul Heckingbottom were in their side. Unfortunately I couldn't even get my boot on, let alone play. Darlington won 3–0.

There was no reason to suspect as much at the time, but this was to prove the beginning of the end for me in the Football League.

Marco was rumoured to be coming to Northampton and I discussed the matter with Brian after the game. He said he would caution against such a move, even though Gabbiadini had just scored against us twice. It seems he was not what you might call a team player, either on or off the pitch. This is a typical trait in someone who scored as many goals as Marco did. He joined the following summer.

A couple of weeks later, I was back in training at Moulton. My toe was fine, but my right knee – ye olde wonky right knee – was hurting again. At first I ignored it and pushed myself further. Training, combined with another visit to piggy-hour at Pizza Hut, made me nod off in front of the television later that afternoon. When I awoke from this nana-nap I stood up and the pain was acute. The knee had visibly swollen up and I called Dennis, who told me to come to the ground. I could just about drive and he sent me from Sixfields to hospital, where I was referred to the highly reputable Droitwich Knee Clinic, which had treated Robbie Fowler, Jamie Redknapp and other wounded superstars of the era.

The consultant did not present me with any welcome news. Because I hadn't done proper rehab all those years ago at Ipswich, my knee remained bent. The cartilage had been taken out when I was nineteen. This meant that bone had been grinding against bone and was why I was told in 1988 that I would never play again. By 2000, the knee was down to the mush and the only option was micro-fracture surgery, more famously undergone by the cricketer Andrew Flintoff a few years later. This involved opening the knee and making a series of small fractures with an awl. Bone marrow then releases cells though the fractures, which rebuilds cartilage and re-calcifies the bone. It's every bit as much fun as it sounds. I then had to wear an electronic device day and night for six weeks to continually move the knee.

I was out for the rest of the season and most of the following one too.

I went home to Sunderland where the same boredom and depression I had felt after sustaining the broken ankle at Elland Road in 1996 returned. Bad news for me, but another boon for The Cavalier.

• • •

More important than my personal tribulations was that North-ampton gained automatic promotion, thanks in no small part to us winning all of our last six games. The arrival of Jamie Forrester on loan from Utrecht late in the season proved important. Most of the victories were narrow and it was similar to what had happened at Sunderland four years earlier.

The fifth from last fixture was at Darlington and I limped down from Sunderland to offer my support. I was accompanied by Elliot, then a month away from his fourth birthday. His speech was really coming along and his vocabulary certainly expanded that day when I took him into the changing room before kick-off. We then sat in the away dugout to watch the game, but not for long. The referee, Roger Furnandiz, spotted Elliot and ordered him from the bench. I had to take him, crutches and all, into the section of Feethams where the Northampton fans stood, which they found hugely entertaining.

The injury still got to me. The final game of the season was away to Torquay United on Saturday 6 May and I travelled to Devon to be part of it, although obviously not to play.

Those of us who could not take part were given permission to have the Friday night out. We played pool at the team hotel with the usual drinkies. While I was playing, Roy Hunter, a midfielder who was also injured, pinched my crutches, wallet and phone for a lark. I knew my wife might ring me and, as we were not rubbing along too well at the time, I didn't want to miss her call. At around one in the morning I thumped on Roy's door and demanded my property back. He denied having any of it, so I barged past him and there before me were my possessions. I gave him verbals at first, but soon upgraded this to a punch in the face and grabbed my stuff. Kevin Wilson, among others, had heard the rumpus, but he waited until breakfast to ask what the hell had been going on. I still wasn't happy and read out the charge sheet against Roy.

Hostilities were put aside by the end of the day. A draw was needed to guarantee promotion. We went one better and won 2–1. This was succeeded by an immense party that began on the team bus and ended God knows when. I was disappointed not to have played since Boxing Day, but reminded myself that I had contributed half a season. Determination and camaraderie had got us back into the Second Division.

• • •

By the summer of 2000, I was off crutches and in very light rehab. At about the same time I had the honour of being best man at my old school friend Eddie Harrison's wedding, which was held at Gretna Green. Nuptials there take months of planning, which rather goes against the original purpose of Gretna Green. It's very popular, so Eddie and his wife-to-be had to wait their turn and while they did so the guests had a suited and booted kick-about. Someone had had the foresight to bring a ball. I joined in and soon felt a burning sensation on the back of my right kneecap, which I put down to the rehab.

Northampton's pre-season tour of Ireland was wonderful. When it emerged that no curfew would be in place we knew what sort of trip this was going to be; it was going to be my kind of trip. My drinking had not suffered.

I still wasn't training properly with the rest of the squad. I would be either in a gym or on a bike. I could still feel a nip behind my kneecap, but as there was no swelling I just plodded on. Back in Northampton, Roy Hunter and I were told by Dennis Casey to make a five-mile cycle ride to the training ground; not a long cycle but mainly uphill. The bike I was given was too small for me and soon Roy was out of sight. By the time I wheeled into the training ground my knee was torturing me. I cursed the knee, cursed the pain, cursed the bike, cursed Dennis, cursed Roy, cursed football and cursed most other things within a million-mile radius. I dismounted the bike and threw the damn thing as far as possible, probably in the direction of Roy.

I was referred to the same consultant at the Droitwich Knee Clinic, who took another scan. This was private care so the results were immediate. He shook his head as he looked at the scan – a desponding sight in itself – and told me that because my knee hadn't healed properly, a hole had been worn in the joint behind the knee-cap where the femur had been rubbing against it: for twelve years.

The only available solution was a bone graft. A piece of my hip was plonked onto my knee (apologies for the medical jargon) and I was out for another six months. It was back to The Cavalier.

• • •

By the end of 2000, my marriage was only in technical existence. After the operation I was on crutches for months and, if I had to quantify such a thing, I was 80 per cent sure that my football career was over. I had moved out of the house in Silksworth for good, asked my wife for a divorce and was now residing permanently in Hunsbury, Northampton. I was injured, depressed and drinking too much. After rehab each day I would call in at the supermarket to buy eight cans and two bottles of wine. I would be out with the lads at the weekend and sometimes during the week. Life was a bit of a kitchen-sink drama at this stage and my friends were all I had; particularly Steve Howard, Richard Hope and Dave Savage. I had an emotional as well as a literal crutch. They helped me through and we remain close today.

But it's always darkest just before dawn and what-not. As my knee got better, so did my life. A major reason for this was that I had met Maz. She was a Northampton girl of Irish stock; her parents were from County Kerry. Cutting a long story short, Maz is now my wife and mother of my two younger sons. We were married in Northampton on 31 May 2003, Joseph was born on 30 July 2004, Christopher on 7 October 2006. To use a completely inappropriate metaphor, she put a spring back in my step. My alcohol intake descended from its quite ridiculous level and I was working hard, morning and afternoon, with Dennis Casey.

I finally played in the first team again on 21 April 2001. It was the first time Maz had seen me play. I replaced Marco Gabbiadini in the eighty-third minute of a 2–0 home win over Colchester United. I had only been on the pitch for a couple of minutes when a long, diagonal pass came into Colchester's penalty area. I met it on the edge of the box with one of the best headers of my career, leaving my ex-teammate Andy Woodman with no chance. I loved it. The crowd loved it. I hoped Maz loved it too.

The referee didn't. He imagined that I had fouled a defender when I struck the ball. I hadn't. The record shows that the ref was one A. R. Hall, which sounds suitably akin to A. R. S. Hole, if you ask me. This buffoon prevented a magnificent goal, a topper header, from standing with his absurd decision. He should never have been allowed on a football pitch again, if not arrested and put on trial for crimes against something-or-other. What a disgrace to the game and to humanity itself. Luckily I'm not one to harbour a grievance.

The bigger issue was playing again, even if I wasn't fully fit. I started the next game at home to Port Vale but had to be replaced at half-time by Chris Carruthers, a seventeen-year-old making his debut. I realised how far off the pace I was. There is a difference between fit and match fit; you can train as hard as you like but you can't replicate matches. I was an unused substitute at Bourne-mouth, but played the whole of our final game of 2000–01 at home to Walsall.

I was supposed to be substitute again, but someone was injured during the warm-up. Initially, player-manager Kevin Wilson was going to pick himself. In fact he was desperate to do so, as he was one short of his 150th Football League goal. However, in addition to being forty years old, he hadn't started a game in sixteen months, so common sense prevailed and I played up front instead. There was nothing to play for. We were safe from relegation and Walsall would finish fourth regardless of the result (they would win the play-offs).

I was partnered by Gabbiadini and had a decent first half. I had one cleared off the line, then I went for a diving header from a corner. To my annoyance, Gabbers went for the same ball with his foot and almost dislodged my head. We contrived to lose what had actually been a very even fixture by three goals to nil. The game was goalless until a Walsall player scored on sixty-three minutes and put away his third only eighteen minutes later.

The name of the hat-trick hero? Brett Angell. A circle had been completed. I congratulated him after the game because he was a great lad and deserved days like this; I only wished he had done it to a team other than mine.

It was my last ever game in the Football League.

• • •

I moved in with Maz and had an important chat with Kevin Wilson. My contract was up on 31 July and my future needed to be sorted. He told me that if I could prove my fitness then I would be offered another contract. That would do me. I visited Elliot and Claudia a few times, had a holiday in Mexico, played in Northampton's pre-season tour of (where else?) Ireland and trained hard. Two weeks before the start of the season Kevin told me that he would be happy to re-sign me, but that we needed to speak to the chairman first. Before that I was called by Gary Bennett, who was managing Darlington. Would I like to sign for him? I appreciated the offer but explained that I was expecting to sign a new contract and that Northampton was now my home.

The chairman, Barry Stonhill, returned from holiday and after Monday training I went to see him, just to make sure that everything was in place. When I asked him about my new con-tract, his eyes widened and he appeared shocked.

'I'm sorry, Lee. There's no budget.'

'What do mean, "no budget"'?

Marco Gabbiadini had arrived a year earlier from Darlington. He was a free transfer, but his salary must have been way in excess of mine and it seems it had devoured the wage budget. I was out.

In rather a daze I left Barry's office and went to train, although I wasn't sure why. There was a short-sided game across the pitch. Gabbers was on my team and was strolling, not giving his all. In little time, I lost my temper and called him a string of unpleasant names. He responded with a mouthful of his own and I began to chase him round the ground, thereby making him move faster than at any other time that morning. I was eventually restrained by some bamboozled teammates. Marco hadn't actually done anything wrong, but my life had taken a turn for the worse again and I was taking it out on him. We've got along well since that day, although he remains wary.

The same day, I was called by Nigel Spink of 1982 European Cup final fame, who had been Northampton's goalkeeping coach. He was now manager of Forest Green Rovers in the Football Conference and asked if I would like to join. It was part-time, but still paid £400 per week. I agreed almost immediately. Here I am compelled to admit that I had muddled Forest Green with Moor Green in Solihull, perhaps because Nigel was from the West Midlands. Moor Green is a fifty-minute drive from Northampton. Forest Green's ground is in Nailsworth, Gloucestershire, and over two hours away along umpteen 'A' roads.

Tony Daley, another former Villa star, was Forest Green's fitness coach as well as a player. He was in charge of warm-ups, among other things. I had to inform him that my warm-ups now consisted of a cup of tea and little more. When the pitches were hard, I would struggle with my knee, especially if there was more than one game in a week. Tony accepted this and I liked him a great deal. We were a middling team in a tight league and I enjoyed my time at the Lawn Ground. I made my debut in a draw at Scarborough (featuring Stephen Brodie). I would play seventeen games in Forest Green's defence and scored a couple of goals. We had a mixed bag of results, but the only game of any real note was in a replay against Macclesfield, a league above us, in the first round of the FA Cup in November 2001.

We came from behind twice at Moss Road to draw the first game

2–2. A young Rickie Lambert scored twice for them, but we should have won. The replay came eleven days later at home and the score was 1–1 after extra time. This led to what was the longest penalty shoot-out in the history of the competition. We had already taken three penalties in the tie – and only scored one of them. We also had a goal dubiously disallowed and their keeper almost punched the ball into his own net in the last seconds.

How I managed to play the whole two hours was something I was unable to explain even to myself. The others were complaining of stiffness. I had gone beyond stiffness and began to suspect rigor mortis. I had to keep jogging to prevent myself from seizing up completely. It was either that or WD-40. I was our eighth penalty taker; each side had missed one (Lambert had failed for Macclesfield) so the score was 6–6. I could barely trot, but happily my spot-kick was a good one. I had decided twenty minutes earlier where I would place my penalty in what seemed the unlikely event of taking one: bottom left. The keeper dived the wrong way but wouldn't have saved it anyway. It was now approaching 11 p.m. Everyone, keepers included, had taken a spot-kick, so we started again. Kevin Langan was the poor sod who put his second kick over the bar before Lee Glover won it for Macclesfield. The shoot-out finished 10–11 and a total of twenty-seven penalties had been taken over the two games. Had we won, we would have gone on to beat Arsenal in the final. I worked it out.

To lose on penalties at any level is an awful experience, but I can confirm that there is a certain relief when your own effort goes in. It's not about scoring, it's about not missing. The scorers are never as well remembered as the missers.

• • •

Forest Green's chairman, Trevor Horsley, had promised to take the players to Spain for a few days if we could beat Macclesfield. After our defeat, he recognised that we couldn't have done much more in the tie and said he would take us anyway, which is just the ticket in January.

I did not make the trip. On 17 January 2002, I was swapped for a Nuneaton Borough winger called Alex Sykes. Alex travelled to Spain with the rest of the Forest Green squad. That's life; it can be a bit of a swizz. What mattered more was that Nuneaton was only forty miles from Northampton. Steve Burr, yet another likeable bloke, was manager. I had just started work on my UEFA 'B' coaching badge and was to be player-coach, although my salary would be the same (with far less spent on petrol). Again, I enjoyed my time there. Two days after signing, I was put straight into the first team for a trip to Yeovil and my partner at centre-back was the experienced Terry Angus. Results varied, but included a 2–1 win at Forest Green, and we finished in the top half of the league.

As part of my coaching badge I spent a fortnight in Potters Bar in Hertfordshire during the summer of 2001. About twenty of us did the course, including Chelsea players such as Gus Poyet, Ed de Goey, Gianfranco Zola and Dennis Wise. Steve Bould and Tony Cottee also attended. Hardly anyone there was on the right side of thirty and we were all knackered at the end of the two weeks. To carry out these coaching exercises we had to draft in players from the local leagues.

Every person was told to coach the others on a given aspect of the game, while everyone else would be 'the players', as it were. The subject that I was to 'teach' a stack of top international players was 'arriving in the box late'. I had to tell Gus Poyet to run early into the penalty area so I could then stop him and 'correct' him to illustrate my profound wisdom. He must have felt very grateful.

I was back at Northampton in the summer of 2002 to coach the under-18s, without pay, as part of the hundred hours' coaching required for my qualification. Kevan Broadhurst had now replaced

Kevin Wilson as manager and he told me that I could be the club's youth development officer (YDO), subject to attaining my coaching badges. I was delighted. Geoff Pike, the former West Ham player then working at the FA, was impressed with the work I had done and recommended that I go for my 'A' licence. All was well. There was a community coach at Northampton, Paul Curtis, who was already qualified and had to be present while I was coaching, as per the rules. He didn't do anything; he just had to be there. Kevan said we just needed to run my appointment past the new chairman, Andrew Ellis.

But the chairman decided that Paul should be YDO as well as community coach as it would save the club a salary. Money issues had forced me out of Northampton Town for the second time in just over a year. It was later realised that the two roles did indeed require two people and Ian Sampson was appointed as YDO, which in time led to him becoming manager. I was pleased for Sammo, but still ponder what might have been.

I still played for Nuneaton and found the Saturday–midweek schedule increasingly arduous. I was thirty-plus, knackered and was being left on the bench more and more. The club was not getting much for their £400 per week and Steve Burr took me aside to explain that I should move on. I understood. My last game for them was in a 3–2 win over Forest Green, who had Gary Owers in the team. This was September 2002.

A couple of weeks later, Kevin Wilson made good on a promise and offered me a position as player-assistant manager at Bedford Town for £150 per week. I took up this role with my usual eagerness, but soon suffered a bad injury during a pre-season warm-up against a Luton Town XI. While chasing the ball in the second half I heard a loud cracking sound and I went down screaming invective at the lad I thought had kicked me. In fact he hadn't. There was no one near me. I had completely torn my Achilles, which was diagnosed easily as my ankle had visibly dropped. A consultant operated on me, but I have never fully recovered from that injury.

In October 2003, Kevin Wilson and I resigned our respective positions at Bedford to do the same jobs at Aylesbury. This was for slightly more money, about £200 per week I think. To justify this mega-salary I attempted to train myself back to full fitness, but I was still some way short, and this created friction.

Aylesbury was not a success and in January 2005 Kevin and I left for Kettering Town at the invitation of their chairman, Peter Mallinger. Peter was a former vice-chairman of Newcastle. Despite this, I liked him a great deal. He was a gentleman and I was sorry when he passed away in 2011. Our coach was Alan Biley, the former Everton and Derby striker and a Rod Stewart lookalike of some prominence. I returned to playing for Kettering as a substitute in a game at Bishop's Stortford. But this was, to say the least, an ill-thought-out decision. I could barely jump or run, and the reality of not being a player any more was mentally registering.

I was only at Kettering for about three months, after which came a bizarre little period for that club. In October 2005, a new chairman shunted Kevin Wilson aside as manager (he declined the offer to become director of football) to make way for a very big name: Paul Gascoigne. The former Arsenal midfielder Paul Davis was his assistant. This made headlines, but the predictable implosion was swift, and Gazza was sacked after thirty-nine days, upon which Kevin was reappointed. While Gascoigne was there, two players, Brett Solkham (who would go on to play many times for Kettering) and a teammate of his whose name eludes me, were told by Gazza a week into his tenure to leave their jobs because they would be offered full-time playing contracts. They were more than happy to comply and resigned from real work immediately. They reported back to their manager two days later to say that they had carried out his instructions.

He didn't have the faintest idea what they were talking about. I think we can guess why. I found this out later when I worked with Brett.

As for me, after a very brief stint for the mighty Long Buckby, it was off to Buckingham Town to be assistant manager to Morell Maison. Morell soon left to become manager of Kettering (who had by then jettisoned Kevin Wilson for a second time after he had returned to replace Paul Gascoigne: don't worry if you're not keeping up, because I'm struggling too) and I was put in charge of Buckingham. I was forced to borrow a couple of academy young-sters from Kettering. My record as manager reads: played seven, lost four, drew three, won bugger all. Beat that.

And still I played on. Aside from my ongoing inability to run, jump, turn or do anything that involved sudden movement – I was dynamite. I played a dozen games in total, headers from a standing position being my speciality.

But the curtain finally descended. My last game as a player came on Tuesday 26 March 2006 in an Eagle Bitter United Coun-ties League Premier Division game for Buckingham Town, on a miserable, wet evening at Ford Sports Daventry at their Royal Oak ground. We lost 5–2. That was it. Finished. No encore. Done. *Fin*. All over. Hang up the boots.

The end.

CHAPTER 15

AND NOW...

My immediate concern after missing out on the YDO job at Northampton in 2002 was finding work. I had attained my UEFA 'B' badge and upon completion sent my CV to all ninety-two Football and Premier League clubs. I did not receive a single reply. The further down the football pyramid I went, the more imperative it became to supplement my salary by any means, because most of the clubs I went to after dropping out of the Football League could not pay me what I needed.

What was I good at apart from football? (Make your own jokes.) Talking. A brief sales career was about to begin with a firm called First For Golf. Subscribers to this organisation would receive a 20 per cent discount on green fees at certain clubs around the country and various other golfing offers. It wasn't a bad job, really, and I visited some very pleasant clubs around England. The problem was the £800 per month wages. As I did this freelance, I also had to pay for my petrol, which took £200 from even that meagre stipend.

Through my work in golf, I became more interested in the hospitality business. I spoke with Marriott and Hilton among other hotels and decided that I could put together travel packages for football clubs. It could be a nightmare job for the manager's secretary to book everything, particularly at smaller clubs, so I left First For Golf to set up a company called Hotels 192 that took over the responsibility. If I arranged for a squad to stay overnight with breakfast and an evening meal, I would make £1,000. If they wanted bed and breakfast I would make £400 and if they just wanted a snack before an evening match I made £250. I did bookings for clubs including QPR, Reading and West Brom. The difficulty was that I could make a fair amount of money, but then go for several weeks without a single booking. On one occasion I was set to make a useful grand out of QPR when they changed their minds about an overnight stay because their manager Ian Holloway was superstitious.

Funds were depleting, and by now Maz was pregnant with Joseph. She sat me down and told me a truth that deep down I already knew. I needed to get a proper job. That was the end of Hotels 192. I was still earning £150 per week at Bedford Town and Maz was working as a nursing assistant at St Andrew's Hospital. I had parted with my BMW and bought a Grand Cherokee… then a VW Passat… then a Ford Orion. By now I was driving a clapped out 1.1 Ford Fiesta Popular with a hole in the footwell through which I could see the road (*'Flintstones, meet the Flintstones…'*).

I thought: 'Right. Who's the biggest employer in Northampton?' That was Barclaycard in Brackmills Industrial Estate, 1234 Pavilion Drive. Such was my distrust of the Fiesta that I cycled there.

It would have brought a tear to Norman Tebbit's eye; I literally got on my bike and looked for work. I asked at reception if there were any jobs available and a pleasant, helpful woman, who looked slightly surprised at the sudden appearance of a sweaty cyclist, made a call. Someone from HR came down and took my details. Within a fortnight I had been interviewed and offered a position in the call centre, selling PDQs for an annual salary of £13,200. I have been in the payments industry ever since.

It soon became apparent that Barclaycard's account managers had better jobs and salaries. Within nine months I was interviewed for such a post and was successful. The Fiesta was sold for about £2.50 (I cycled to work anyway) and I bought an Audi A3. After a few jobs at different organisations within the industry, I was offered a job back in the North East in 2008, and we moved into our home in County Durham.

I shall spare you the details, but I left Mastercard in 2017 and am now Director of Business Development at Judopay, which enables payments for mobile apps. If you made a card transaction in a UK pub while I was at Mastercard, there was a fair chance that I'd be involved somewhere along the line facilitating the payment. Between 2011 and 2017, I worked from Canary Wharf. I had always wondered what went on in there. It was my own enthusiasm that brought me to this point. I am as motivated now as I ever was as a footballer. It's my nature to make the most of what I have.

Much as I enjoy my work, I still scratch my head when I think of how I came to do it. Football did not open any doors for me in the financial sector. On many occasions, colleagues have discovered what I used to do and been shocked. This was especially true in the call centre when I was in my thirties and most of the others there were at least ten years younger than me. Northampton is more of a rugby town and I wasn't David Beckham, so there was no instant recognition. But my name nudged a few memories and I would be Googled. This would be followed by the looks of disbelief I still receive to this day. The often-asked question of 'What are you doing here?' arises from the misconception that anyone who played in the Premier League, even in 1996–97, must be a multi-millionaire. Regularly, people I have worked with for some time have been visibly jarred to discover my 'secret' past.

Leaving football is very difficult and many an ex-pro, very wealthy ones included, has had difficulty adapting. The games, training, travelling, companionship, bonding, shared emotions and experiences, the recognition and the adrenalin provided by playing before thousands of people is abruptly taken away. A huge, huge, huge void descends on your life and it's something that has to be experienced to be understood.

I miss football, but mine is a happy life. I have a career while Maz does the hard work. This was a conscious decision that we will stick to until our sons are of a certain age. I have four kids that I love, but the situation with my older children, Elliot and Claudia, continues to be difficult.

My brother and I have not communicated for some years. We had been in-and-out as friends ever since the Newcastle–Sunderland game of 1997. At the time of writing there has, by mutual agreement, been no verbal contact since 2011. Apologies for not elaborating, and the intention is not to create a false mystique. But it really is better that I say no more about him. He has his own past, his own private life and his own problems, some of which he has gone public with. I have my own thoughts.

Let us leave the subject on a positive note: Steven Howey was a good footballer. His England caps were given on merit.

It is often said that football today is a completely different game compared to years ago. They were saying this when I was a kid.

That doesn't mean it isn't true. My career wasn't *that* long ago, but the differences are stark; better in some ways and worse in others. One major reason is money. I shall give you an example that is not massively significant in isolation, but still very telling and indicative.

In November 2000, Northampton took Mark Maley on loan from Sunderland. Mark was then a promising nineteen-year-old full-back. His opportunities at Sunderland were limited by the talent at the club (they finished seventh for the second successive time in the Premier League that season) and he would only ever play twice in their first team. Both appearances were in the League Cup. He picked up a thigh injury in the first half of only his second game for Northampton and returned to Wearside. A similar thing had happened to him a few weeks earlier during another loan to Blackpool. His last action in the Football League was a third loan at York City where he made seventeen appearances. That loan – and his playing career – was ended in bizarre circumstances in April 2002 when he was accidentally shot in the eye with an airgun by his Sunderland teammate John Oster. They were mucking about with the gun, which they both thought was unloaded. Regrettably, Mark Maley's time in football was brief and not a notable success.

He still earned a fortune.

I knew him vaguely and decided to make him welcome when he arrived at Northampton, especially as he was so young and nervous. He was staying at the Westone Hotel where we had a drink and a chat, in the course of which he mentioned that he was buying a place on the Newcastle quayside; an expensive place to live. I don't know what his basic salary was but, although he barely featured for Sunderland, he was in Peter Reid's squad and that was enough to put him on a win bonus of around six grand per victory – ten times bigger than any bonus I had ever known. This information made my jaw descend and I realised that in financial terms, my season in the Premier League, only three-and-a-half years earlier, was not propitiously timed however much I had enjoyed it. It was now that the real money was being made. Though not exactly the lynchpin of the team during Sunderland's 1996–97 campaign, I had been on either the bench or the pitch in twenty of the thirty-eight games. Mark was never even named as a substitute in a league game, yet here he was, aged nineteen and able to buy and sell me.

The wages in the top tier were becoming mad. As you know, they would become even madder. Forget for now the salaries of the very highest earners. What would a player, at any Premier League club, on either the bench or the pitch in twenty of the thirty-eight games in a season, earn today? A figure somewhere between 'eye-watering' and '*HOW MUCH!!?*' would seem to be the answer.

The cash, as well as the profile, the foreign imports and the influence of social media has led to the aloofness of footballers. At separate times in the past decade I have lived next door to two Sunderland players; not superstars but reasonably well known and both British. One of them would draw the curtains rather than run the risk of making eye contact. The other one was a little more amenable, but still reclusive. They seemed scared to be normal. I didn't want to go on holiday with them, or tap them for a loan: a simple 'good morning' would have done.

This is sad for all concerned and contrasts sharply with the heroes of my childhood – Gary Rowell, Stan Cummins and the rest – who would stop and chat with fans. It was the same at every club. Footballers were part of the community. Later, when I was at Sunderland, we would often be in pubs with supporters who might be happy, frustrated, depressed or downright angry because of us. Whatever their mood, we always mixed with them and didn't think anything of it.

By the time I played in my only ever game for Sunderland against Newcastle in 1997, there was bewailing at how many foreign footballers were in England. But of the twenty-seven players used that day, twenty-two were from the UK and nine of them were from the North East. A few years before that, when I was watching as a schoolboy, a foreign footballer was still a novelty. The novelty today is when someone local is on the pitch. Fans will sing 'He's one of our own' when a native is representing his boyhood team, as it's now such a deviation from the norm.

Over time, the money has built metaphorical and actual walls between players and fans. The connection has gone and the Premier League is a global brand like EMI, Facebook or Nissan. Still, it should be said that the severed connection between players and fans becomes less of an issue the further from the top flight you are. The Premier League is a business run for the whole world; it just so happens that its actual football matches are played in England. Hence the thirty-ninth game idea: it would generate even more income – and detach more of football's soul.

We all want a few more quid, but I don't resent missing out on the millions because I was born in 1969 and not 1989. The compensation for being paid a relative pittance during my time was the laughter, bonhomie with colleagues and fans and the enormous amount of fun we had. I refer especially, though not exclusively, to the 1995–96 season at Sunderland. The drunken fun in Chaplin's after we had won the league is a special memory that I shall take to the grave. They were the best times of my life and I'm not sure that today's players will ever experience anything quite like it. Of course, the biggest consolation for the passing of my time as a player is provided by the following thought:

At least I had my time.

I earned decent money by normal standards. But I remember a plumber friend of mine at the time who was earning the same as me, the difference being that he had to work much harder for it. I was being paid to do something I loved, which is everyone's fantasy. Then there were the fringe benefits, such as being ushered into nightclubs, gliding past the queue, entering free of charge then being lionised; treated like a film star merely because I played for our beloved local football club. Not every day was wonderful, but overall I had a magnificent time as a footballer and will never apologise for that.

And unlike today when players are essentially teetotal athletes – and I'm not saying that is a bad thing – we were allowed to drink and experience the joys of being silly, normal young men. Normality has apparently been banned since then.

Had I earned the big money, bought a pile of property and not needed to work again, it would not necessarily have been a positive thing. I have already mentioned the void that retirement from football can create. I filled the void with work and family. But had there been no *need* to earn money, the void could have been filled with booze, boredom, depression and an array of other negatives. However, I like to think that this wouldn't have happened and that I would have done something productive. Anyway, regardless of income, the opportunity always exists to become a full-time arsehole and I have never taken it. Self-respect is everything.

So I don't begrudge today's players their money, any more than I begrudge them their ridiculous full heads of hair and their stupid flat stomachs.

For the main part I am fit and well. I enjoy my cycling immensely and take it quite seriously. I do it with friends: Tim Connors, Steve Norton, Ian Dodd, Ben Robinson and Mickey Crowe. Every year we do the 144-mile Coast-to-Coast ride from Whitehaven to Sunderland for charity. It gives me an adrenalin surge that would otherwise be missing. However, I'm some way short of physical perfection and certain bits of me have by necessity been screwed back on.

Because of the pressure on my knee, my left thigh is bigger than my right. My right calf is massive compared to the left due to my Achilles injury. My legs look as though they have been drawn by a toddler of limited artistic ability, even among the toddling community. And as for my back…

Common consensus is that the soul has been removed from the game. But I still love football and always will. I coach kids between the ages of eight and thirteen and derive great pleasure from this.

I am as much a Sunderland fan today as I ever was, despite the perennial frustrations and anger I occasionally feel. I remain a bloke from Thorney Close who sometimes has to let off steam when his team lets him down.

On 21 January 2017, I travelled to the Hawthorns to watch Sunderland turn in an abject performance against West Brom. Standing (because you can't use your seat) in the Smethwick End, where over two decades earlier I had scored the winner, I was particularly annoyed by our full-back Patrick van Aanholt, whose 'effort' and commitment to the cause were pitiful (although perhaps explained by his big-money move to Crystal Palace a week later). I'm normally quite calm, but this motivated me at the end of the game to lean over a barrier and scream my opinions at him.

I could have gone on and on and on and on and…

INDEX

van Aanholt, Patrick 348
Adams, Tony xii, 229, 255, 257, 267
Adamson, Damian 20
Adamson, Tony 20–21
Agnew, Steve 174, 192, 200, 204, 206–7, 213, 214, 220, 225, 235, 250, 251, 254, 256, 267–8, 280, 294
Aiston, Sam 189
Ajax AFC 267, 294
Alderson, Trevor 87
Aldridge, John 211, 238, 239
Allardyce, Sam 259–60
Allison, David 112, 114
Anderson, John 96
Angell, Brett 175–9, 183, 186, 194, 203, 334
Annabel's (nightclub) 227–8
Ards FC 107
Armstrong, Gordon 25, 86, 94, 98, 105–6, 124, 134, 156, 186, 194, 324
Arsenal FC 10, 38, 121, 229, 254–7, 266–7, 336
Asanović, Aljoša 253
Aston Villa FC 28, 40, 144, 192, 204, 258–9, 269, 295, 335
Athlone Town FC 190, 191
Atkins, Ian 28, 104, 125, 126–7, 304, 316, 317, 322, 328
Atkins, Mark 212
Atkinson, Brian 99, 106, 137, 240, 328
Atkinson, Dalian 40–44

Ball, Kevin xii, xiv, 99, 101, 131, 135–6, 141, 143–4, 150, 156, 158, 164, 183, 189, 194, 206, 210, 213, 225, 226, 234–5, 237, 243, 250, 251, 252, 265, 266, 272, 273, 276, 292
Barber, Graham 223
Barmby, Nick 160, 166, 258, 282
Barnes, John 196, 251, 276, 291
Barnes, Paul 297, 300, 301
Barnsley FC 23, 178–9, 199–200, 230–31
Barton, Warren 142, 275
Beardsley, Peter 251, 323
Beck, Mikkel 278–9
Beckham, David 206, 208, 250, 343
Bedford Town FC 302, 338–9
Benitez, Rafael 53

Bennett, Gary 91, 105–6, 126, 166–7, 170, 186, 189, 334
Beresford, Marlon 297, 300
Bergkamp, Dennis 267
Beys, Frank 65
Bingham, David 48–9
Birch, Paul 171
Birmingham City FC 4, 47, 52, 109, 116–18, 120, 122, 204, 227, 232, 233, 245, 317, 323
Bishop Auckland FC 85, 87, 89, 92, 93, 95, 103, 145, 166, 298
Blackburn Rovers FC 217, 219, 233, 270, 279
Blair, Tony 282
Blatherwick, Steve 297, 300, 301, 314, 319
Blatter, Sepp 13
Blyth Spartans FC 49
Bolton Wanderers FC 183, 259
Bolton, Joe 10, 260
Boniek, Zbigniew 192
Bono 293
Bosman, Jean–Marc 79–81, 128
Bosnich, Mark 258–9
Bould, Steve 255, 256, 337
Bournemouth, AFC 129, 133, 333
Brabant, Fernand 59, 69, 74
Bracewell, Paul 93, 187–8, 195, 196, 197, 208, 213, 221,222, 235, 253, 267, 271, 288, 294, 306, 323
Bradford City FC 45, 46, 271
Branco 279
Brass, Chris 297, 301, 304
Brazil, Alan 28
Breen, Gary 233
Brennan, Mark 198
Brentford FC 101, 301, 304, 307
Bridges, Michael 221, 224, 225, 230, 231, 233, 256–7, 272, 273, 288
Brief History of Time, A 29
Bristol City FC 93, 155–6, 157, 159, 165, 174, 183, 186, 304, 306
Bristol Rovers FC 100, 307
Broadhurst, Kevan 317, 322, 337
Brock, Kevin 91
Brodie, Stephen 91, 186, 335
Brown, Grant 25

Bruce, Steve 96, 187, 205
Buckingham Town FC xi, 340
Bull, Steve 171
Bungalow Cafe (Sunderland) 125–6
Burley, George 28, 46
Burnley FC 11, 62, 124, 155, 187, 267, 290, 294–320, 324–5
Burr, Steve 337, 338
Bury FC 11, 186, 307, 308, 312
Butcher, Terry 28, 33, 35–6, 46, 73, 89, 92, 94–5, 97, 100–106, 108, 111, 115, 117, 123–8, 129, 130–32, 140, 179, 184, 198
Butler, Eddie 161
Butt, Nicky 206, 207
Butters, Guy 98
Buxton, Mick 124–5, 129–31, 140, 146, 150, 154–5, 156, 157, 159, 160–61, 165, 171–2, 175–7, 179, 182, 184, 193, 228
Byrne, Chris 293
Byrne, John 86

Cairns, John 101
Callaghan brothers 84
Campbell, Glenn 192
Campbell, Sol 168–70
Cantona, Eric xiii, 117, 206–8
Cardiff City FC 53
Carlisle United FC xii, 139–41, 160, 196, 307, 319
Carman QC, George 279–80
Carruthers, Chris 333
Carruthers, John 27, 49, 89–90
Carter, Jimmy 213
Carter, Tim 124
Carver, John 53
Casey, Dennis 327, 331, 332
Celtic FC 105, 272
Chamberlain, Alec 104, 107, 108, 110, 111, 158, 167, 194, 206–8, 217–18, 221, 232, 240
Chaplin's (pub) 236, 347
Charles, Gary 48
Charlton Athletic FC 23, 25, 46, 90, 93, 171, 232, 290
Charlton, Bobby 14
Charlton, Jack 26
Chelsea FC 4, 38, 86, 90, 100, 186, 270, 271, 337
Chester City FC 111, 123
Chesterfield FC 47, 306, 317, 319
Ciney, RUW 67, 70, 71
Clamot, Daniel 66, 67
Claridge, Steve 249
Clark, Gary 89
Clark, Lee 187, 274, 290, 292–3, 323
Clarkson, Ian 326
Clothes Show, The 27
Clough, Brian 14, 279
Coatsworth, Gary 23, 41
Colback, Jack 187
Colchester United FC 47, 317, 332
Cole, Andy 93, 206, 208
Cole, Michael 30, 41, 45
Coleman, Chris 323

Collymore, Stan 130, 146, 202, 251, 323
Common, Jonathan 12, 13, 18, 20, 25
Conroy, Mr 8
Consett AFC 151
Cooke, Andy 297
Cooper, Colin 130
Cooper, Paul 28, 33
Corazzin, Carlo 321–2, 325
Coton, Tony 245, 248, 256, 258, 261–2, 263, 264
Cottee, Tony 337
Coventry City FC 4, 89, 254, 288–9
Cowans, Gordon 295, 297, 307
Cowie, Ronnie 264, 297
Coxall, Philip 21, 25
Craddock, Jody 290, 294
Crichton, Paul 324–5
Cronin, Gareth 107
Crook Town FC 151
Crosby, Malcolm 88–9, 99, 129
Crossley, Mark 251
Crowe, Mickey 265, 348
Crystal Palace FC 112, 202, 204, 205, 219, 249, 302, 348
Cullip, Danny 306
Culot, David 63–4
Cummins, Stan 10, 346
Cunnington, Shaun 98, 186
Curbishley, Alan 145

D'Avray, Mich 28, 46
Daish, Liam 254
Daley, Tony 335
Dandy, David 47–8
Danson, Paul 256
Darlington FC 20, 23, 25, 54, 85, 328, 329, 334
Davenport, Peter 95, 124
Davies, Barry 257
Davis, Evan 168, 170
Davis, Paul 339
Deane, Brian 259–60
Defoe, Jermain 119
Demaerschalk, Daniel 67
Derby County FC 4, 17, 109–11, 116, 117, 130, 183, 209, 210, 225, 227, 233, 249, 252–4, 259, 266, 283, 339
Derbyshire, Victoria 168, 170
Dick, Alistair 18
Dillon, Kevin 4, 11
Dipper, Ian 25
Dixon, Lee 255–6
Docherty, Mick 314
Docherty, Tommy 315
Docquier, Roland 74–7
Doncaster Rovers FC 90, 133
Dowell, Davey 151, 273
Dozzell, Jason 41
Drogheda United FC 190
Dryden, Richard 116
Duncan, James 20
Duncan, John 47, 48, 74, 200–202
Dunn, Harry 85, 92

Durban, Alan 25, 239
Durham City FC 89–90
Durie, Gordon 106
Duxbury, Mike 96

Earl, Robbie 142
Edge, The 293
Edmondson, Darren 139
Ehiogu, Ugo 259
Elleray, David 252
Elliott, Robbie 251, 274
Elliott, Shaun 10
Ellis, Gordon 261, 263–4
Ellis, Kenny 54–6, 59
Ellis, Sam 310–11, 314, 315–16, 324
Emerson 258, 279
Emmerson, Neil 30, 37, 110
Eriksson, Jan 269–70
Escape To Victory 222
Euell, Jason 288
Everton FC 45, 175–8, 181, 187, 252, 266, 282–3, 291, 339
Eyres, David 297, 299

Fashanu, John 142–4
Feathersone, John 127, 177
Ferdinand, Les 251, 323
Ferdinand, Rio 252
Ferguson, Alex 206–8
Ferguson, Bobby 27, 45–6, 89, 94, 104, 198, 239
Ferguson, Derek 108–9, 110, 111, 116, 126, 139, 144, 156, 158, 162, 175, 186
Ferguson, Duncan 282, 284–5
Festa, Gianluca 279
Finnan, Steve 323
Fino's (nightclub) 227
Flowers, Tim 217
Football Echo 65, 117
Football Focus 161, 165
Ford, Mark 259, 297, 301–2
Ford Sports Daventry xi, 340
Forest Green Rovers FC 335–7, 338
Forrest, Craig 30
Foster, Neil 25
Fowler, Robbie 196, 251, 276–7, 291, 328
Frain, John 321
Freestone, Chris 321
Fry, Barry 232
Fulham FC 30, 133, 293, 294, 306, 322
Furnandiz, Roger 330

Gabbiadini, Marco 111, 121, 209, 225, 253, 328, 332–5
Gallagher, Dermot 287
Gamble, John 84, 85
Gascoigne, Paul 26, 48, 73, 339–40
Gates, Eric 28, 46, 198
Gateshead FC 51, 53–4, 56, 79
Gemine, Louis 55–6, 60, 71, 72, 74, 77, 79, 92
Gemine, Stéphane 55–6, 60, 61, 64, 68–9, 70, 71, 77

Gemmill, Scott 130
Gerrard, Paul 226
Gibb, Ali 305
Giggs, Ryan xiii, 206
Gillingham FC 133, 299, 306
Ginola, David 251, 275–6
Given, Shay 217–19, 222, 230, 231
Gleghorn, Nigel 46
Glentoran FC 107
Glover, Lee 336
Goddard, Paul 90
De Goey, Ed 337
Gogglebox 249
Goldie (exotic dancer) 285, 287
Golightly, Steve 84
Goodman, Don 93, 94, 98, 105, 112, 117, 122, 126, 139, 146, 155, 171, 174, 186, 211–12
Gough, Richard 106
Gray, Martin 98, 108, 125, 128, 191, 195, 328
Gray, Micky 125, 149, 162–5, 196, 206, 209, 223, 226, 232, 235, 237, 240, 250, 270, 275, 282, 285, 286, 288–9
Gray, Phil 104, 105, 108, 115, 122, 126, 134, 146, 148, 149, 155, 158, 162, 167, 168, 189, 191, 200, 204, 207, 208, 214, 225, 240
Gregory, Neil 222
Griffiths, Carl 213
Grimsby Town FC 1, 25, 89, 205, 210, 225, 304
Gritt, Steve 145–6

Håland, Alf-Inge 251
Hall, A. R. 333
Hall, Gareth 38, 214, 219, 253–4, 267, 281
Hall, Paul 213
Hamed, Naseem 285–6
Hamilton, Gary 108
Hansen, Alan 161
Hardy, Billy 285–6
Harford, Mick 4, 11, 95
Harrison, Eddie 20, 89, 92, 107, 331
Harrison, Gerry 298
Hartlepool United FC xiii, 54, 133
Hartley, Trevor 129, 161, 182, 188
Hartson, John 255, 257
Hateley, Mark 106
Hayles, Barry 323
Hazard, Eden 72
Hazard, Mick 4, 11
Hazard, Thierry 72
Hearts FC 109, 270
Heath, Adrian 294
Heckingbottom, Paul 189
Hell (Norway) 151
Hemptinne, AS 56–61, 64, 66, 70, 72, 74, 77, 79, 80, 83, 85, 92, 135, 166, 298
Hendon, Ian 321, 326, 327
Herd, George 25–6
Heskey, Emile 219
Heysel disaster 181
Hill, Colin 219, 321
Hill, Jimmy 161, 289

Hindmarch, Rob 10
Hirst, David 43
Hislop, Shaka 276
Hitchin Town FC 302
Hodgson, Dougie 321
Holdsworth, David 38
Holdsworth, Dean 38, 142, 287, 288
Holloway, Darren 269
Holloway, Ian 342
Hooper, Mike 203
van Hooijdonk, Pierre 272
Hope, Richard 150, 321, 322, 326
Horsfield, Geoff 323
Horsley, Trevor 336
Houghton, Ray 151
Hoult, Russell 225
Howard, Steve 150, 321, 326
Howells, David 167
Howey, Christopher (son) 332
Howey, Claudia (daughter) 241, 320, 334, 344
Howey, Elliot (son) 238, 244, 291, 329–30, 334, 344
Howey, Joseph (son) 332, 342
Howey, Maz (wife) 332, 334, 342, 344
Howey, Norman (father) 1–2, 5, 10, 13, 14–17, 21, 22–3, 27, 31, 32, 35, 51, 54, 65, 81, 88, 90, 96, 144, 239, 264, 274, 297, 301, 323
Howey, Steven (brother) 6–9, 11, 14, 16, 20, 52–3, 58, 96–7, 137–8, 150, 187, 251, 275, 323, 344
Howey, Tom (uncle) 17–18
Howey, Yvonne (mother) 1–2, 4, 6, 22, 51, 65, 68, 74, 79, 81, 138, 161, 273
Huddersfield Town FC 124, 230
Hughes, Mark 96
Hunt, Andy 91
Hunter, Roy 330, 331
Hurley, Charlie 237

Ipswich Town FC 27–49, 55, 71, 89, 90–92, 94, 100, 103, 104, 110, 145, 197, 198, 200, 204, 222, 254, 255, 298, 302, 305, 317, 328
Irwin, Denis 205

Jailhouse Rock 132
James, David 38
James, Julian 223
Jepson, Ronnie 311
Joachim, Julian 219
John Paul II, Pope 18
Johnston, Allan 270, 274, 280, 283
Jones, Rob 196, 291
Jordan, Joe 89, 156
Judopay xii, 343
Juninho 258, 278, 279

Kavanagh, Graham 301
Kay, John 116, 120–22
Keane, Robbie 217
Keane, Roy 206, 215
Keegan, Kevin 93, 96–7, 185, 323
Kelly, Alan 183

Kelly, David 171, 189, 202–3, 210, 234, 258, 294
Kelly, Gary 123
Kendall, Howard 232
Keown, Martin 255
Kettering Town FC 339–40
Kidd, Ryan 195
Kirton, Trevor 34
Kiwonya, Chris 255
Klinsmann, Jürgen xiii, 166–7, 171
Knight, Alan 214
Kristensen, Bjørn 91
Kubicki, Dariusz 144, 156, 192–3, 247, 252–4, 294

Lambert, Rickie 336
Lambert, Stephen 249
Lampard, Frank 252
Langan, Kevin 336
Lawrence, Jamie 132
Lawrence, Lennie 223
Ledwith, Gavin 20
Lee, Rob 93
Leeds United FC 123, 133, 259–60, 261, 286, 297
Leicester City FC 23, 25, 99, 193, 196, 210, 218–20, 249, 275
Lennon, Neil 275
Let There Be Light 279
Lincoln City FC 25, 128, 256, 298, 326, 327
Lineker, Gary 73
Lindstedt, Ray 22
Little, Glenn 312, 315
Live Aid 30
Liverpool FC 2, 39, 86, 93, 178, 196–7, 202, 208, 249, 251, 276–7, 291
Long Buckby FC 340
Lord of the Flies 19
Lormor, Tony 96
Lowe, David 47
Lukic, John 123
Luton Town FC 4, 104, 108, 118, 132, 223, 255, 338
Lyall, John 91
Lynam, Des 161
Lyttle, Des 272

Mabbutt, Gary 160
McAllister, Gary 123
Macari, Lou 233
McAteer, Jason 291
McAuliffe, Jimmie 11, 16, 99
McCall, Steve 28
McCall, Stuart 106
McCarthy, Mick 204. 205
McClair, Brian 96, 206
McClaren, Steve 73
McClements, John 235, 264, 301
McCoist, Ally 106
McCreery, David 96
McGavin, Steve 47
McGhee, Mark 193
McKeag, Gordon 235

McKee, Gina 248
McLeary, Alan 145–6
McManaman, Steve 178, 196, 251, 276, 277
McMenemy, Lawrie 88
McNally, Lee 12
McQueen, Gordon 267
McStay, Paul 18
Madness (band) 22
Maison, Morrell 340
Makin, Chris 226
Maldini, Paolo 166
Maley, Mark 344–5
Manchester City FC 87, 158, 181, 218, 245, 247
Manchester United FC 2, 5, 40, 96, 99, 184, 197, 205–8, 210, 218, 245, 249, 250, 267, 270, 280, 292
Mariner Paul 28
Marriner, Vincent 11, 12, 20, 21, 89
Marshall, Aidy 246, 262, 285
Martindale, Dave 99
Marwood, Brian 299
Match of the Day 161, 165, 250, 257, 279
Mathie, Alex 197
Matteo, Dominic 178–9
Mawson, David 189
Mayhew, Danny 27
Melville, Andy 108, 110, 126, 148, 150, 158, 166, 175, 189, 191, 196, 211, 213, 226, 227, 238, 244, 245, 255, 259, 267, 269, 271, 290, 323
Mendonca, Clive 23, 25, 37, 290
Merson, Paul 38, 229, 255
Messi, Lionel 296
Middlesbrough FC 52, 108–9, 132–7, 140, 258, 259, 267–8, 277–80, 281, 289
Miller, Kevin 116
Millwall FC 38, 96, 179, 204–5, 209, 215, 220, 230, 246
Milošević, Savo 269
Milton, Simon 222
Mimms, Bobby 217, 219
Mitchell, Kenny 83, 84
Mohamed Al-Fayed 279, 322
Mohan, Nicky 134
Mooney, Brian 91
Moore, Bobby xii, 37–8
Moore, Neil 297, 302, 309, 310
Mourinho José 128, 184
Mowbray, Tony 222
Mühren, Arnold 28
Mulhall, George 252
Mullin, John 186, 267, 270, 291, 294
Murdoch, Rupert 134
Murray, Bob 89, 108, 124, 126–7, 147, 175, 177, 179, 193, 245, 280
Murtagh, Ian 107

Naisbett, Phil 258
Neal, Phil 89
Neville, Gary 205
Neville, Phil 206
Nevin, Pat 99

Newcastle United FC 2–3, 4, 19, 26–27, 52, 53, 66, 73, 83, 89, 91, 93–5, 96–7, 119, 133, 138, 141, 158, 185, 187–8, 202, 248, 273–6, 277, 292–3, 323, 344, 346
Nielson, Alan 91
Norman, Tony 126, 173, 186, 230
Northampton Town FC 150, 184, 186, 241, 304–6, 316–18, 321–38, 344–5
Norwich City FC 9, 86, 111, 194, 208, 210, 297
Nottingham Forest FC 130, 132, 146, 147, 202, 250–51, 271–2, 289, 297
Notts County FC 100–102, 111, 146, 161, 322
Nuneaton Borough FC 337, 338

O'Donnell, Chris 30
O'Neill, Martin 193, 218
Olabode, Joe 53
Oldham Athletic FC 209, 226–7, 230
Olson, Danny 30, 55, 57
Ord, Richard xiv, 25, 91, 142–3, 150, 156, 189, 193, 210, 220, 227, 235, 243, 247, 251, 252, 254, 258, 259, 262, 263, 265, 266, 267, 269, 270, 273–5, 276, 281, 284, 285, 288–90, 294, 295
Osman, Russell 28, 46
Østenstad, Egil 258, 281
Oster, John 345
Owen, Brian 27, 49, 198
Owers, Gary 25, 94, 101, 113, 124, 156, 157, 159, 186, 322, 338
Oxford United FC 108, 140
Oyston, Owen 259

Pallister, Gary 205
Parlour, Ray 255, 257
Parnaby, Dave 51, 53
Parnaby, Stuart 52
Partridge, Adrian 192
Patton 130–131
Peacock, Gavin 90
Peacock, Keith 90
Peake, Trevor 118
Pearce, Stuart 130
Pears, Stephen 134
Pembridge, Mark 111
Pérez, Lionel 246–7, 258, 271, 275
Peschisolido, Paul 323
Pethick, Robbie 214
Phillips, Kevin 203, 290, 292, 293
Pike, Geoff 338
Pilkington, Kevin 205–8
Plains Farm WMC FC 83–5, 87, 92, 94, 95, 103, 122, 144, 166, 173, 206, 241, 305
Platt, David 255
Poll, Graham 258
Pollock, Jamie 135
Popescu, Gheorghe 160, 167
Port Vale FC 11, 171, 196, 212, 221, 333
Portsmouth FC 98–9, 110, 130, 212–16, 222, 276, 322
Powell, Chris 225
Power, Lee 111

Poyet, Gus 337
Preece, David 189, 244, 258, 269
Premier Passions xiv, 23, 188, 248–9, 281
Preston North End FC 193–6
Pringle, David 25

Queen's Park Rangers FC 323, 342
Quinn, Jimmy 209
Quinn, Niall xiv, 247–8, 250, 251, 254, 262, 264–5, 271, 281, 290, 293–4, 296, 310

Răducioiu, Florin 252
Rae, Alex 246, 248, 262, 272
Rangers FC 46, 47, 94, 105–6, 108, 117, 118, 284
Rankine, Mark 113, 211
Ravanelli, Fabrizio xiii, 258, 267–8, 278–9
Reading FC 209, 317, 342
Redknapp, Harry 252
Redknapp, Jamie 196, 328
Redman, Paul 12, 25
Reed, Mike 167
Reid, Peter xiv, 23, 110, 127, 181–90, 193, 195, 203, 204, 205, 214, 215, 217, 221, 226, 228, 234, 238, 240, 241, 243, 245, 247, 248, 251, 252, 253, 256, 259, 265, 269, 270, 271, 278, 281, 283, 290, 292, 295, 245
Rennie, Uriah 211
Rice, Pat 257
Richardson, Lee 226
Rideout, Paul 18
Robinson, Ben 348
Robinson, Keithy 83–4
Robinson, Mickey (a) 20, 25, 55
Robinson, Mickey (b) 55
Robson, Bobby 28
Robson, Bryan 35, 89, 96, 132, 267, 279
Rochdale FC 208
Rodgerson, Ian 108–9
Roeder, Glenn 96, 295, 298, 299, 307
Rogan, Anton 91, 94, 124
Ross, Ian 151
Rotherham United FC 25, 166, 304
Rowe, Rodney 301
Rowell, Gary 10, 320, 346
Ruddock, Neil 38–40
Rush, Ian 259
Russell, Craig 91, 125, 134, 146, 156, 152, 183, 189, 195, 200, 204–5, 206–7, 213, 219, 222, 223, 225, 230–31, 232, 234, 235, 256, 258, 266, 288

St Aidan's Secondary School 19–21, 30, 53, 166, 299
St Cuthbert's Primary School 11–13, 17–19
St Leonard's Primary School 7–8
St Patrick's Athletic FC 190
Salako, John 323
Salmon, Mike 90
Sampson, Ian 128, 304, 321, 338
Sanchez, Laurie 142
Sandford, Lee 233

Sansom, Kenny 96
Saunders, Dean 272
Savage, Dave 150, 321, 332
Saxton, Bobby xiv, 188, 190, 197, 203, 221, 232, 250, 256, 259
Scales, John 142
Scarborough FC 122, 335
Schmeichel, Peter xiii, 205, 208
Scott, Chris 312
Scott, Martin 156, 192, 223, 238, 251, 256, 262, 265, 267, 290
Scunthorpe United FC 124
Seaham Red Star FC 83, 85
Seaman, David 255, 267
Sedgley, Steve 222
Segers, Hans 142
Sharpe, Lee 96, 206, 207
Shawshank Redemption 19
Shearer, Alan xiii, 53, 178, 248, 251, 274–6
Sheffield United FC 177, 183, 232, 294
Sheffield Wednesday FC 40, 43, 135, 266, 270, 297
Shelbourne FC 293–4
Sheringham, Teddy 160, 166–7, 171
Sherwood, Steve 45, 46
Shilton, Peter 252
Shirtliff, Peter 171
Shoot! 3, 5
Short, Craig 110
Shrewsbury Town FC 319
Sigurðsson, Lárus 233
Simpson, David 12, 20
Sinclair, Ronnie 175
Sky Television 134, 208, 304
Slater, Stuart 222
Small, Mike 111
Smith, Denis 88, 121, 129
Smith, Jamie 173
Smith, Jim 96
Smith, Martin xiv, 125, 134, 140, 149, 162, 163, 168, 169, 183, 189, 196, 209, 235, 244–5, 285
Smith, Mick 4
Smith, Simon 53
Smith, Tony 124
Solkham, Brett 339
Southall, Neville 282, 283
Southampton FC 39, 258, 280–81, 282, 289
Southend United FC 37, 175, 223–4, 328
Southgate, Gareth 259
Spedding, Duncan 317, 321
Speed, Gary 123
Speedie, David 100
Spink, Nigel 335
Sproates, John 6
Stelea, Bogdan 243
Stevens, Gary 106
Stewart, Paul 189, 197, 199, 225–6, 230, 232, 235, 245, 256, 258, 271, 277, 280, 282–3, 294
Stewart, Ray 11, 13, 18
Stimson, Mark 91
Stockport County FC 175, 295, 299

Stockwell, Mick 222
Stoke City FC 133, 174–5, 203–4, 218, 233–4, 294, 301, 316
Stone, Steve 130
Stonhill, Barry 334
Storey, Geoff 82, 214
Stowell, Mike 171
Strachan, Gordon 123
Sturridge, Dean 225
Styles, Rob 302
Suggett, Colin 2, 26
Summerbee, Nicky 290
Sunderland Echo 21, 82, 170, 214, 244
Surnadal FC 151
Swan, Peter 311
Swindon Town FC 4, 10, 73, 111, 159, 190, 217, 228
Sykes, Alex 337
Symons, Kit 323

Tarrico, Mauricio 22
Taylor, Graham 230
Teasdale, Frank 307
Ternent, Stan 307–16, 318–20
Thijssen, Frans 28
Thomas, Geoff 6, 112–15, 143, 167, 171, 173–4, 196, 203
Thomas, Michael 291
Thompson, Alan 91
Thompson, Andy 212
Thomsen, Claus 222
Thorne, Peter 301
Thorpe, Lee 326–7
Todd, Kevin 84, 85
Torquay United FC 330
Tottenham Hotspur FC 39, 160–61, 165–7, 168
Townsend, Andy 259
Tranmere Rovers FC 89, 99, 205, 211, 238–9, 241, 294
Trevivean, Peter 27
Tye, Charlie 84

Venison, Barry 93
Vickers, Steve 135
Viera, Patrick 255

Waddle, Chris 13, 135, 271, 272, 273, 275, 276, 277, 278, 283, 288, 294–6, 297, 300, 301, 303–7
Walker, Jack 219
Wallace, Ray 203
Wallace, Rod 123
Walsall FC 333
Walsh, Paul 98
Walters, Mark 171
Warburton, Ray 305
Wark, John 28, 222
Warnock, Neil 89
Watson, Dave 282
Watson, Paul 66, 73
Watson, Steve 91, 274

Weah, George 166
Welch, Keith 156, 243
Weller, Paul 309
Wenger, Arsène 257, 323
West Bromwich Albion FC 177–8, 203–4, 234, 236, 237, 240, 342, 348
West Ham United FC 90, 99, 252, 338
Whelan, Jonathon 12
Wigan Athletic FC 47, 306
Wilkins, Ray 323
Wilkinson, Paul 321
Williams, Darren 266, 278–9, 284, 290
Williams, Mike 297, 298, 314, 319
Wilson, Kevin 304, 317, 321, 322, 328, 330, 333, 334, 338, 339, 340
Wilson, Mark 74
Wimbledon FC xii, 4, 40, 96, 121, 140, 141, 142–4, 250, 286–9
Winstanley, Mark 310, 314, 319
Winterburn, Nigel 255
Wise, Dennis 337
de Wolf, John 171–4, 203, 212
Wolf, Wolfgang 172
Wolfsburg FC 172
Wolverhampton Wanderers FC 111–13, 115, 155, 171–4, 196, 202, 203, 204, 211–12, 294
Woodman, Andy 321, 332
Woods, Charlie 27
Woods, Chris 271, 280, 294, 295, 297, 307
Woods, Neil 47
Wright, Ian xiii, 255, 256
Wright, Mark 291
Wright, Philip 172
Wright, Richard 222
Wright, Tommy 91
Wycombe Wanderers FC 47

Yallop, Frank 198
Yeanshire, John 51
Yeanshire, Superintendent Steph 51
Yeovil Town FC 310, 337
York City FC 266, 300–301, 312–14, 317, 319, 344
Yorke, Dwight 259
Young, Kevin 11
Young, Martin 30, 37

Zoetebier, Edwin 293
Zola, Gianfranco 337